T0305356

Global Real Estate Investment Trusts

To my wife and our twin teenagers.
May the future with Susan, Elliot and Victoria
recompense for that foregone.

Global Real Estate Investment Trusts

Investment Trusts

People, Process and Management

David Parker

Professor of Property
University of South Australia

WILEY-BLACKWELL

A John Wiley & Sons, Ltd., Publication

First edition published by Blackwell Publishing 2008

Library of Congress Cataloging-in-Publication Data

Parker, David, professor.
  Global real estate investment trusts : people, process and management / David Parker. – 1st ed.
     p.   cm.
  Includes bibliographical references and index.
  ISBN 978-1-4051-8722-0 (hardback)
1. Real estate investment trusts–Management.   I. Title.
  HG5095.P37 2012
  332.63'247068–dc23

                                                          2011035003

A catalogue record for this book is available from the British Library.

This book is published in the following electronic formats: ePDF 9781444398793; ePub 9781444398809; oBook [ISBN]

Set in 10/13pt Trump Mediaeval by SPi Publisher Services, Pondicherry, India

1   2011

Contents

About the Author

David Parker is an internationally recognised real estate industry expert and highly regarded real estate academic, being a director and adviser to real estate investment groups including listed real estate investment trusts, unlisted funds and private real estate businesses (www.davidparker.com.au).

Professor Parker is currently the inaugural Professor of Property at the University of South Australia, an Adjunct Professor of Property at the University of Queensland, a Visiting Fellow at the University of Ulster and an Acting Commissioner of the Land and Environment Court of New South Wales.

With over 25 years experience in all aspects of property fund management, portfolio management, asset management and property management as well as in property valuation, Professor Parker previously held senior executive positions with Schroders Property Fund and ANZ Funds Management.

Professor Parker consults widely to REITs and real estate funds, having developed *Clarity*®, a proprietorial research-based real estate investment decision making process linking corporate vision to individual real estate assets.

Holding BSc, MComm, MBA and PhD degrees, Professor Parker is a Fellow of the Royal Institution of Chartered Surveyors, the Australian Institute of Company Directors, the Australian Property Institute, the Australian Institute of Management and the Financial Services Institute of Australasia. He is a member of the Society of Property Researchers, the American Real Estate and Urban Economics Association and the European, American and Pacific Rim Real Estate Societies.

The author of numerous papers published in academic and industry journals, Professor Parker is a regular conference presenter around the world and Editorial Board Member for the highly ranked *Journal of Property Research*, the *Pacific Rim Property Research Journal* and *Property Management*.

David Parker may be contacted by email at davidparker@davidparker.com.au.

Foreword

This very interesting book is the first to analyse how decisions are, and more importantly should be, made in Real Estate Investment Trusts. REITs are one of the world's fastest growing stock exchange sectors; one of the major means by which commercial property assets are owned and managed, and through which these assets have access to the capital markets. Would that it had been written earlier for it might have provided a statement of how things should be done in a sector that managed to accentuate, rather than damp down, the volatility of financial markets in the crisis of 2008 to 2010!

REITs were invented in Australia, one of the many achievements of the great real estate visionary Dick Dusseldorp, the founder of Lend Lease. They spread to the United States, and then to Europe. They were the chosen means in Japan to reinvigorate property markets in the early 2000s; and have been adopted in many Asian jurisdictions. They need to be seen against the way in which the real estate investment sector has become an important capital market over the last 40 years.

Australia is also important here for it, along with the United Kingdom, had quite active pension fund and insurance company investment in property from the mid-1970s. This did not happen in the United States until ten years later, and in much of Europe until the late 1990s. In the early years property investment was largely achieved through direct ownership of assets by pension funds and insurance companies themselves.

The model of institutional ownership of high grade commercial property is now universal in the developed world. During this major shift in the capital ownership of the sector, new means have been invented to hold and administer the assets. Principals no longer own the assets themselves but contract this responsibility to either fund managers who administer funds or shares in funds on their behalf; or to listed property companies, which are now largely organised as REITs. They gain expertise, liquidity, and reach in the process.

David Parker's book gives a step-by-step guide to running a REIT, and about getting top quartile performance from the effort. While this is, essentially, to work out where a REIT wants to go, how to go about getting there in a sensible way and then to measure whether they got there…life is of course more complicated than this. You need to know about the particularities of commercial real estate and its many oddities; you have to appreciate the economics of the cycle and its extreme proneness to volatility; and in the new world of fiduciaries you have to be a competent manager and financier.

The strength of this book seems to me to be that it pulls no punches. It explains in crystal clear terms the steps that need to be gone through and thought about if you are going to operate in this sector. The sensible motif of setting up a straw man, a large diversified REIT, and showing what it should be doing works well: but mostly the book may be characterised by clear application of management, financial, economic and property theory to a real estate portfolio. The book is as valuable to a chief executive of a REIT, or an experienced chairman appointed to the sector for the first time as it is to a student wanting to make their career in this area. It is notably low on anecdote but describes sequentially how a sensible person would go about managing a REIT taking advantage of the tools and expertise now available.

As the book clearly shows, robust, rigorous property data is one of the foundations of effective decision making. From strategic asset allocation through tactical asset allocation to performance monitoring and attribution analysis, reliable property data is essential if sound decisions are to be made. At IPD, we specialise in creating property data and measuring performance which is, to some degree, the outcome of doing a whole host of other things. I learned a lot from this text about how this data could and should be used!

I particularly like the focus on post audit and recursion, which are each so important but so easily overlooked. Embracing the idea of stepping back and looking at whether what you forecast has come to pass, then taking such action as maybe required, is a sure sign of a mature, well managed REIT.

To be successful in property you need to combine insight and experience with process. While doing each of these steps in the right order is vitally important to good decision making, so too are the roles of the analytically focused research team, strategy team and portfolio management team in balancing the contributions of the more outgoing capital transactions team and a dynamic CEO.

David Parker is a recognised authority on REITs, and is well placed to write this scholarly work. He has however done the sector a tremendous service in outlining the sequence of decision making that needs to be made to succeed. I hope it will be widely read by lawyers, directors, REIT managers and regulators and others who work to build a sustainable REIT sector worldwide.

This is a great handbook for anybody wanting to know how a well governed REIT should be properly run.

Rupert Nabarro
Chairman IPD
London
June 2011

Preface

Real estate investment trusts or REITs are now an accepted form of real estate investment worldwide, having grown exponentially in the second half of the twentieth century. Despite there being hundreds of REITs investing thousands of millions of dollars in real estate globally, remarkably little research has been undertaken about how REITs make real estate investment decisions.

There are numerous substantial books that consider real estate investment decision making in general, but not in the specific context of REITs. Similarly, there is a range of books that consider specific aspects of REITs, but not their approach to real estate investment decision making generally.

The shameful stock market performance of some REITs during the global financial crisis may provide painful evidence, if any further evidence were needed, of the inadequacies of the opaque, curious and *ad hoc* investment decision making processes adopted by those REITs.

Following the experience of the global funds management industry in the management of equities funds, to gain sustained commitment from sophisticated international institutional investors it is essential to be able to demonstrate a transparent, explicit and above all repeatable investment decision making process.

Based upon original up to date research, this book seeks to explain not only how REIT real estate investment decision making should be undertaken in practice, but also how it is undertaken and the real estate theory, capital market theory and finance theory underlying each part of the real estate investment decision making process. Accordingly, this book is aimed at REIT managers and those involved in the REIT industry including real estate practitioners, researchers, lawyers, accountants and bankers around the world.

Following the global financial crisis, there is a major challenge for some REITs to regain both credibility with and the confidence of sophisticated international institutional investors. Bringing rigor and consistency to their real estate investment decision making process in order to offer transparency, explicability and the prospect of repeatability would be a commendable starting point.

David Parker
Adelaide, February 2011

Acknowledgments

The author gratefully acknowledges the general contribution of delegates at American, European and Pacific Rim Real Estate Society Conferences over the past few years in providing feedback to research papers and the specific contribution through review of draft chapters by Professor Andrew Baum of the University of Reading, Dr Malcolm Frodsham from IPD and Professor Colin Lizieri of the University of Cambridge.

Introduction

From the latter half of the twentieth century, *real estate investment trusts* or REITs have grown to become a substantial sector in the world's stock markets, being now well established in the USA and Australia, growing in Asia and emerging in Europe.

Starting as an amalgam of a few individual properties, REITs have now become not only substantial, structured real estate portfolios but also large business enterprises. As such, management of the modern REIT requires a combination of professional skills from the real estate sector, portfolio management skills from the finance and capital markets sectors and management skills akin to those required for the successful operation of other global enterprises. Accordingly, this book views REITs primarily as major international enterprises for which the core business is investment in and development of real estate.

This book seeks to explain how a REIT converts $1 of unitholder capital into $1 of investment real estate; including the roles of the key participants in the process, the theory behind the practice of the various steps involved, the alternative tools used and the important role of intuition and judgment.

Based on up to date, original academic research, including structured interviews with the managers of a wide range of different types of REITs as well as the research and publications of others as referenced, together with drawing on the author's 25 years experience in REIT management, this book seeks to provide a theoretically robust and practically relevant up to date guide to the real estate investment decision making process for REITs. As such, this book fuses not only how REITs should undertake real estate investment decision making, based on how they do undertake it, but also why each part of the decision making process is important.

Presenting new insights, this book breaks the REIT real estate investment decision making process down into three phases comprising six stages with 30 sequential steps. Each chapter focuses on one stage of the real estate investment decision making process, introduces the key people in the REIT management team relevant to the activities in that chapter with the theory and principles considered and illustrated by application to Super REIT, a $15 billion diversified REIT.

In addition to explaining the more familiar steps in the real estate investment decision making process such as Strategic Asset Allocation and Due Diligence, the book also emphasises the importance of such steps as Post Audit and Transformation, together with such activities as recursion and attribution analysis, in the effective management of risk-return within a REIT environment.

As a process, real estate investment decision making is viewed as being capable of application in principle within any jurisdiction around the globe. Thus, within this book, the REIT real estate investment decision making process is considered using generic terms (such as Governing Entity) that are capable of application anywhere in the world, though it is acknowledged that this may cause some confusion where individual jurisdictions adopt specific terms (such as Trustee or Director in the USA or Manager or Responsible Entity in Australia).

Significantly, REIT real estate investment decision making is viewed as a cyclical, ongoing process combing a variety of activities in monthly, quarterly, half-yearly, annual, two-yearly and five-yearly cycles. Accordingly therefore, once started the REIT real estate investment decision making process is effectively unending.

1

Envisioning

This book seeks to explain the real estate investment decision making process by which a *real estate investment trust*, or REIT, converts $1 of unitholder capital into $1 of investment real estate. Focusing equally on the people and the process, the contributions of the key participants in the real estate investment decision making process are described and analysed with a particular emphasis on both the overlap between their roles and their interaction.

The process of real estate investment decision making is a fusion of the 'how' and the 'why'. In this book, the *how* is based on the results of new, original academic research, including structured interviews with the managers of a wide range of different types of REITs, as well as the research and publications of others as referenced, together with the author's 25 years experience in REIT management. The *why* is drawn from the real estate theory, capital market theory and finance theory that underpins real estate investment management.

While the real estate investment decision making process draws on a range of tools, such as the Capital Asset Pricing Model, the role of intuition and judgment remains vital. Spreadsheets, sensitivity analysis and scenarios all have an important role to play in real estate investment decision making but need to be balanced with the intuition and judgment that come from years of practical experience.

Real estate investment decision making is presented in this book as comprising three Phases with six Stages and 30 Steps, being an ongoing, cyclical process. The first Phase, the Preparing Phase, comprises the Envisioning Stage and the Planning Stage wherein the REIT articulates where it is going and how it is going to get there, providing unitholders with a clear understanding of the risk-return profile to expect from the managers investment of their funds. The second Phase, the Transacting Phase, comprises the Dealing Stage and the Executing Stage, wherein the REIT implements the outcomes of the Preparing Phase through the creation of a tangible real estate portfolio. The third and final Phase, the Observing Phase, comprises the Watching Stage and the Optimising Stage, wherein the REIT ensures that its performance will achieve its goals and so attain its vision, thereby completing the cyclical process of REIT real estate investment decision making.

The six chapters of this book address each of the Stages of the REIT real estate investment decision making process sequentially, introducing and explaining the contribution of the relevant members of the REIT management team to that Stage. For each Stage, the relevant supporting theory, or the *why* for the *how*, is explained in detail and illustrated by application to Super REIT, a $15 billion diversified REIT.

REITs are a continuously evolving real estate investment product. Similar to listed equities investment funds, many REITs started through association with an entrepreneur who was the sole decision maker focusing on specific assets and evolved over time into a team approach focusing on a portfolio of assets. However, whereas the dominance of sophisticated international institutional investors in listed equities investment funds has pressured portfolio managers to adopt more transparent, explicable and repeatable investment decision making processes which are independent of individual decision makers, this has been less evident in REITs where the investment decision making process often appears to be opaque, curious and *ad hoc*.

This book seeks to increase the transparency and explicability of the real estate investment decision making process by REITs, thus contributing to the potential for repeatability, by shifting from a greater emphasis on people to a greater emphasis on process, so contributing to the continued evolution of REITs as a real estate investment product.

Extensive research over the last 25 years has shown that real estate investment is not necessarily different to other forms of investment. While many aspects of real estate investment can be explained by the application of theories and principles developed for other forms of investment, some aspects of real estate investment remain specific to the real estate sector. Similarly, many of the skills required to manage a REIT can be drawn from disciplines other than real estate while some skills remain firmly rooted in the real estate discipline. As the highly successful US real estate investor, Sam Zell, observed:

> REITs are no longer different from any other industry that is dependent on access to capital markets,

and

The successful REITs are the ones that can be characterised as operating companies versus a collection of properties. (Garrigan and Parsons, 1997)

This is a view echoed by Geltner et al. (2007):

Shares of the major REITs are publicly traded in the stock exchange. Viewed by Wall Street as operational firms, that is, actively managed corporations, they are valued as such (i.e. not as passive portfolios of properties). Thus, REITs are valued in essentially the same way other publicly traded firms are valued ... (Geltner et al., 2007)

This book seeks to view the REIT holistically as a major business enterprise which combines roles and skills common to all major business enterprises with roles and skills specific to the real estate sector. Similar to mining enterprises having CEOs as well as geologists or airline enterprises have CFOs as well as pilots, a REIT may be considered as just another type of business enterprise where the CEO and CFO work in a business team with dealers and developers. This reflects the increasing trend around the world for the CEO and various members of a REIT senior management team to increasingly be experts in a discipline other than real estate and for those with expertise in the real estate discipline to decreasingly occupy positions inside the C-suite.

With a REIT sector now forming part of the stock market of the US, Australia, numerous Asian countries and an increasing number of European countries, this book seeks to provide principles of real estate investment decision making that are capable of application in all countries (subject to local laws, regulations and rules) rather than focusing on decision making within the context of a specific country's laws, regulations and rules.

For clarity, this book adopts the hierarchy whereby a REIT may comprise a group of funds and each fund may comprise a group of portfolios and each portfolio may comprise a group of properties. Also, the term *'appraisal'* is used instead of *'valuation'* though it is acknowledged that *valuation* is commonly used in Commonwealth countries.

Further, this book focuses the application of the REIT real estate investment decision making process on the acquisition of a property, though it is acknowledged that the process is equally applicable to the disposal of a property or other major transaction such as a large lease renewal or the letting of a substantial area of vacant accommodation.

Finally, where individual authors have contributed ideas specifically referred to in a chapter such authors are acknowledged individually in the text, with those authors contributing ideas generally referred to in a chapter being acknowledged in the references at the end of that chapter to which the reader is referred for greater detail.

This chapter seeks to outline REITs in principle with an overview of the REIT real estate investment decision making process and the key participants. Accordingly, by the end of this chapter, the reader should understand:

- the relevance of **commercial** and **legal principles** underlying a REIT and its characteristics;
- the importance of the **structure** and **composition** of a REIT management team for effective control of a large and often international business; and
- the significance of the **Phases**, **Stages** and **Steps** comprising the REIT real estate investment decision making process.

1.1 People and process

As the title *Global Real Estate Investment Trusts: People, Process and Management* indicates, this book focuses on both the people and the process involved in real estate investment decision making with the consideration of people intentionally coming first. This reflects the current emphasis on people relative to process in REIT real estate investment decision making which, as referred to above, is expected to reverse as REITs continue their evolution to a greater emphasis on process.

1.1.1 People

Over the last 40 years, the global REIT sector has developed from a small adjunct to the stock markets of several countries to a significant sector of the global equities market. REITs themselves have grown from small businesses collecting rents from a handful of buildings to massive multinational conglomerates undertaking a wide range of activities related to real estate.

The evolution from being small, localised entities into being large, international entities has been accompanied by an evolution in both people and real estate investment decision making processes. Accordingly, REITs today are major business enterprises, with management structures that mirror other major business enterprises, but happen to have a principal business undertaking a wide range of activities related to real estate.

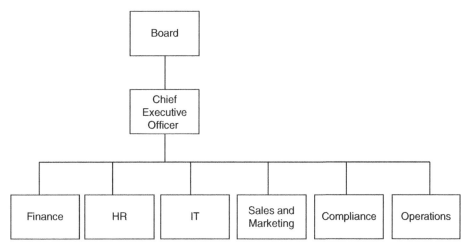

Figure 1.1 Typical management structure of an international enterprise.

As small, localised entities, REITs were often lead by an individual and managed by a small team who, between them, fulfilled all the roles necessary for the REIT to function. As is common in small business, the respective roles may not have been defined and may have overlapped.

As large, international entities, REITs have evolved to adopt that management structure common to many international enterprises as illustrated in Figure 1.1. Though such line management functions as Finance, HR and IT are common to both REITs and major enterprises in other sectors such as banking, retail and so forth, REITs may be considered to have evolved the sales and marketing and operational line management functions to reflect the nature of the REIT business.

The sales and marketing line management function has evolved to comprise an investor interface function including marketing, sales and investor relations. For a business that specialises in real estate, the operational line management functions have evolved most specifically in REITs and so exhibit the greatest difference, as may be expected, to line management functions in other enterprises.

The operations line management functions for a large REIT reflect the various line management layers involved in the fund level, portfolio level, asset level, property level and facility level management of a REIT as illustrated in Figure 1.2. Those people comprising each of the management functions illustrated in Figure 1.2 contribute to the real estate investment decision making process within a REIT and are considered in the chapter outlining that part of the real estate investment decision making process with which they are most closely associated. Accordingly, the Portfolio Management, Strategy and Research Teams are

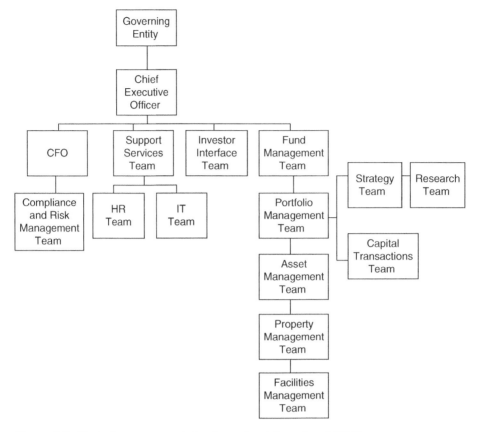

Figure 1.2   Typical management structure of an international REIT.

considered in Chapter 2 (Planning Stage), the Capital Transaction Team is considered in Chapter 3 (Dealing Stage), the Investor Interface Team is considered in Chapter 4 (Executing Stage), the Compliance and Risk Management Team is considered in Chapter 5 (Watching Stage), the Asset Management, Property Management and Facilities Management Teams are considered in Chapter 6 (Optimising Stage) with the Governing Entity, CEO, CFO, Support Teams and Fund Management Team considered in this chapter (Envisioning Stage).

While generic names have been adopted for the various management roles, it is accepted that names may vary in different countries and for different REIT models. It is also accepted that only the largest international REITs may separate all of the various roles considered, with smaller REITs and domestic REITs combining roles to suit operational requirements.

1.1.2 Process

The real estate investment decision making process outlined in this book is based on new, original academic research, including structured interviews with the managers of a wide range of different types of REITs and the research and publications of others as referenced, as well as drawing on the author's 25 years experience in REIT management.

While this book focuses on the steps involved in real estate investment decision making in the context of a large sectorally and geographically diversified REIT, the principles of the steps may be equally applied to small REITs and to sectorally or geographically focused REITs.

However, rather than the size or nature of the REIT, a potentially greater challenge to the effective implementation of the steps in the real estate investment decision making process comprises the willingness of REIT management teams to evolve their approach to decision making which may be succinctly summarised as:

> To some degree, the quest to upgrade the quality of real estate decisions is perhaps a classic exposition of the aphorism: "You can lead a horse to water, but you can't make him drink".' (Roulac in Pagliari, 1995)

Real estate investment decision making is the synthesis of theory, history, content, context, process and methodology (Roulac, 2001). This book breaks the REIT real estate investment decision making process down into three phases comprising six stages with 30 sequential steps as summarised in Table 1.1.

The Preparing Phase comprises the:

- **Envisioning Stage** – in which the REIT clearly articulates its destination together with a high order route map by which to get to the destination and some measurable outcomes to determine whether or not the REIT has arrived at the destination (considered in detail in this chapter); and the
- **Planning Stage** – in which the REIT converts its destination into the identification of a target list of specific real estate assets for potential acquisition that meet the stock selection criteria and may be mis-priced (considered in detail in Chapter 2).

Accordingly, on completion of the Preparing Phase, the REIT has articulated where it is going and how it is going to get there, providing unitholders with a clear understanding of the risk-return profile to expect from the managers investment of their funds and is positioned to undertake the Transacting Phase.

Table 1.1 Phases, Stages and Steps in the REIT real estate investment decision making process.

Phase	Stage	Steps	Steps	Steps	Steps	Steps
Preparing	Envisioning	Vision	Style	Goals	Strategic Plan	Objectives
	Planning	Property P'folio Strategy	Strat. Asset Allocation	Tactical Asset Allocation	Stock Selection	Asset Identification
Transacting	Dealing	Preliminary Negotiation	Preliminary Analysis	Structuring	Adv. Fin Analysis	P'flio Impact Assessment
	Executing	Governance Decision	Transaction Closure	Documentation	Due Diligence	Independent Appraisal
Observing	Watching	Settlement	Post Audit	Performance Monitoring	Performance Measurement	Portfolio Analysis
	Optimising	Asset Managem't	Prop. & Fac. Management	Transformation	Portfolio Rebalancing	Disposal

The Transacting Phase comprises the:

- **Dealing Stage** – in which the REIT converts the target list of specific assets for potential acquisition into an in-principle transaction for the acquisition of a nominated asset (considered in detail in Chapter 3); and the
- **Executing Stage** – in which the REIT verifies all information relied upon and assumptions made in the pricing process and reflects this in the documentation necessary to protect the interests of unitholders at settlement (considered in detail in Chapter 4).

Accordingly, on completion of the Transacting Phase, the REIT has implemented the outcomes of the Preparing Phase through the creation of a tangible real estate portfolio and is positioned to undertake the Observing Phase.

The Observing Phase comprises the:

- **Watching Stage** – in which the REIT monitors the portfolio to determine whether or not the objectives, goals and hence the vision for the REIT will be achieved (considered in detail in Chapter 5); and the
- **Optimising Stage** – in which the REIT takes such action as may be necessary to ensure the objectives, goals and hence the vision for the REIT will be achieved (considered in detail in Chapter 6).

Accordingly, on completion of the Observing Phase, the REIT has ensured that its performance will achieve its goals and so attain its vision, thereby completing the cyclical process of REIT real estate investment decision making.

While the complete cyclical process of REIT real estate investment decision making is only likely to be undertaken sequentially by a newly formed REIT at inception or by an existing REIT facing transformational change or restructure, respective stages or individual steps may be undertaken by existing, operational REITs on an ongoing basis or as required. For example, while an existing operational REIT may be expected to undertake the Watching Stage on an ongoing basis, it may only be expected to undertake the Dealing Stage when required for the acquisition or disposal of a property or other major transaction within the portfolio.

Reflecting the fiduciary nature of REIT management, individual steps within a given stage should be completed sequentially in order to avoid a significant omission. For example, an existing, operational REIT undertaking the Dealing Stage when required should complete the five steps of the Dealing Stage sequentially and not omit a step, such as the Portfolio Impact Step, as this will result in important data then being missing from the real estate investment decision making process and a potentially suboptimal decision then resulting which may not be in unitholders' best interests.

To illustrate the REIT real estate investment decision making process, a fictitious existing and operational REIT, named Super REIT for convenience, is used by way of example for each Phase, Stage and Step. Super REIT is a $15 billion diversified REIT which implements the real estate investment decision making process to invest in Superman Tower in the fictitious city of Metropolis.

The approach to REIT real estate investment decision making described in this book is premised on a normative approach of sequential Steps undertaken by rational participants in a methodical manner with access to all the information, data and tools that may be required to make logical, optimal decisions in an unproblematic environment. Significantly, while the approach is described as normative, being how an investor should behave, it is based on and supported by new, original academic research (including structured interviews with the managers of a wide range of different types of REITs, as well as the research and publications of others as referenced) providing a descriptive approach, being how an investor actually behaves.

Interesting research is currently underway around the world, drawing from the disciplines of cognitive psychology and behavioural finance, that fundamentally challenges the premis of such a normative approach, arguing that real estate investment decision making is neither sequential, rational, methodical, informed, logical nor optimal and often undertaken in a problematic environment, being:

> '*undertaken by imperfect players in imperfect markets using imperfect information*' (Roberts and Henneberry, 2007).

Ongoing research suggests that the real estate investment decision making process may be influenced by the individual decision maker, their decision making environment (which may be complex, dynamic and chaotic) and the extent of information available, with a propensity for the decision maker to '*collapse down*' the decision making process and take short cuts, potentially leaving the decision making process open to the influence of multiple biases, perceptions, beliefs, preferences, judgment and sentiment (MacCowan and Orr, 2008; French and French, 1997; French, 2001; Gallimore et al., 2000; Gallimore et al., 2000a; Gallimore and Gray, 2002; Roberts and Henneberry, 2007).

Such research is consistent with the long accepted view that real estate investment decision making is more than an explicit process, including '*... the implicit decision-making apparatus of judgment, hunch, instinct, intuition, faith, and gut feel.*' (Pyhrr et al., 1989), so underlining the vital connection between people and process.

1.1.3 People and process

This book seeks to explain the real estate investment decision making process by which a real estate investment trust, or REIT, converts $1 of unitholder capital into $1 of investment real estate.

While focusing equally on the people and the process, as the book title indicates, the REIT real estate investment decision making process is dependent upon the combination of and interaction between people and process, being incapable of effective operation in the absence of either and sub-optimal in the event that either is compromised.

1.2 REITs: an introduction

The original role of a REIT, which remains the core role of many REITs today, was to unitise and securitise otherwise illiquid investment real estate. As individual buildings increased in value and became denominated in billions of dollars rather than just in millions, the ability of and wisdom for investors to own such a building in its entirety came into focus.

By acquiring a billion dollar building and offering a billion one dollar units tradeable on a stock exchange, the REIT provides an intermediation role allowing a building for which there may otherwise be a limited market of possible purchasers to be owned indirectly by investors who would otherwise be unable to own such real estate.

The same intermediation principle is applicable to buildings in different real estate sectors, different states and different countries. In each case, the REIT offers the opportunity for bricks and mortar investment real estate to be broken down into small paper units tradeable on a stock exchange.

Further, the same intermediation principle is applicable to either individual buildings or to a very large number of buildings. As the number of buildings owned by a REIT grows or as the REIT expands into different sectors, states or countries, the REIT may group the buildings, sectors, states or countries through the creation of funds and portfolios based on such characteristics or upon other characteristics such as income, capital growth and so forth.

The evolution of REITS varies between countries with, for example, US REITs based in specific enabling legislation, Australian REITs based in trust law and other countries adopting varying combinations of both. While the details of governing documents may vary between countries, a common feature of REITs worldwide is that they enjoy some form of beneficial tax treatment in their local jurisdiction requiring very close adherence to local laws, regulations and rules in order to qualify for and maintain the tax benefit.

In the US, REITs were shaped through successive legislation including the Real Estate Investment Trust Act (1960), the Tax Reform Act (1986) and the REIT Modernisation Act (1999). US REITs have to fulfil a variety of criteria including a specified proportion of assets invested in real estate, mortgage loans, shares in other REITs, cash or government securities and deriving a specified proportion of gross income from rents, mortgage interest or gains from the sale of real estate (Block, 2002; Chan et al., 2003). From a taxation viewpoint, US REITs pay no corporate taxes provided that they distribute at least 90% of taxable income to unitholders who then pay tax at their individual tax rate (Block, 2002; Chan et al., 2003).

Comparatively, in Australia, REITs were initially shaped by the equitable principles of trust law generally and latterly by corporations and taxation legislation specifically. Australian REITs have comparatively few criteria to fulfil, with the nature of investment determined by those investments authorised under a financial services licence (Booth, 2006). From a taxation viewpoint, Australian REITs pay no corporate taxes provided that they distribute all relevant income to unitholders who then pay tax at their individual tax rate (Booth, 2006).

With REITs now existing not only in the US and Australia but also growing across Asia and emerging in Europe, the range of differing laws, regulations and rules for the REIT sector in the respective countries is vast and beyond the scope of this book to address. Readers seeking further detail of REIT laws, regulations and rules in those countries with an active REIT sector are referred to the comprehensive overview provided by Rachel Booth in *Real Estate Investment Trusts: A Global Analysis* (2006).

In addition to the common feature of some form of beneficial tax treatment, REITs across the world are also gradually converging on more transparent governance while gradually diverging on the nature of REIT models developed.

1.2.1 Transparency in governance

While there is a trend to greater transparency in the governance of entities listed on stock exchanges around the world, the details of acceptable levels of transparency vary significantly between countries.

For the purposes of this book, a high level of transparency in governance is assumed though it is acknowledged that this may be in excess of the level required in certain jurisdictions. In this sense, the level of openness and explicitness in the principles of real estate investment decision making outlined in this book may be considered aspirational targets rather than a required threshold in some countries.

1.2.2 *REIT models*

The variety of REIT models developed is only limited by investment banker creativity, investor demand and local jurisdictional laws, regulations and rules. REIT models have evolved around the world to provide a wide range of combinations of focus, sector and geography.

REITs may focus on being real estate owners and/or real estate developers and/or real estate fund managers and may be internally managed or externally managed. Similarly, REITs may be sector specific and provide real estate investment opportunities in established sectors such as office, retail and industrial real estate as well as emerging sectors such as healthcare, self-storage and prison real estate. Further, REITs may be city specific, state specific, country specific or international real estate investors. Conversely, REITs may be diversified and provide real estate investment opportunities in more than one sector and/or more than one geography.

For the purposes of this book, it is not proposed to consider a specific REIT focus, sector or geography but to outline the principles of the real estate investment decision making process that may be capable of application by any REIT focus, sector or geography.

1.2.3 *REITs: summary*

The REIT sectors in the US, Australia, Asia and Europe are continuously evolving at such a pace that a fully up to date understanding may only be maintained through daily monitoring of the financial media and the reports of global investment banking houses such as UBS and Morgan Stanley.

The exponential development of REIT sectors around the world over the last half century has resulted in a level of variety of REITs globally that is beyond consideration in this book. Accordingly, therefore, this book seeks to focus on the principles of REIT real estate investment decision making that may be capable of application by any variety of REIT.

1.3 Preparing Phase

The Preparing Phase comprises the:

- **Envisioning Stage** – in which the REIT clearly articulates its destination together with a high order route map by which to get to the destination and some measurable outcomes to determine whether or not the REIT has arrived at the destination (considered in detail in this chapter); and the
- **Planning Stage** – in which the REIT converts its destination into the identification of a target list of specific real estate assets for potential

acquisition that meet the stock selection criteria and may be mis-priced (considered in detail in Chapter 2).

Accordingly, on completion of the Preparing Phase, the REIT has articulated where it is going and how it is going to get there, providing unitholders with a clear understanding of the risk-return profile to expect from the managers investment of their funds. The REIT is then positioned to undertake the second Phase of the REIT real estate investment decision making process, the Transacting Phase, which then leads to the third and final Phase, the Observing Phase, of the real estate investment decision making process.

1.4 Envisioning Stage

This chapter outlines the Envisioning Stage of the REIT real estate investment decision making process comprising the Steps of development of a Vision, Goals, Style, Strategic Plan and Objectives for the REIT.

The Envisioning Stage may be conceptualised through the conversation between Alice and the Cheshire Cat:

> *'Would you tell me, please, which way I ought to go from here?'*
>   *'That depends a good deal on where you want to get to,'*
>   *said the Cat.*
> *'I don't much care where-' said Alice.*
>   *'Then it doesn't matter which way you go,' said the Cat.*
> *'-so long as I get* somewhere,' *Alice added as an explanation.*
>   *'Oh, you're sure to do that,' said the Cat, 'if you only*
>   *walk enough.'*
>
>   (Carroll, 1999)

In the context of REITs, Garrigan and Parsons (1997) succinctly note:

> *'The management of a modern real estate operating company creates an entirely different dynamic than that of a passively managed group of properties.'*

Such differences may be manifest in two essential features of REITs that distinguish them from unlisted real estate portfolios or directly held real estate assets:

- the REIT is a **corporate and/or trust entity** which is more than a portfolio of properties or an individual property. The REIT brings together not only the real estate portfolio but also specialist management skills, capital budgeting expertise and a range of other corporate activities into an operating business. Accordingly, the REIT as a business should be capable of generating synergistic value in excess of that of the carried assets, recognised by the market through the REIT trading at a premium to the net value of its real estate portfolio; and
- as a **listed entity**, the REIT has a standard of transparency and accountability comparable to other listed entities and potentially considerably greater than that for unlisted entities. Further, unlike unlisted entities or individual properties where unit pricing might be monthly, quarterly or annually, a REIT is priced by the minute through the stock market as an indicator of the success or otherwise of the operating business.

By undertaking the Envisioning Stage, the REIT is able to focus resources on activities that will contribute to attaining its Vision, operating as an effective business and providing investors with confidence through defined direction and demonstrably measurable Goals which should be positive for the REIT's unit price. As Goleman (1999) observes:

> '*An organisational mission statement serves an emotional function: articulating the shared sense of goodness that allows us to feel what we do together is worthwhile.*'

and

> '*Clarity about an organisation's values, spirit, and mission leads to a decisive self-confidence in corporate decision making.*'

though care is required to avoid 'decisive self-confidence' being undermined by behavioural influences such as biases and irrational preferences, or by being unable to deal with complexity where more than three or four variables require simultaneous consideration (Pyhrr et al., 1989).

However, by undertaking the Envisioning Stage explicitly, the REIT faces a conundrum. On the one hand, if every REIT is explicit about its Vision, Goals and Strategic Plan, competitive advantage may be at risk. On the other hand, relative to the stock market as a whole, the REIT sector is small and individual REITs may benefit from homogeneity and only a minor point of difference (Geltner et al., 2007).

Also, knowing where other REITs are planning to go provides boundaries for the development of Goals and minimises the business risk of sub-optimal decisions (Baum, 2002), with the repeated statement of Vision and Goals by all REITs providing each with an incentive to achieve as failure is public (Hudson-Wilson and Wurtzebach, 1994).

On completion of the Envisioning Stage, the REIT should have a clearly articulated destination together with a high order route map by which to get to the destination and some measurable outcomes to determine whether or not the REIT has arrived at the destination.

Having completed the Envisioning Stage, the REIT then moves into the Planning Stage of the REIT real estate investment decision making process comprising the Steps of development of the Property Portfolio Strategy, Strategic Asset Allocation, Tactical Asset Allocation, Stock Selection and Asset Identification, considered in Chapter 2.

Completion of the Envisioning Stage and the Planning Stage mark the completion of the first of the three Phases, the Preparing Phase, wherein the REIT articulates where it is going and how it is going to get there, providing unitholders with a clear understanding of the risk-return profile to expect from the managers investment of their funds.

Accordingly, by end of this chapter, reader should understand:

- the **interdependency** between a REIT's Vision and investment management Style;
- the **interpretative process** by which a REIT's Vision is converted into action through Goals and the Strategic Plan; and
- the key role of Objectives in **aligning employee motivation and performance** with the attainment of the REIT's Vision.

1.5 People

The Envisioning Stage is principally undertaken by the REIT Governing Entity, the CEO, CFO and the Fund Management Team. As with any major business enterprise, the Support Teams of HR and IT underpin all aspects of the business and so are also considered in this chapter.

In common with other major business enterprises, some REIT models and sizes may suit certain roles being outsourced where the laws, regulation and rules in that jurisdiction permit. The decision to use outsourced service providers or in-house staff is usually based on a broad range of considerations including:

- **cost** – outsourced service provider costs may be substantial in terms of fees, some of which may be recoverable from tenants and other parties. However, the remuneration and on-costs for in-house staff in terms of HR, IT, workspace and so forth together with costs associated with staff turnover may also be substantial;

- **control** – the use of outsourced service providers may result in an actual or perceived loss of control by a REIT compared to the use of in-house staff;
- **management** – the management and motivation of outsourced service providers may be challenging to achieve due to the extent of intermediaries relative to an employer/employee relationship;
- **communication** – balancing the amount, quality and timeliness of information provision to decision makers within the REIT by an outsourced service provider relative to in-house staff;
- **expertise** – considering the nature of skills required and the extent to which such skills are required on an ongoing basis may favour use of an outsourced service provider or in-house staff;
- **flexibility** – the cost and time taken to address underperformance and to replace non-performers may vary between outsourced service providers and in-house staff; and
- **conflict of interest** – the use of outsourced service providers may result in an actual or perceived conflict of interest by a REIT compared to the use of in-house staff.

As individual situations differ, there is no simple guide to the decision whether to use outsourced service providers or in-house staff. Generally, a REIT may be expected to use a combination of outsourced service providers and in-house staff with the proportion varying over time as the REIT grows in size and/or complexity.

1.5.1 Governing Entity

The term Governing Entity has been adopted for the purposes of this book to acknowledge that, despite the wide diversity of governance structures adopted by REITs in different jurisdictions around the world, each has a person or a group that, ultimately, provides governance to the REIT concerning the real estate investment decision making process.

In the US, a Governing Entity may be the Trustee(s) or Director(s) whereas, in Australia, a Governing Entity may be the Manager or Responsible Entity (Booth, 2006). While specific requirements for and obligations of a Governing Entity will vary depending on local law, regulations and rules, there are some generic requirements for and obligations of a Governing Entity which may be commonly applicable in most jurisdictions and which are considered in this chapter. Further, the Governing Entity will be assumed to be a body of people (such as a board or committee) rather than an individual person, though the principles considered may be applicable to both.

For the purposes of this book, a high level of transparency in governance is assumed though it is acknowledged that this may be in excess of that level required in certain jurisdictions. In this sense, the level of openness and explicitness in the principles of real estate investment decision making outlined in this book may be considered aspirational targets rather than a required threshold in some countries.

The role of the REIT Governing Entity is to represent the interests of unitholders, with the principal purpose of the role being to focus on the future while overseeing the present and the scope of the role comprising the entire business, including all funds and portfolios.

The REIT Governing Entity usually reports to the unitholders in the REIT, with the direct report comprising the CEO. The principal contribution of the REIT Governing Entity is stewardship, with the functions of the role including:

- **effective corporate governance** – ensuring the maintenance of high standards of accountability, transparency, independence and effectiveness through an appropriately sized governance group with skills, age and gender diversity and complementarity and an appropriate mix of independent, non-executive and executive members. The Governing Entity should not replicate the real estate skills or other skills of management and should contribute skills in governance, business, strategy, finance and law to ensure a range of perspectives, representation of REIT constituencies and representation of the interests of unitholders. The Governing Entity also appoints, works with, retains, motivates and removes the CEO, with an obligation to ensure qualified management and a management succession plan;
- **focus on the future** – the Governing Entity evolves the Vision for the future direction of the REIT, from which the Goals, Strategic Plan and Objectives are developed. Consistent with a focus on the future, the Governing Entity works closely with the CEO on corporate activity, including mergers, acquisitions, making bids and responding to bids;
- **oversight of the present** – with a particular emphasis on risk management, the Governing Entity supervises operations through management reporting and the appointment of Committees to identify risk areas, require policy development for approval, implementation and monitoring in order to ensure compliance with relevant laws, regulations and rules for areas such as occupational health and safety and environmental issues. Consistent with a focus on the future, the Governing Entity also monitors government policy and real estate industry trends for emerging risk management issues such as green building regulation or carbon pricing law;
- **monitor solvency** – monitoring of monthly management accounts and cash flow together with consideration and approval of annual statutory accounts and appointment of and receipt of the report of the external auditor. The Governing Entity is generally responsible for the statement of fair value of assets in the accounts of the REIT under International

Financial Reporting Standards and so should be closely involved with the appraisal policy for all investment real estate assets including the basis and frequency of appraisal and independence of the appraiser;

- **continuous disclosure** – the Governing Entity should ensure full disclosure of information to relevant stakeholders, including the approval of the annual report and the conduct of the annual general meeting. With the increasing concentration of unitholder power in institutional investors and growing activism of small unitholders world-wide, the annual general meeting, media releases and continuous communication are ideal opportunities to engage with and enfranchise unitholders; and

- **setting values and shaping culture** – the Governing Entity sets the values of the REIT and determines acceptable levels for ethical conduct in areas such as honesty, fiduciary responsibility, prudence, care and diligence, acting in the best interests of unitholders, conflict of interest, related party transactions, alignment of the interests of management and unitholders, openness and transparency, insider trading, giving and receiving gifts, government relations and so forth, usually through the development and communication of a code of ethics, values statement or similar clear, written commitment (Garrigan and Parsons, 1997; Jarchow, 1988).

Tricker (1994) conceptualises the complex interactions involved in effective REIT governance as requiring the balancing of outward and inward roles (such as the outward provision of accountability role, as well as the inward monitoring and supervising role) with backwards/compliance and forwards/performance roles (such as the backward/compliance role of monitoring and supervising, the forward/performance role of policy making), with the central interaction for effective REIT governance being a positive working relationship between the Governing Entity and the CEO, as illustrated in Figure 1.3.

While there is no simple formula to ensure such a positive working relationship, which is heavily dependent on the personalities of the participants, the prospects for a positive working relationship are enhanced where there is a clear understanding of the respective roles and responsibilities, mutual respect, sharing of knowledge and expertise and open and honest communication between the participants.

1.5.2 *Chief Executive Officer (CEO)*

The role of the REIT Chief Executive Officer is to manage the REIT as a business, with the principal purpose of the role being to optimise unitholder returns and the scope of the role comprising the entire business, including all funds and portfolios.

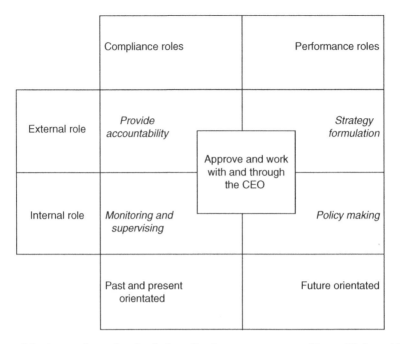

Figure 1.3 Interactions involved in effective governance. From Tricker (1994). *International Corporate Governance: Text, Readings and Cases* (Figure 4.1, p.149). © 1994 Prentice Hall Asia, a Pearson company. Reproduced by permission.

The CEO usually reports to the Governing Entity, with direct reports including the CFO and each of the Support Team, Investor Interface Team and Fund Management Team.

The principal contribution of the CEO is the development of the Vision for the REIT as a whole, in consultation with the Governing Entity, with the functions of the role including:

- being the **public face** of the REIT comprising the management of the interface with unitholders, the financial markets and the capital markets (with a focus on equity capital management), both through management of the Investor Interface Team and through direct involvement including media activities and unitholder, banker and regulator presentations;
- leadership of the business and regular communication with all REIT staff to imbue a **common sense of purpose** and develop a REIT-wide commitment to deliver the Vision, Goals, Strategic Plan and Objectives;
- management of the finance, fund management, HR and IT aspects of the business through the **management of the CFO, Support Teams and Fund Management Team** direct reports;
- monitoring of all aspects of **risk management and compliance** through membership of the relevant compliance and investment committees;

- making **recommendations to the Governing Entity** on REIT acquisitions, disposals, large transactions and major capital expenditure consistent with achieving the REIT's Goals and thus attaining its Vision; and
- periodic **management reporting** at the REIT level to the Governing Entity.

Reflecting the evolution of REITs, the nature of the REIT CEO role tends to be clearest at the extreme. Where a REIT is associated with an entrepreneur who is the sole decision maker as CEO at one extreme and where a major international REIT with a CEO who controls a massive global management structure is at the other extreme, the role of the CEO is clear. However, for those REITs in transition from an entrepreneur structure to a corporate structure, for those REITs growing or contracting rapidly or for those REITs facing some form of major change or transformation, the nature of the CEO role may fall between the two extremes and so be far less clear.

1.5.3 Chief Financial Officer (CFO)

The role of the REIT Chief Financial Officer is to manage the financial affairs of the REIT, with the principal purpose of the role being to maintain solvency and the scope of the role comprising the entire business, including all funds and portfolios.

The CFO usually reports to the CEO, with direct reports including the Compliance and Risk Management Team together with accounting, internal audit, finance, treasury and tax managers as well as being the point of contact for the REIT's external, independent auditors.

The principal contribution of the CFO is the provision of financial transparency, with the functions of the role including:

- management of **accounting for all purposes** including management accounts, statutory accounts, taxation and payroll at the REIT, fund, portfolio and property levels and budgeting, forecasting, performance measurement and analysis at the REIT level;
- management of **reporting** at the REIT, fund, portfolio and property levels;
- **capital management** with a focus on debt management (but including equity management), distribution management, capital budgeting and capital raising together with relationship management with major lenders and institutional investors;
- **cash management, currency management** and **derivatives management** for foreign exchange and interest rate management;
- **risk management** and **compliance** management including supervision of internal auditors and external, independent auditors and insurance together with management of the Compliance and Risk Management Team; and

- **corporate real estate management** including the REIT's own offices, data centres and so forth.

Given the REIT-wide view of the business held, the CFO is often the second highest ranking executive in the REIT management team after the CEO and so may also be the Deputy CEO or Acting CEO in the CEO's absence.

1.5.4 Support Teams

The role of the REIT Support Teams is to provide the infrastructure necessary for the REIT to operate as a business, with the principal purpose of the roles being to provide human resources (HR) and information technology (IT) services to the business and the scope of the roles comprising the entire business, including all funds and portfolios.

The HR Team usually reports to the CEO without any direct reports but with responsibility for managing a range of external service providers including recruitment consultants, remuneration consultants, training providers and so forth.

The principal contribution of the HR Team is the administration of people within the business, with the functions of the role including:

- **recruitment, development, promotion** and **termination** of employees;
- design and administration of the REIT **remuneration policy** including base salary levels, short and long term incentive packages, stock ownership incentive packages and perquisites, to align the Objectives of employees with the Goals of the REIT and the motivations of the differing personality types of employees in the various Teams;
- maintenance of **employee records** including development and maintenance of position descriptions to clearly define roles, responsibilities and expectations;
- co-ordinating a periodic cycle of individual employee **performance plans** and performance reviews, to align the Objectives of employees, the Goals of the REIT and the REIT remuneration policy and to promote employee productivity, satisfaction and retention;
- design and management of employee **development programmes**, including continuing professional development for role specific learning, training programmes for generic skills development, graduate rotation programmes, career track enhancement initiatives and so forth; and
- design and administration of all relevant **HR policies** including occupational health and safety, equity and so forth.

The IT Team usually reports to the CEO without any direct reports but with responsibility for managing a range of external service providers including software developers, hardware providers, recovery specialists and so forth.

The principal contribution of the IT Team is the administration of technology within the business, with the functions of the role including provision and maintenance of:

- **hardware** infrastructure for the business locally, nationally and internationally on an interconnected, current time basis;
- **software** infrastructure for the business including generic packages for word processing, spreadsheeting, email and so forth for all employees as well as specific packages such as SAP™ for the CFO's team, Peoplesoft™ for the HR Team, DYNA™ for the Portfolio Management Team etc.;
- **databases** for the business to suit specific requirements, including CRM packages for the Investor Interface Team, research databases for the Research Team and so forth;
- **security** for the IT system including the management of periodic back-up and offsite data centres;
- the REIT **website**, which is increasingly becoming the first point of contact with a REIT for many stakeholders as well as being a repository of vast amounts of REIT specific information for both external and internal users; and
- **telephony**, video conferencing and related technology applications.

In common with many major business enterprises, the contribution of Support Teams is often both invisible and undervalued, with greater attention paid to a Support Team when something occasionally goes wrong rather than when most things usually go right.

1.5.5 Fund Management Team

The role of the Fund Management Team is to manage the respective funds comprising the REIT, with the principal purpose of the role being to optimise the risk-return balance at the fund level and the scope of the role usually comprising either one or a small number of funds per fund manager.

The Fund Management Team usually reports to the CEO, with direct reports including the Portfolio Management Teams for the respective portfolios within the funds comprising the REIT.

The principal contribution of the Fund Management Team is the selection of investment management Style and development of the Goals and Strategic Plan, in consultation with the CEO and CFO, for each of the respective funds comprising the REIT, with the functions of the role including:

- business **planning** for each of the respective funds comprising the REIT;
- **budgeting and forecasting** at the fund level;

- **performance measurement** and analysis at the fund level;
- **capital management** at the fund level including equity, debt and cash management and capital expenditure management;
- **foreign exchange management** at the fund level, where relevant;
- **distribution management** at the fund level;
- periodic **management reporting** at the fund level to the CEO and Governing Entity; and
- **relationship management** with joint venture partners and co-owners, where necessary.

For a REIT comprising a number of funds, the position of the Fund Management Team is particularly challenging, requiring not only regard to the performance of individual funds but also regard to the performance of all other funds and the potential cumulative impact on the performance of the REIT as a whole.

1.5.6 People

Each of the Governing Entity, CEO, CFO, Support Teams and Fund Management Team are closely associated with the holistic process of the Envisioning Stage. The Governing Entity and the CEO determine the Vision for the REIT which then cascades down to the CEO, CFO and Fund Management Team to develop the Goals and Strategic Plan which, if achieved, will attain the Vision. Achievement of the Goals is then facilitated through achievement of the Objectives of each employee in the REIT facilitated by the requisite people and technology infrastructure provided by the Support Teams.

1.6 Vision

The first Step of the Envisioning Stage comprises the development of the Vision which is a public statement by the REIT, considered interdependently with Style, from which the Goals, Strategic Plan and Objectives of the REIT may then be developed. The Vision should be reviewed regularly but, in recognition of its long term nature, such review should not be more frequent than five yearly. The Vision for a REIT is developed by the Governing Entity with support from the CEO.

The Vision is a clear statement of where the REIT is going; usually being a qualitative statement of how the REIT intends to create value for unitholders, with both financial and non-financial emphases. The nature of a REIT as a real estate business usually results in a greater emphasis on the financial aspects rather than the non-financial aspects with some variation on wealth maximisation common.

An emphasis on wealth maximisation is consistent with the later Stages and Steps of the REIT real estate investment decision making process which focus on earning abnormal returns and the use of decision rules which lead to wealth maximisation. Wealth maximisation may be expressed in a variety of ways but usually focuses on an income return emphasis, a capital return emphasis or a total return emphasis pre-tax as, in most jurisdictions, post-tax wealth maximisation is then a matter for the unitholder rather than the REIT. Similarly, wealth maximisation may be expressed as an absolute concept or relative to something such as a benchmark or index.

Non-financial emphases in a REIT Vision may include intangible or psychological benefits such as the sense of security or self-esteem engendered by a REIT with a Vision to invest only in absolutely prime locations or in buildings only leased to tenants with the highest possible credit rating.

There should be a stated time horizon for the Vision which may be explicit (*'within ten years'*) or implicit (*'eventually'* or *'ultimately'* or expressed through the identified Goals). A stated time horizon is particularly important in the context of the stated risk-return relationship with a Vision emphasising short term, high risk, high return characterising a REIT very differently from a Vision emphasising long term, low risk, low return.

Reflecting the interdependence with Style, the Vision requires a risk framework. The Governing Entity, with support from the CEO, thoroughly considers the nature or types of risk and the level of risk that are acceptable to the REIT and develops a stated risk tolerance to underlie the Vision and which must be consistent with the nature of activities of the REIT.

Consistency is essential between the Vision and:

- **governance** – with the composition of the Governing Entity being consistent with the Vision. For example, a REIT with a Vision for steady returns from low risk investment may be consistent with a Governing Entity comprising older, reflective, low risk tolerance individuals whereas a REIT with a Vision for speculative returns from high risk development may be consistent with a Governing Entity comprising younger, more aggressive, high risk tolerance individuals;
- **values and culture** – with the Vision being consistent with the stated values and culture of the REIT. For example, a Vision to be a lean organisation may be inconsistent with stated values such as employee retention and a culture of employee participation; and
- **brand and image** – with the Vision being consistent with the brand and image of the REIT. For example, a brand or image that emphasised long term security may be inconsistent with a Vision focused on short term profit.

For a new REIT, the Vision may be developed without the constraints of an existing real estate portfolio or REIT management structure. However, where the REIT is operational, the Vision needs to be developed within the constraints of the existing real estate portfolio and REIT management structure.

Accordingly, the development of the Vision provides the REIT Governing Entity and CEO with another conundrum – the Vision should be aspirational whilst also being attainable with regard to the constraints of the existing real estate portfolio and REIT management structure. The REIT Governing Entity and CEO need to balance the expectations of unitholders and anticipated trends and changes that may affect the REIT's environment with the challenge of implementation through the capacity of the existing real estate portfolio and REIT management structure to deliver and their capacity for change management.

Bringing independent thinking and an objective mindset to the process, the REIT Governing Entity is able to have a dialogue with the CEO, listening and questioning, being cognisant of the REIT's competitive advantages and any parenting advantages that it may enjoy, before stepping back and forming an often relatively simply stated overview of the current environment in the context of which the Vision may be developed:

> *Confronting knowledgeable, experienced and committed organisational people with challenging questions in a receptive environment can be the conduit to (these) new strategic perspectives.*

and

> *'This needs to be coupled with new perspectives that prise open invisible but restricting assumptions that limit the organisation's growth, capability and field of vision'* (Management Today, March 2010).

Accordingly, the REIT's Vision provides a clear statement of where the REIT is going over a stated future period from which the Goals, Strategic Plan and Objectives can then be developed to transform the Vision into action and outcomes.

1.7 Style

Style is a public statement by the REIT, considered interdependently with the Vision, from which the Goals, Strategic Plan and Objectives of the REIT may be developed. Consistent with the Vision, Style should be reviewed regularly but not more frequently than five yearly. The Style adopted by a REIT is developed by the Fund Management Team with the support of the CEO and Governing Entity.

Style is a clear statement of the approach to real estate investment management to be adopted by the REIT reflecting the stated risk tolerance underlying the Vision. Style is usually expressed as a combination of generic Style (active or passive, top down or bottom up, value or growth) and specific Style (core, value added or opportunistic) often with little explanation of how the REIT interprets such generic and specific Style in the context of its own real estate investment management. Reflecting the interdependence of the Vision and Style, the stated time horizon for the Vision will generally also be applicable to Style.

1.7.1 *Active* vs. *passive*

An active Style of real estate investment management or a passive Style of real estate investment management is an expression of generic Style. A passive Style is an investment management style where a manager seeks to replicate or follow a benchmark or index and so approximate the risk-return of the benchmark or index. An active Style is an investment management style where the manager seeks to actively manage an individual investment or portfolio in order to add value and enhance returns above those achieved by a benchmark or index within a stated risk tolerance.

REIT real estate investment management is generally an active Style reflecting:

- the relative **informational inefficiency** of the real estate market and the ability to identify assets that offer the opportunity to earn abnormal returns; and
- the **heterogeneity** of the real estate market which limits the ability of a manager to construct a real estate portfolio that replicates a benchmark or index.

The key issue for attention then becomes the specific Style adopted by a REIT within a generic active Style, being either core, value added or opportunistic, which is considered further below.

The Style of REIT management as a form of investment management at the portfolio level should be distinguished from the Style of property asset management which may also be active or passive. In terms of property asset management, certain types of real estate investment suit a low-involvement or passive approach to property asset management by the investor, such as early and mid term ground leases or UK properties leased on 25-year full repairing and insuring leases. Conversely, certain types of real estate investment suit a high involvement or active approach to property asset management such as the implementation of transformational initiatives to enhance returns including refurbishment or partial redevelopment of a real estate investment.

1.7.2 *Top down* vs. *bottom up*

A top down Style of real estate investment management or a bottom up Style of real estate investment management is an expression of generic Style. A top down Style is an investment management Style where a manger sequentially considers the global economy, national economy, regional economies and local economies and then considers the global real estate market, national real estate market, regional real estate markets and local real estate markets to identify optimal geographic areas and/or real estate sectors for investment, then seeking assets within such areas and sectors for acquisition. A bottom up Style is an investment management Style where the manager seeks to specifically consider the investment attributes of a nominated individual asset and their acceptability as the basis for acquisition, potentially disregarding other than local economic and real estate market conditions.

REIT real estate investment management is generally a top down Style reflecting the portfolio focus of REIT real estate investment management. The distinction between a top down Style and a bottom up Style is central to the distinction between the management of the REIT as a portfolio of properties rather than as an amalgamation of individual property assets. Historically, REITs often evolved out of the real estate holdings of an individual or an entity which had generally been acquired with a greater emphasis on the individual property in a transactional approach (the '*art of the deal*'; Wurtzebach et al., 1994) rather than upon the portfolio impact, reflecting a bottom up Style. REITs have now evolved to focus primarily on the portfolio role of individual property assets with the top down Style permeating the entire REIT real estate investment decision making process through the Steps of Strategic Asset Allocation (wherein the entire real estate market is analysed through a range of risk-return lenses to identify target sectoral and geographic weightings), Tactical Asset Allocation (wherein target markets offering significant potential outperformace are identified) and Stock Selection (being the process of identifying portfolio asset criteria).

The key issue for attention then becomes the specific Style adopted by a REIT within a generic top down Style, being either core, value added or opportunistic, which is considered further below. It should be noted that an opportunistic Style may incorporate aspects of a bottom up Style, as an opportunistic Style places a greater emphasis on individual property opportunities within the framework of the REIT real estate investment decision making process.

1.7.3 *Value* vs. *growth*

A value Style of real estate investment management or a growth Style of real estate investment management is an expression of generic Style. A value Style is an investment management Style where the manger consistently

Table 1.2 Principal characteristics of specific Styles.

Features/Style	Core	Value added	Opportunistic
Property type	Traditional	Mix between non-traditional and traditional	Mix between non-traditional and traditional
Asset size/ quality	Predominantly large, high quality	Mix between large and small and impaired assets	Mix between large, but predominantly small and impaired assets
Markets	Primary markets	Primary/secondary markets	Domestic and international markets
Diversity	Fully diversified	Limited diversification	Diversification is not a consideration
Leverage	None to low (0–30%)	Moderate – high (50–70%)	High – very high (70%+)
Income/capital component	Relatively high income component	Balance between income and capital	Relatively high capital component
Holding period	Multiple market cycles (at least one)	Generally limited to period for active management strategies to be implemented	Generally limited to period for active management strategies to be implemented

Source: de Francesco (2010). Reproduced by permission of IPD.

focuses on seeking assets that are significantly mis-priced and offer the potential for abnormal income, capital and/or total returns over a defined future timeframe. A growth Style is an investment management Style where the manager consistently focuses on constructing a portfolio comprising assets that offer the potential for growing income, capital and/or total returns over an undefined but usually longer future timeframe.

REIT real estate investment management is generally a growth Style reflecting the focus on the portfolio, though Tactical Asset Allocation may include elements of a value Style. The key issue for attention then becomes the specific Style adopted by a REIT within a generic growth Style, being either core, value added or opportunistic, which is considered further below.

1.7.4 Core, value added and opportunistic

Core, value added and opportunistic Styles of real estate investment management are expressions of specific Style. Reflecting the relatively recent adoption of terms for specific Style in real estate investment management, the definitions of core, value added and opportunistic vary with one interpretation of the principal characteristics provided in Table 1.2.

Core Style

A core Style seeks to provide a risk adjusted return that is approximately equal to the market but through the holding of only a small portfolio of high quality properties with limited leverage. Outperformance may be generated within a core Style through the acquisition of individual assets with high risk adjusted returns but low correlation with other assets in the portfolio (Pagliari, 1995).

Value added Style
Sometimes also referred to as the *core plus Style*, the value added Style seeks to achieve outperformance by identifying opportunities to add value using mixed quality real estate assets and moderate leverage. This may include selecting markets where development to address undersupply may generate outperformance or individual assets where transformation refurbishment, remodelling or focused, active asset management may generate outper-formance (Pagliari, 1995).

Opportunistic Style
The opportunistic Style to generating outperformance includes a wide spectrum of multiplicative risk approaches including higher risk real estate assets and greater leverage. These may range from identifying opportunities arising from the prospect of reletting partial vacancy in a building to a con-trarian approach of acquiring empty buildings in temporarily over-supplied markets where confident of long term economic growth (Pagliari, 1995).

1.7.5 Style

Having developed the Vision to provide a clear statement of where the REIT is going over a stated future period and adopted an interdependent Style reflecting the stated risk tolerance underlying the Vision, the REIT is now in a position to develop the Goals, Strategic Plan and Objectives that will transform the Vision through the Style into action and outcomes.

1.8 Goals

Goals are a public statement by the REIT, consistent with the Vision and the Style, from which the Strategic Plan and Objectives of the REIT may be developed. Goals should be reviewed regularly during the life of the Vision to ensure continued relevance with review every two to three years optimal. Goals for a REIT are developed by the CEO and the Fund Management Team.

Goals are stated measures or steps of significance to which management efforts are directed and which, if achieved, will attain the Vision. The Goals are usually a quantitative statement of the Vision and so mirror the contents of the Vision. Accordingly, if the Vision has a financial emphasis, the Goals will be quantitative financial measures such as a target level of return, target relative to a benchmark or index or a specified risk tolerance, such as a target for volatility of returns. If the Vision has a non-financial emphasis, the Goals will be quantitative non-financial measures such as the proportion of portfolio revenue from highest credit rating tenants.

To be effective, Goals should be:

- **relevant** – demonstrating a clear alignment with the Vision so that the achievement of Goals can clearly be seen to contribute to the attainment of the Vision;
- **few** – being up to around six Goals, facilitating clear focus on those matters which are critical for achievement if the REIT is to attain its Vision;
- **independent** – being capable of individual achievement without one Goal being dependent on another and with care required to avoid conflict between Goals;
- **clear** – unequivocal, simple, succinct statements that are not open to misinterpretation;
- **measurable** – capable of easy and indisputable quantification;
- **attributable** – providing clarity as to whom within the REIT management team will be responsible for achievement;
- **timely** – having a specified time horizon within which achievement is required, acknowledging that all years are not going to be the same, that specific risk exists through the properties comprising the portfolio and that appraisal timing has an impact on performance;
- **marketable** – being framed to provide confidence to investors and the market;
- **achievable** – while providing a challenge to management to achieve, Goals should not be manifestly unachievable or they will be disregarded by management and become counter-productive; and
- **manageable** – being capable of dissection by management and interpretation as Objectives which, if achieved, will achieve the Goal (Baum, 2002).

Given the relative longevity of Goals, care is required to avoid deviation from stated Goals in the development and implementation of the Strategic Plan and Objectives. An apparent need to reshape the Strategic Plan or Objectives to achieve something other than specified Goals is usually indicative of a change in the REIT environment, warranting a review of the continued relevance of the achievement of the stated Goals to the attainment of the Vision.

In the event that the Goals include financial measures such as a target level of return relative to a benchmark or index, clarity is required in the choice of benchmark or index to ensure relevance in composition and the time period over which measurement is to occur having regard to the status of the REIT relative to those other REITs comprising the benchmark or index. Further, consideration should be given to the choice of a specific numeric Goal (such as a return of 100 basis points above a nominated index) or a Goal specified as a relative measure (such as a return within the top quartile of a nominated index). In each case, a Goal concerning a clear statement of risk tolerance is also required for effective risk-return management.

Having developed a clear Vision and a small number of specified Goals, the REIT is now in a position to develop a Strategic Plan and Objectives to achieve the Goals and so attain the Vision.

> A survey of 215 commercial real estate investment groups in Sweden found their top three ranking goals to be long term return on equity, value appreciation and regular return on equity. (Brzeski et al., 1993)

1.9 Strategic Plan

The Strategic Plan is a public statement by the REIT, consistent with and outlining the pathway to the Goals, through the Style to the Vision. The Strategic Plan, developed by the Fund Management Team, should be reviewed regularly, consistent with the Goals which it seeks to achieve, with review every two to three years optimal.

The Strategic Plan provides a route map to the achievement of Goals by the REIT, being based on the rational analysis of alternative routes in the context of the REIT's current and expected environments. Reflecting the evolution of the REIT sector, several strategic models have developed which may provide a template for the REIT Strategic Plan, such that a REIT may need to undertake part or all of the strategic planning process.

1.9.1 Strategic models

With REITs having now operated in various countries around the world for over 40 years, a series of strategic models have evolved as summarised by Geltner et al. (2007):

- **financial strategic model** – by seeking capital more often from the market in order to grow, being a strategic model that suits a capital intensive industry such as real estate;
- **specialisation strategic model** – being the choice between sector or geographic specialisation and diversification;

- **vertical integration strategic model** – also known as the development strategy and the funds management strategy, whereby the REIT seeks to control and derive returns from all stages of the real estate lifecycle including land acquisition, real estate development, part or whole transaction into a related fund, ongoing management, leasing and so forth within either the REIT or a related fund;
- **economy of scale strategic model** – where a REIT seeks to grow larger to benefit from lower operating costs and lower costs of capital, being particularly effective for sector specialised REITs;
- **branding strategic model** – building a brand name recognition and reputation among the REIT's space using customers, also being particularly effective for sector specialised REITs; and
- **power in the space market strategic model** – where a REIT uses its size and access to capital to corner a market by concentrating its space ownership within a geographically confined space market and so has market power as the dominant space owner.

Depending on the environment surrounding a REIT at a given point in time, one of the above strategic models may provide a template for the REIT Strategic Plan.

1.9.2 Strategic planning process

The Strategic Plan provides a route map to the achievement of Goals by the REIT, being based on the rational analysis of alternative routes in the context of the REIT's current and expected environments.

Strategic environment

A comprehensive and detailed analysis of the strategic environment will determine exactly where the REIT is now, providing an assessment of current and potential issues facing the REIT in a wide range of different dimensions, for comparison to where the REIT wants to be to achieve its Goals and so attain its Vision.

A variety of popular management tools are commonly used to analyse the strategic environment including a SWOT analysis (identifying the REITs strengths, weaknesses, opportunities and threats), consideration of Porter's five forces (being competitive rivalry, barriers to entry, threat of substitutes, customer power and supplier power; Porter, 1994), together with other tools such as balanced scorecard, core competence agenda, value chain analysis and moral purpose framework. The use of external consultants with strategic planning expertise may facilitate discussion and self-examination in the strategic planning process, leading to a more objective view and encourage '*out of left field thinking*' by management which should be rewarded where productive.

Such analysis should provide a clear understanding of the current internal and external environment of the REIT together with the potential future internal and external environment facing the REIT. The REIT's current internal environment, being issues such as employee skill levels or availability of capital, may impact the REIT's strategic planning with critical self-assessment by the REIT, particularly around issues of culture and values, being an essential foundation for strategic planning.

Similarly, the current external environment, being issues such as the state of the economy or the real estate market for a particular sector, may also impact the REIT's strategic planning. By then analysing the potential future internal and external environments, the REIT may also identify a range of factors in the short to medium term future that may have an impact on the strategic planning process such as the potential availability of certain types of investment real estate for acquisition or the potential for legislative change impacting the REIT.

Strategic alternatives

Having clearly established the current environment, being where the REIT is now and the Vision, being where the REIT wants to go, the REIT management team has a starting point and end point for the journey and now needs to determine the optimal route, being usually one route from a range of possible routes which each offer differing advantages and disadvantages.

For an existing REIT portfolio, the identification of the optimal route for strategic planning needs to accommodate individual projects already underway and current or anticipated property specific issues. For example, if a redevelopment project is partially complete or a whole building lease to a major tenant is due for renewal in six months' time, these issues cannot be disregarded in the strategic planning process and must be accommodated in the identification of the optimal route. Similarly, the choice of the optimal route may be influenced by medium term expectations such as upcoming major capital expenditure for plant replacement or the impact of a competing development.

In order to determine the optimal route, the use of scenario analysis is common whereby a range of distinctly different but plausible potential routes or strategic alternatives are identified as scenarios for individual assessment. Each scenario may be initially assessed by testing against the following five criteria:

- **comprehensibility** – being whether the strategic alternative can be clearly understood;
- **appropriateness** – being the extent of fit with the Goals and Vision;
- **sustainability** – including economic, environmental and social responsibility;

- **feasibility** – being the readiness and ability of the REIT to implement the strategic alternative; and
- **accountability** – being the ability for quantitative and qualitative reporting and accountability mechanisms to be developed for the strategic alternative.

Such initial testing may result in the range of strategic alternatives being narrowed to, ideally, two or three for detailed analysis through cash flow modelling at the REIT level. By testing the impact on earnings, distributions, debt covenants and so forth, each remaining strategic alternative may be analysed and the optimal strategic alternative derived.

Before adoption, the optimal strategic alternative should be further analysed through sensitivity analysis, whereby key inputs are varied and the sensitivity of earnings, distributions, debt covenants and so forth, monitored. Such sensitivity analysis is commonly based on three possible states for the REIT, being the most likely, optimistic and pessimistic, with attached probabilities.

Accordingly, in developing the Strategic Plan at the REIT level through the selection of the optimal strategic alternative, the strategic planning process considers the return outcomes of each strategic alternative in the context of the risk profile resulting and the extent to which each may be consistent with and likely to achieve the REITs Goals and so attain the REIT's Vision.

1.9.3 Strategic Plan

Having considered the applicability of strategic models and undertaken the strategic planning process, the REIT has developed a Strategic Plan which provides a route map to the achievement of Goals by the REIT.

With a clear Vision and a small number of specified Goals capable of being achieved through the Strategic Plan, the REIT is now in a position to develop Objectives with which to align REIT management executive motivations with fulfilment of the Strategic Plan.

1.10 Objectives

Unlike the Vision, Style, Goals and Strategic Plan which are public statements, Objectives are a non-public or internal statement by the REIT. Objectives should be reviewed annually or bi-annually in line with the performance plans of those REIT executives tasked with the achievement of the Objective in order to ensure alignment. Objectives are developed by the respective line managers and then discussed and agreed with each relevant REIT management executive as part of the periodic performance planning process administered by the HR Team.

With the Strategic Plan conceptualised as the route map to the achievement of Goals by the REIT, Objectives comprise the checkpoints along the route adopted. Unlike Goals, Objectives may be many but otherwise meet the same criteria for effectiveness including relevance, independence, clarity and so forth.

Objectives may be likely to be smaller, discrete items for achievement which, when fulfilled in aggregate across the REIT, achieve the stated Goals and which are capable of reward for achievement at the individual REIT management executive level. Accordingly, an individual REIT management executive may have a series of Objectives for which achievement results in satisfactory performance of the role and exceeding results in some form of remuneration linked incentive such as the payment of a bonus, as well as contributing to the achievement of a Goal at the REIT level.

In summary, therefore, achievement of Objectives by individual REIT management executives contributes to the fulfilment of the Strategic Plan which, in turn, results in the achievement of the stated Goals which, in turn, results in the attainment of the Vision. Thus, through the careful implementation of each Step in the Envisioning Stage, a REIT may align the motivations and actions of all employees with the attainment of its Vision.

1.11 Super REIT

The implementation of the Envisioning Stage may be illustrated by application to Super REIT, a $15 billion diversified REIT. As a large REIT, Super REIT considers itself to be a sector leader and reflects this in the development of its Vision:

> *'Super REIT's vision is to be the premier diversified REIT on the stock exchange.'*

As such, Super REIT's Vision is both aspirational and a qualitative statement, with *'premier'* being undefined and lacking either a financial or non-financial emphasis. Consistent with its risk tolerance and interdependent with its Vision, Super REIT's adopted generic Styles are active, top down and growth with its adopted specific Style being value added or core plus, reflecting its relatively large portfolio of good quality assets and moderate leverage of 40%.

Having adopted its Vision, Super REIT identifies four Goals to indicate how it intends to attain its Vision, having financial and non-financial emphases:

Goal 1   to be within the top quartile **return** performance of the stock exchange REIT index every year;

Goal 2   to be within the lowest **tracking error** quartile of REITs in the stock exchange index every year;

Goal 3   to be an **employer of choice** with five appropriate candidates for each career opportunity offered within two years; and

Goal 4   to be a **green real estate investor** with 25% of buildings in the portfolio green star rated within five years.

The principal Goal of top quartile return performance of the stock exchange REIT index every year is consistent with wealth maximisation which, when combined with Goal 2 concerning risk and the adopted Style, provides a stated time horizon and defines *'premier'* in the Vision in a financial context. Similarly, Goal 3 and Goal 4 define *'premier'* in a non-financial context. Accordingly, Super REIT may contend that the achievement of each of its stated Goals would result in the attainment of its Vision to be the premier diversified REIT on the stock exchange.

Having regard to its current portfolio, its current internal and external environment and its expectations about its future internal and external environment, Super REIT adopts an economy of scale strategic model and undertakes scenario analysis and sensitivity analysis to develop a Strategic Plan. Focusing on return optimisation at the REIT, portfolio and property level, measures for effective risk management at each level, steps to significantly improve the appeal of the REIT as an employer and a commitment to substantial capital expenditure to improve the environmental friendliness of several identified properties within the portfolio, the Strategic Plan includes a detailed strategy for each Goal committed to writing and supported by a large number of specified Objectives encompassing all REIT management executives in the respective Teams.

By way of example, the Objectives for the return optimisation aspects of the Strategic Plan include:

- budget debt interest cost reduction Objectives for members of the Fund Management Team;
- budget capital expenditure Objectives for members of the Portfolio Management Team;
- budget major rent review income Objectives for members of the Asset Management Team;
- budget net income Objectives for members of the Property Management Team; and
- energy cost reduction Objectives for members of the Facilities Management Team.

Each of which are linked to achievement in the performance planning process for the respective REIT management executives with exceeding achievement tied to a remuneration incentive.

Accordingly, if the members of the Property Management Team achieve their Objectives for budget net income this will help achieve the REIT Goal of being within the top quartile return performance of the stock exchange REIT index every year which, in turn, will help attain the Vision to be the premier diversified REIT on the stock exchange.

By replicating such a cascading approach from the Vision through the Goals, Strategic Plan and Objectives, Super REIT may effectively align the motivations and actions of all REIT management executives with the attainment of its Vision.

Having completed the Envisioning Stage, Super REIT has a clearly articulated destination together with a high order route map by which to get to the destination and some measurable outcomes to determine whether or not it has arrived at the destination. In order to convert its Vision into an identified target list of specific real estate assets for potential acquisition that meet the stock selection criteria and may be mis-priced, Super REIT must now embark on the Planning Stage of the REIT real estate investment decision making process.

1.12 Summary

While REITs may have an unusual legal or commercial structure to preserve their tax status and facilitate their tax effectiveness, they otherwise have much in common with other large business enterprises. The management structure of a large REIT resembles that of any other large business, with the exception of the sales and marketing and operational roles that have evolved into an investor interface role and the various line management roles involved in the fund level, portfolio level, asset level, property level and facility level management of the REIT portfolio.

The REIT real estate investment decision making process, whereby $1 of unitholder capital is converted into $1 of investment real estate, comprises three Phases, six Stages and 30 Steps. The first Phase is the Preparing Phase, comprising the Envisioning Stage (considered in this chapter) and the Planning Stage (considered in Chapter 2), with the second and third Phases comprising the Transacting Phase and the Observing Phase, respectively.

The Envisioning Stage comprises five sequential Steps, being Vision, Style, Goals, Strategic Planning and Objectives, whereby the REIT determines where it is going, how it is going to get there and how it will know when it has arrived at its destination. The Vision comprises an aspirational statement of a future state for the REIT, which is interdependent with the risk tolerance of the REIT expressed through the investment management

Style adopted. Key aspects of the Vision are translated into measurable outcomes through the identification of Goals to which management efforts may then be directed for achievement. Strategic Planning provides the link between the Vision and action through the identification of a range of activities which, when undertaken, will result in achievement of the Goals. Objectives then connect each REIT management executive with Goals through the Strategic Plan with defined responsibilities for achievement which are then recognised by remunerative reward.

Through undertaking the Envisioning Stage, the REIT creates a sequence of effective action whereby achievement of Objectives by individual REIT management executives contributes to fulfilment of the Strategic Plan which, in turn, achieves the Goals which then results in the Vision being attained for the REIT. Having completed the Envisioning Stage, the REIT has a clearly articulated destination together with a high order route map by which to get to the destination and some measurable outcomes to determine whether or not the REIT has arrived at the destination.

Completion of the Envisioning Stage positions the REIT to undertake the Planning Stage, wherein the REIT's Vision is converted into an identified target list of specific real estate assets for potential acquisition that meet the stock selection criteria and may be mis-priced.

Completion of the Envisioning Stage and the Planning Stage mark completion of the first of the three phases, the Preparing Phase, wherein the REIT articulates where it is going and how it is going to get there, providing unitholders with a clear understanding of the risk-return profile to expect from the manager's investment of their funds. This leads to the second phase of the REIT real estate investment decision making process, the Transacting Phase, completion of which then leads to the third and final phase, the Observing Phase, of the real estate investment decision making process.

1.13 Key points

- REITs are major **business enterprises** where the increasing dominance of institutional investors may be expected to pressure REIT managers to adopt more transparent, explicable and repeatable real estate investment decision making processes.
- REITs provide an **intermediation role** to unitise otherwise illiquid investment real estate, having unusual legal and commercial structures generally associated with the maintenance of their beneficial tax status.
- The **management structure** of REITs mirrors that of other major business enterprises but with operational line management functions reflecting the real estate investment management nature of the REIT business.

- The REIT real estate investment decision making process converts $1 of unitholder capital into $1 of investment real estate, comprising **three Phases, six Stages** and **30 Steps**.
- The first Phase of the REIT investment decision making process is the **Preparing Phase**, comprising the Envisioning Stage and the Planning Stage, followed by the Transacting Phase and the Observing Phase.
- The **Envisioning Stage** is a sequential process comprising the Steps of development of a Vision, adoption of an investment Style, identification of Goals and development of a Strategic Plan together with the specification of Objectives.
- Principal participants in the Envisioning Stage are the **Governing Entity**, **CEO**, **CFO**, **Support Teams** and the **Fund Management Team**, each contributing to the development of the REIT-wide Vision, Style, Goals and Strategic Plan.
- The **Vision** provides the foundation for all REIT activities and serves as the basis for development of strategic direction, being an aspirational statement for stakeholders and the market of where the REIT is going and how it intends to create value for unitholders.
- The investment management **Style** comprises the statement of risk tolerance for the REIT interdependent with and underlying the Vision, comprising a combination of generic and specific styles.
- **Goals** are stated measures or steps of significance to which the REIT management team efforts are directed and which, if achieved, will attain the Vision.
- The **Strategic Plan** is the route map to the achievement of Goals by the REIT.
- The **Objectives** are the checkpoints along the route map comprising the Strategic Plan, being linked to individual employee responsibility and remuneration.
- Achievement of Objectives will contribute to fulfilment of the Strategic Plan which, in turn, will achieve the Goals which will then result in **attaining the Vision** for the REIT.
- Completion of the Envisioning Stage may result in the REIT having a clearly articulated **destination** together with a **high order route map** by which to get to the destination and some measurable outcomes to determine whether or not the REIT has arrived at the destination.
- The Envisioning Stage is followed by the **Planning Stage**, where the REIT Vision is converted into an identified target list of specific real estate assets for potential acquisition that meet the stock selection criteria and may be mis-priced, with completion of the Envisioning Stage and the Planning Stage completing the first Phase, the Preparing Phase, so positioning the REIT to then enter the second Phase, the Transacting Phase.

References

Further information concerning issues considered in this chapter may be found in the following texts:

Baum, A.E. (2002) *Commercial Real Estate Investment*, Estates Gazette, London.

Block, R.L. (2002) *Investing in REITs*, Bloomberg Press, Princeton.

Booth, R. (ed.) (2006) *Real Estate Investment Trusts: A Global Analysis*, Globe Law and Business, London.

Brzeski, W. J., Jaffe, A. J. and Lundstrom, S. (1993) Institutional Real Estate Investment Practices: Swedish and United States Experiences, Journal of Real Estate Research, **8**(3), p.293.

Carroll, L. (1999) *Alice in Wonderland and Through the Looking Glass*, Wordsworth Classics, London.

Chan, S.H., Erickson, J. and Wang, K. (2003) *Real Estate Investment Trusts: Structure, Performance, and Investment Opportunities*, Oxford University Press, New York.

de Francesco, A. (2010) *The Role of Property Industry Research*, Pacific Rim Real Estate Society Conference, Wellington.

French, N. (2001) Decision Theory and Real Estate Investment: An Analysis of the Decision Making Processes of Real Estate Investment Fund Managers, *Managerial and Decision Economics*, **22**(7), p.399.

French, N. and French, S. (1997) Decision Theory and Real Estate Investment, *Journal of Property Valuation and Investment*, **15**(3), p.226.

Gallimore, P. and Gray, A. (2002) The Role of Investor Sentiment in Property Investment Decisions, *Journal of Property Research*, **19**(2), p.111.

Gallimore, P., Gray, A. and Hansz, J.A. (2000) *Sentiment in Property Investment Decisions: A Behavioural Perspective*, Pacific Rim Real Estate Society Conference, Sydney.

Gallimore, P., Hansz, J.A. and Gray, A. (2000a) Decision Making in Small Property Companies, *Journal of Property Investment and Finance*, **18**(6), p.602.

Garrigan, R.T. and Parsons, J.F.C. (Eds.) (1997) *Real Estate Investment Trusts*, McGraw Hill, New York.

Geltner, D.M., Miller, N.G., Clayton, J. and Eichholtz, P. (2007) *Commercial Real Estate Analysis and Investment*, Thomson South-Western, Mason.

Goleman, D. (1999) *Working With Emotional Intelligence*, Bloomsbury, London.

Hudson-Wilson, S. and Wurztebach, C. (1994) *Managing Real Estate Portfolios*, Irwin, Burr Ridge.

Jarchow, S.P. (1988) *Real Estate Investment Trusts*, John Wiley & Sons, Inc., New York.

MacCowan, R.J. and Orr, A.M. (2008) A Behavioural Study of the Decision Process Underpinning Disposals by Property Fund Managers, *Journal of Property Investment and Finance*, **26**(4), p.342.

Management Today (2010) *Management Today*, Australian Institute of Management, Eveleigh.

Pagliari, J.L. (ed.) (1995) *The Handbook of Real Estate Portfolio Management*, Irwin, Chicago.

Porter, M. (1994) *Competitive Strategy: Techniques for Analyzing Industries and Competitors*, The Free Press, New York.

Pyhrr, S.A., Cooper, J.R., Wofford, L.E., Kapplin, S.D. and Lapides, P.D. (1989) *Real Estate Investment: Strategy, Analysis, Decisions*, John Wiley & Sons, Inc., New York.

Roberts, C. and Henneberry, J. (2007) Exploring Office Investment Decision Making in Different European Contexts, *Journal of Property Investment and Finance*, **25**(3), p.289.

Roulac, S. (2001) *Stephen Roulac on Place and Property*, Property Press, California.

Tricker, R.I. (1994) *International Corporate Governance: Text Readings and Cases*, Prentice Hall, New York.

Wurtzebach, C.H., Miles, M.E. and Cannon, S.E. (1994) *Modern Real Estate*, John Wiley & Sons, Inc., New York.

2

Planning

Chapter 1 outlined the Envisioning Stage of the REIT real estate investment decision making process comprising the Steps of development of a Vision, Goals, Style, Strategic Plan and Objectives for the REIT. On completion of this Stage, the REIT should have a clearly articulated destination together with a high order route map by which to get to the destination and some measurable outcomes to determine whether or not the REIT has arrived at the destination.

Having completed the Envisioning Stage, Super REIT has developed a Vision to be the premier diversified REIT on the stock exchange, interdependent with its adopted generic and specific investment management Style which is active, top down, growth and value added, respectively. To attain this Vision, Super REIT has identified four Goals including to be within the top quartile return performance with lowest quartile tracking error of the stock exchange REIT index every year. Consistently, Super REIT's Strategic Plan focuses on return optimisation at the REIT, portfolio and property level together with effective risk management, supported by a large number of specified Objectives encompassing all REIT management executives in the respective teams and so aligning the motivations and actions of all REIT management executives with the attainment of Super REIT's Vision.

The REIT now enters the Planning Stage of the REIT real estate investment decision making process which is the subject of this chapter. The Planning Stage comprises the Steps of development of the Property Portfolio Strategy, Strategic Asset Allocation, Tactical Asset Allocation, Stock Selection and Asset Identification.

Completion of the Planning Stage may result in the conversion of the REIT's Vision into the identification of a target list of specific real estate

Global Real Estate Investment Trusts: People, Process and Management,
First Edition. David Parker.
© 2011 David Parker. Published 2011 by Blackwell Publishing Ltd.

assets for potential acquisition that meet the Stock Selection criteria and may be mis-priced, leading into the Dealing Stage of the REIT investment decision making process, which is considered in the next chapter.

Completion of the Envisioning Stage and the Planning Stage mark completion of the first of the three phases, the Preparing Phase, wherein the REIT articulates where it is going and how it is going to get there, providing unitholders with a clear understanding of the risk-return profile to expect from the manager's investment of their funds.

This leads to the second phase of the REIT real estate investment decision making process, the Transacting Phase, which then leads to the third and final phase, the Observing Phase, of the real estate investment decision making process.

Accordingly, by the end of this chapter, the reader should understand:

- the **conceptual and practical issues** involved in converting a REIT's Vision into a Property Portfolio Strategy capable of implementation;
- the rational and logical approach required of a **fiduciary** to the process of identifying potential assets for acquisition;
- the relevance of **modern portfolio theory** to Strategic Asset Allocation and the role of the Capital Asset Pricing Model in the pricing process of real estate assets;
- the significance of achieving acceptable risk adjusted returns in Tactical Asset Allocation, acknowledging the **idiosyncratic and unsystematic risk** accepted as a result;
- the **generic and specific characteristics** that comprise the determination of suitability in Stock Selection; and
- the role of **market efficiency and information processing**, both current and forecast, to indicate potential mis-pricing in Asset Identification.

2.1 People

The activities undertaken in the Planning Stage principally involve the Portfolio Management Team with support from the Strategy Team and Research Team. As the Planning Stage moves into the Dealing Stage, the Portfolio Management, Strategy and Research Teams will also be supported by the Capital Transactions Team.

2.1.1 Portfolio Management Team

The role of the REIT Portfolio Management Team is to manage the respective portfolios which, together, comprise the funds that comprise the REIT, with the principal purpose of the role being to optimise the risk-return balance at the portfolio level and the scope of the role usually comprising either one or a small number of portfolios per Portfolio Manager.

The Portfolio Management Team usually reports to the Fund Management Team, with direct reports including the Strategy Team, Capital Transactions Team and Asset Management Team.

The principal contribution of the Portfolio Management Team is to develop the Property Portfolio Strategy to achieve the Goals and so attain the Vision for the REIT, with the functions of the role including:

- **business planning** for each of the respective portfolios comprising the fund, including interpretation of Property Portfolio Strategy in a form that can be communicated to and implemented by the respective teams;
- **budgeting and forecasting** at the portfolio level;
- performance measurement and analysis at the asset and portfolio level, including commissioning and management of the **independent appraisal** process;
- **capital expenditure budgeting** and management at the portfolio level, including redevelopment and refurbishment;
- co-ordination of the various types of **insurance** for the portfolio;
- involvement in the negotiation, documentation and advanced financial analysis of real estate **acquisitions and disposals**; and
- periodic **management reporting** at the portfolio level to the Fund Management Team.

During the last two decades of the twentieth century, a range of portfolio management software programmes were developed around the world including Argus™, DYNA™ and Circle™ (www.argussoftware.com) and Cougar™ (www.cougarsoftware.com).

The impact of such software on property portfolio management, real estate appraisal and forecasting has been profound leading to a greater standardisation of approach to each, particularly in the content, layout and mathematics of discounted cash flow valuation. For the real estate funds management industry to use Argus™ terms as a currency of information and to attach Cougar™ cash flow forecasts to sale contracts is testimony to the centrality that the role of such software has come to occupy in real estate portfolio management.

As with software programmes and companies in general, real estate portfolio management software is in a constant state of development and the software developers are in a constant state of corporate activity. Accordingly, it is not proposed to focus on such software in detail and readers are referred to the respective web sites for further information.

As referred to above, the activities involved in the Planning Stage principally involve the Portfolio Management Team but require the support of the Strategy Team and the Research Team.

2.1.2 Strategy Team

The role of the REIT Strategy Team is to recommend fund and portfolio strategy, with the principal purpose of the role being to determine the target risk-return balance at the fund and portfolio level and the scope of the role usually comprising all portfolios and all funds comprising the REIT.

The Strategy Team usually reports to the Portfolio Management Team, with direct reports including the Research Team.

The principal contribution of the Strategy Team is to determine the Strategic Asset Allocation, Tactical Asset Allocation and Stock Selection criteria for the portfolios and funds for recommendation as the Property Portfolio Strategy to achieve the Goals, with the functions of the role including:

- the development and recommendation of **Property Portfolio Strategy**;
- the development and recommendation of **Strategic Asset Allocation** targets and **Tactical Asset Allocation** targets;
- the development and recommendation of **Stock Selection** criteria;
- **monitoring** Strategic Asset Allocation and Tactical Asset Allocation exposures;
- monitoring the **currency and relevance** of Stock Selection criteria;
- continual focus on the **systematic and unsystematic risk** aspects of the portfolios and funds; and
- maintenance of **rigour, discipline and focus** in all aspects of Property Portfolio Strategy.

In addition to the Strategy Team, the activities involved in the Planning Stage also require the support of the Research Team.

2.1.3 Research Team

The role of the REIT Research Team is to provide quantitative and qualitative information, with the principal purpose of the role being to source and analyse data for use in determining the target risk-return balance at the property, portfolio and fund level and the scope of the role including all properties, all portfolios and all funds comprising the REIT.

The Research Team usually reports to the Strategy Team, but may often be a resource for use by all parts of the business including preparation of market commentaries for the Governing Entity, presentations for the CEO, comparable sales data for the Capital Transactions Team, vacancy rate graphs for the Asset Management Team and so forth. While the Research Team does not have any direct reports, it may draw on the entire REIT business for information and manage a wide range of external data and information providers.

The principal contribution of the Research Team is information and data, with the functions of the role including:

- source, analysis and provision of **real estate market information** for occupancy and investment by sector and geography;
- source, analysis and provision of **economic information**, including data on inflation, employment, retail sales, manufacturing and so forth;
- source, analysis and provision of **capital and financial markets information**, including data on the long term central government bond rate, equity market performance, REIT sub-market performance and so forth;
- preparation of **real estate market forecasts** and commentaries, including vacancy, rental, capitalisation rate and discount rate;
- preparation of **economic, capital market and financial market forecasts** and commentaries;
- **econometric modelling** to support rental and capital value forecasts;
- provision of **special purpose analysis** and reports to address specific issues such as the impact of a new tax across all portfolios and funds or the rental and capital value consequences of a proposed transformation for a particular real estate asset;
- provision of a **conduit** for the movement of information around the REIT as a business enterprise; and
- maintenance of **rigour, discipline and focus** in all aspects of and a continual focus on the integrity of the research process, with the process being of comparable importance to the outcome.

During the last two decades of the twentieth century, the role of research in real estate investment management grew exponentially. Building on the foundations of existing research conferences and publications in various countries, the establishment of the International Real Estate Society (IRES, www.iresnet.net) family of research societies around the world provided a catalyst for the dissemination of real estate research and thought leadership globally.

Table 2.1 comprises IRES affiliated societies which now host an annual conference for real estate researchers and collectively publish a wide range of academic research journals, complementing those produced by professional publishers. Greater discussion of ideas at conferences and dissemination through publication of research findings in journals have contributed to raising the standard and standing of real estate research globally and further cemented the vital links between academic and industry researchers.

While the Planning Stage principally involves the Portfolio Management Team with the support of the Strategy Team and the Research Team, as the Planning Stage moves into the Dealing Stage, the Portfolio Management, Strategy and Research Teams will also be supported by the Capital Transactions Team as considered further in Chapter 3.

Table 2.1   IRES affiliated societies.

Continent	Society and Internet address	Abbreviation
Europe	European Real Estate Society (www.eres.org)	ERES
North America	American Real Estate Society (www.aresnet.org)	ARES
South America	Latin American Real Estate Society (www.lares.org.br)	LARES
Australasia	Pacific Rim Real Estate Society (www.prres.net)	PRRES
Asia	Asian Real Estate Society (www.asres.org)	AsRES
Africa	African Real Estate Society (www.afres.org.za)	AfRES
Middle East	Middle East North Africa Real Estate Society (www.menares.org)	MENARES

2.2 Property Portfolio Strategy

Having completed the Envisioning Stage, a REIT will have developed a Vision to be attained through the adoption of an investment management Style, achievement of identified Goals and fulfilment of an adopted Strategic Plan. Accordingly, the REIT should have a clearly articulated destination together with a high order route map by which to get to the destination and some measurable outcomes to determine whether or not the REIT has arrived at the destination.

The Property Portfolio Strategy is then developed to be consistent with the Vision, Style, Goals and Strategic Plan and to provide a detailed route map linking the Vision to an operational real estate portfolio with identified assets for acquisition that will contribute to achieving the Goals and so attaining the Vision.

Development of a Property Portfolio Strategy within the context of a wealth maximisation motive requires consideration of such issues as target risk-return performance, a focus on portfolios rather than properties, issues associated with new REIT portfolios compared to existing portfolios and the iterative process required to be undertaken.

2.2.1 Targeting risk-return performance

The REIT's Vision and Goals may include a focus on achieving return and/ or risk performance consistent with or in excess of an index or benchmark. If in excess, this may be specified as a relative or absolute level, such as '*capital return within the top quartile of the stock exchange REIT index*' or '*capital return 150 basis points above the stock exchange REIT index*'.

For the former, it is challenging to develop a Property Portfolio Strategy to achieve a Goal of top quartile performance without knowing what range of performance the top quartile may comprise. The challenge is magnified by the relevant index being a share price index which, by definition, is based on movements in or performance of share prices. As such performance is yet to occur, reliance has to be placed on forecasts of share prices or values requiring some form of assessment of how competing REITs may perform. Effectively, this is akin to the performance forecasting undertaken by equity fund managers or real estate securities fund managers who may endeavour to select REITs to form a portfolio that will outperform an index or peer group.

The extensive reports prepared for equity fund managers and real estate securities fund managers by equity analysts in broking houses may provide a range of views concerning forecast earnings and distributions for competing REITs, together with stock unit valuations and twelve month price estimates. Consideration of a range of such reports provides the REIT management team with guidance as to which REITs may be likely to comprise the top quartile and a broad guide as to the likely level of performance that such REITs may achieve.

While such an approach cannot account for the impact of unexpected significant changes on the equity market, such as terrorist activity or an unexpectedly high monthly inflation result, such systematic factors should impact all REITs. Further, in periods where certain factors are unusually volatile, such as interest rates on debt, a REIT management team may make an assessment as to which competing REITs are more or less likely to be impacted by such changes and performance forecasts considered accordingly.

Similarly, such an approach also cannot account for the impact of unexpected changes idiosyncratic to a specific REIT. Shock changes in management or a sudden, unexpected vacancy on lease expiry by a major tenant may impact a specific REIT's performance but is unlikely to be built into equity analyst's forecasts. A REIT management team may form a view, based on personal knowledge of competing REITs, as to which are more or less likely to be impacted by such changes and performance forecasts considered accordingly.

This approach may provide the REIT management team with an indication of the potential range within which the top quartile performance of the stock exchange REIT index may lie. A similar review may be undertaken of equity market analysts forecasts for the REIT itself which, together with the REIT's own forecasts, will provide an indication of the likelihood or otherwise of being within the top quartile for performance and, if unlikely, the extent of the performance gap to be addressed. Effectively, such an approach provides an indication of the goal posts of performance at which the REIT needs to aim and within the context of which any potential real estate acquisitions, disposals or significant transactions will need to be considered.

Risk-return accretive acquisitions

At a general level, potential real estate acquisitions, disposals or significant transactions should be risk-return accretive in principle and substantially accretive if a performance gap is to be addressed to achieve a high target such as top quartile performance. Accordingly, potential real estate acquisitions, disposals or significant transactions are most likely to be considered when risk neutral with a forecast return equal to or greater than that for the existing portfolio. However, consideration of a potential real estate acquisition, disposal or significant transaction becomes more challenging if it appears likely to be risk neutral but mildly performance dilutive in the short term before becoming substantially performance accretive in the medium term, particularly if such potential real estate acquisition, disposal or significant transaction is substantial. Similarly, if a potential real estate acquisition, disposal or significant transaction is not substantial but is likely to increase or decrease portfolio risk, the determination of an acceptable level of return is also challenging.

Such potential real estate acquisitions, disposals or significant transactions may contribute to outperformance through Strategic Asset Allocation and portfolio structure, Tactical Asset Allocation, Stock Selection or Asset Identification. Portfolio structure, considered within Strategic Asset Allocation below, might include seeking outperformance through the addition of retail real estate to a portfolio comprising office and industrial real estate or the addition of real estate in the southern states to a portfolio comprising real estate in the northern states. In such cases, it is relevant to consider the appropriateness or otherwise of sectoral and geographic classifications and the accuracy of data and forecasts for same together with the capacity of the Research Team in terms of time and expertise to provide analysis and forecasts of the required quality (Baum, 2002).

Stock Selection and Asset Identification, considered below, might include seeking outperformance through the addition of specific properties that meet the Stock Selection criteria and indicate potential for greater growth or lower risk and the propensity for mis-pricing. While a focus on Strategic Asset Allocation and Tactical Asset Allocation may be more consistent with a top down approach, it may be contended that fiduciary obligations dictate that the REIT manager should still ensure that location, building quality, tenant quality and so forth are appropriate not only in a portfolio context but also for the building itself on a stand-alone basis (Baum, 2002).

Indexation

The REIT's Vision and Goals may include a focus on achieving return and/ or risk performance consistent with an index or benchmark. Theoretically, a REIT manager could seek to replicate the real estate portfolio composition of those REITs comprising an index or the top quartile of the index in order to achieve broadly similar performance. In practice this would be very challenging to achieve unless there was considerable homogeneity among such REITs. If, for example, all such REITs were diversified and generally held portfolios comprising the same sectoral and/or geographic compositions, it may be possible for a REIT to invest in similar allocations and so target an index level performance. Further, by investing proportionately more of the portfolio in sectors or geographies forecast to outperform, a REIT could tilt the portfolio in an endeavour to achieve outperformance.

However, the heterogeneous nature of real estate would render it effectively impossible to replicate the portfolios of those REITs in the index, the likelihood of each REIT having consistent sectoral and geographic allocations is low and the prospect of all such REITs in the index being diversified, rather than sector specific, is practically non-existent (Baum, 2002). Accordingly, while theoretically possible, an index approach to real estate portfolio construction may be likely to be challenging to achieve in practice.

2.2.2 *Properties* vs. *portfolios*

The evolution of REITs may be considered to reflect a paradigm shift in the real estate portfolio management process. In the, effectively, pre-REIT era up to 1960 and the following first decade of the REIT era, real estate portfolio management may have been characterised as a real estate specific process. Commonly associated with an entrepreneur, the REIT portfolio would likely comprise an amalgam of individual properties acquired or developed in a piecemeal fashion over a period of time. Investment decisions would have been made on the basis of an individual property's fundamental characteristics such as location, building quality, tenancy profile and so forth with regard to the local market supply and demand conditions. Effectively, the portfolio composition was determined by the *ad hoc* selection of assets that met real estate specific criteria. As such, the portfolio was simply the result of the amalgamation of a series of properties acquired on common specific real estate criteria (Pagliari, 1995).

Since the 1980s, the real estate specific approach to real estate portfolio management has largely been replaced in the REIT sector by the portfolio approach. This trend may be considered consistent with the need to restore credibility lost in various real estate industry and market collapses, the move from entrepreneurs to fiduciaries as REIT managers (being evolutionary in some countries, such as Australia, or effectively mandated through statute in other countries, such as in the USA through the Employee Retirement Income Security Act, 1974 with the introduction of the *'prudent man'* rule), the increasing sophistication of REIT investors and the growing use of capital market theory and finance theory in portfolio construction together with more readily available data and significant improvements in computing power. Property portfolio management has effectively been reversed with the portfolio being designed first and properties then acquired to meet the requirements of the portfolio rather than the properties being acquired first and the portfolio then resulting (Pagliari, 1995).

Such a paradigm shift has a profound impact on the real estate investment decision making process, moving from an additive process to a multiplicative process. Rather than simply adding individually acceptable properties to the portfolio, the process now has specific regard to the multiplicative impact of the property proposed to be added to the portfolio in terms of the risk-return profile of the portfolio as a whole. Accordingly, it is now unacceptable to add a property to a REIT portfolio just because it is a 'good' property without a clear understanding of the impact of the property on the forecast risk-return of the portfolio.

The individual property still remains an important element in the portfolio construction process, it is now simply at the end of the process rather than at the beginning. While the real estate investment decision making process must be disciplined and rigorous, reflecting the fiduciary nature of REIT management, it also needs to maintain flexibility. A rigorous and disciplined process provides a consistent framework within which to comprehend and assess changes in the economy, capital markets and real estate markets in the context of the REIT portfolio, providing a superior position from which to then consider opportunities and risks. However, reflecting the limitations in real estate market data and some of the analytical tools and techniques adopted, a level of flexibility is required in implementation through the application of the REIT manager's skill and experience through judgment. This is particularly so in the context of individual properties where a range of quantitative and qualitative issues may need to be balanced within the real estate investment decision making process (Pagliari, 1995).

Economies of scale
With an economy of scale strategy being one of the alternative strategic models considered above, the REIT industry has many common processes and fixed costs that can be operated for a portfolio of, say, 50 properties for little more cost than for a portfolio of, say, 15 properties. REIT Support Teams together with head office accommodation all comprise fixed costs

that can be scaled over a larger portfolio. Similarly, services such as air conditioning maintenance or cleaning and supplies such as toilet requisites or fluorescent light tubes may all be secured at lower cost when bought in bulk. At the REIT management level, efficiencies may also be achieved through control of larger portfolios at each of the Asset Management Team and Property Management Team levels, particularly where high levels of sectoral or geographic (especially city or state) concentration is evident within a REIT portfolio.

The highest level of operating and management efficiency through scale may be achieved in sector specific REITs. For example, a super-regional shopping centre REIT with a large portfolio would benefit not only from the ability to make bulk purchases of general real estate related services and supplies but also such sector specific supplies as bulk purchases of advertising space in print and media. Further, REIT management costs could be reduced by spreading the cost of marketing over a greater number of centres while also having the scale to develop branding, cross promotional strategies and significant specialist in house expertise in super regional shopping centre management, marketing and development.

Accordingly, as portfolio size grows, operating and management efficiencies may increase leading to lower costs and potentially higher net real estate income and REIT earnings. Coupled with the development of higher levels of specialist expertise which may be applied to further enhance real estate income and REIT earnings, a focus on the portfolio may provide a virtuous spiral if effectively managed.

2.2.3 *New* vs. *existing portfolios*

The Planning Stage differs significantly between that for a new REIT portfolio and that for an existing REIT portfolio. Essentially, additions to an existing REIT portfolio are constrained by the nature of the existing portfolio whereas a new REIT portfolio does not face such constraints, being able to implement the various Steps of the Planning Stage outlined below unfettered and unconstrained.

Such constraints arising from an existing portfolio are particularly significant where the REIT has been underperforming for a sustained period. If, for example, a REIT had been within the lowest quartile performance of the stock exchange REIT index for a sustained period, designing and implementing a Property Portfolio Strategy to achieve top quartile performance would be challenging. Not only might a high level of disposal and reinvestment be required, but the Vision may need to be qualified and the Goals restated to reflect a particular time frame, such as a nominated acceptable number of years to be committed to improving performance before reaching top quartile (Hoesli and MacGregor, 2000).

Further, in the event of the adoption of a new Vision or the appointment of a new REIT manager for an existing REIT portfolio, it is appropriate to review the composition and structure of the portfolio. Undertaking the Strategic Asset Allocation and Tactical Asset Allocation Steps outlined below to identify an optimal portfolio for comparison to the existing portfolio will identify those real estate sectors, geographic areas or real estate types that are sub-optimal for attention (Baum, 2002).

Reshaping existing portfolios
Addressing such sub-optimal aspects may then, however, be challenging. Scope for changing the composition of the REIT may be limited by the availability of capital, particularly if new equity raising is impractical (such as after a period of sustained lowest quartile performance) and/or the sale of existing properties from the portfolio may be likely to be problematic or slow. Even in relatively buoyant markets, the time taken to complete a property sale given the complexity of a real estate transaction means that reshaping portfolio composition can be a process lasting from months into years. Such delay may be compounded where the properties for disposal suffer from any disadvantageous characteristics (such as a secondary location or imminent vacancy) or are in a market or sector that is either small or inactive (Baum, 2002).

The impact of delay, together with the transaction costs and taxation issues that accompany the disposal of real estate by a REIT, may compound to adversely affect performance for a considerable period. Accordingly, the timing of such disposal is important with skilled forecasting required to anticipate market movements in an endeavour to transact at the most advantageous time (Baum, 2002).

Lot sizes are also a much more significant issue in the reshaping of an existing REIT portfolio than in the creation of a new REIT portfolio. Following the process outlined below, a new REIT portfolio may acquire assets within target lot size ranges in order to ensure lot size balance across the portfolio, with no individual asset dominating the portfolio and thus potentially skewing both return and risk. However, as the process of disposal and acquisition is spread over a long period of time, an existing REIT may face periods when individual assets become a disproportionately large part of the portfolio and so potentially skew return and risk.

Also, an existing REIT seeking to acquire assets will need to have regard to lot size not only in the context of that which suits target allocations and maintains portfolio balance, but also that which is practically achievable in the market. For example, a target allocation of $50 million to super-regional retail real estate may result from the Strategic Asset Allocation process, considered further below, but may be impractical to invest in a direct real estate interest (Baum, 2002).

2.2.4 *Iterative process*

The practice of implementing the Planning Stage generally results in an iterative process. Following the Steps outlined below may suggest that a target portfolio is identified and then instantly acquired in a simple linear process. However, in practice, it is rare to be able to acquire exactly the right sectors, profiles of asset and lot sizes at the same time to comprise the target portfolio.

For example, there may simply be no assets currently available for acquisition in the target sector and a 6-12 month search period may be required or, when identified, assets may be 20% smaller or larger than targeted or have a slightly higher or lower credit rated tenant than targeted. In each case, the REIT management team will need to revisit the Steps of the Planning Stage to determine the impact of acquiring that property which is available on forecast portfolio return and risk, compared to the target allocation.

As such, the implementation of the Planning Stage becomes iterative with each asset acquired that does not exactly match the target then resulting in changes to the portfolio and so to the target profile for further acquisitions. While such changes may be reduced by adopting a wider range for key criteria, too wide a range undermines the rigour and integrity of the asset allocation process. For example, when targeting an asset of $50 million, a range of $47.5–52.5 million might be contemplated with relatively limited effect on return and risk forecasts, but adopting a range of $25–75 million may render the risk-return forecasts from the asset allocation process meaningless (Baum, 2002).

Simultaneously, the economy, capital markets, financial markets and real estate markets are continuously changing, resulting in the input data used for variables in the modelling process also continuously changing. Thus, not only is the Planning Stage iterative due to acquisitions, disposals or significant transactions not exactly matching the targets but it is also iterative reflecting the continuous change in the economy, capital markets, financial markets and real estate markets. Within such a dynamic process, it is important that the Vision and Goals of the REIT remain visible through the morass of data and calculations inherent in a seemingly unending iterative process.

Decision to do nothing

Further, the delays resulting from the process itself may be compounded by the additional delay that results from the rejection of a transaction which almost but not closely enough meets the target. The resulting period of extended delay is effectively a decision to do nothing for a given time period which will have risk-return impacts on portfolio performance. When rejecting an asset in the hope of finding a closer match to the target it is, therefore, appropriate to explicitly consider the impact on the achievement of the Goals and Vision of the resulting period of delay or inactivity. Following such explicit consideration, it may be appropriate to review the targets slightly for the future to facilitate transactions rather than suffer the potentially adverse risk-return impact of an extended period of inactivity (Hoesli and MacGregor, 2000).

Unlike the construction of an equity portfolio, where higher levels of divisibility and liquidity result in the ability to precisely specify target allocations, the limited divisibility and liquidity of the real estate asset class render it challenging to achieve precise target allocations in a direct real estate portfolio. This results in REIT portfolios effectively being in a constant state of imperfection, whereby exact target allocations are rarely, if ever, achieved and the performance of the REIT portfolio at best only approximates the risk-return forecasts of the target allocations though, with the majority of REITs being in the same position, this problem is relative.

2.2.5 Property Portfolio Strategy

Property Portfolio Strategy comprises the process by which a REIT's Vision is converted into the identification of assets for potential acquisition which will contribute to the achievement of Goals and so to attaining that Vision.

With the entire real estate market available for investment, the REIT management team may potentially be overwhelmed with opportunities provided by excitable, commission driven sales agents keen to do a deal. The temptation to revert back to historic practices of individual property by property acquisitions, from which a portfolio then results, while appealing must be firmly and persistently rebuffed.

Four key Steps
Reflecting its fiduciary obligations and with so many options to consider, the REIT management team needs to adopt a rational and logical approach to the process of identifying potential transactions. Accordingly, the balance of the Planning Stage comprises four key Steps in the process of identifying potential assets for transaction, before the Dealing Stage commences during which the REIT management team endeavours to secure the preferred transaction for the portfolio.

The four key Steps, as illustrated in Figure 2.1, comprise a rigorous process, supported by both quantitative and qualitative analysis, which gradually breaks down the entire real estate market into investable and non-investable sections within which the profile of target assets may be specified.

Strategic Asset Allocation: overview
The first of the four key Steps comprises Strategic Asset Allocation, wherein the entire real estate market is analysed through a range of risk-return lenses, including the different real estate sectors (such as office, retail,

Step1
Strategic Asset Allocation
↓
Step 2
Tactical Asset Allocation
↓
Step 3
Stock Selection
↓
Step 4
Asset Identification

Figure 2.1 Property Portfolio Strategy – four key steps.

industrial, etc.) or different geographic areas (such as northern states, southern states, etc.), to identify the proportion of funds to be invested in each. Following completion of the analysis comprising Strategic Asset Allocation, the Strategy Team may recommend investment of nominated percentages of the portfolio in specified sectors and/or geographies.

Such analysis may, by necessity, be focused at a city level. In most states, there is one major city and potentially several minor cities. While this principle may be globally applicable, the scale of application may vary. For example, in the USA the major city of the State of Texas is Houston with a population of approximately 2.3 million and with the minor cities of San Antonio and Dallas having populations of approximately 1.4 million and 1.3 million, respectively. Comparatively, in China, the major city of Guangdong Province is Shenzhen with a population of approximately 8.6 million, with the minor cities of Dongguan and Guangzhou having populations of approximately 6.9 million and 6.0 million, respectively.

Tactical Asset Allocation: overview
Having rationally identified the sectors and geographic areas in which to target investment, the second of the four key Steps for a REIT management team in the process of identifying potential transactions is to determine if any of the target markets offer sufficient potential outperformance to warrant a Tactical Asset Allocation, being an increased level of investment for a limited time period.

For example, through comparative city by city analysis, it may be determined that a particular market in a particular city appears likely to generate outperformance for a definable upcoming period; such as the office market in a city where demand is forecast to exceed supply for several years resulting in the prospect of significant rental growth as various expanding occupiers compete for a limited amount of vacant office accommodation.

Following completion of the analysis, the Strategy Team may recommend a Tactical Asset Allocation of a nominated percentage of the portfolio to an identified city for a specified period. Effectively, the REIT is overweighting its portfolio to a nominated market in order to benefit from forecast short term outperformance, with the specified holding period anticipating benefit from rising rental levels with sale before new office buildings are completed and supply increased.

Stock Selection: overview

Having completed a rigorous analysis to determine Strategic Asset Allocation and Tactical Asset Allocation, the third of the four key Steps for a REIT management team in the process of identifying potential assets for acquisition is to determine the characteristics for Stock Selection. This Step comprises the identification and specification of property characteristics such as lot size, preferred location, real estate style, asset age, tenant profile and so forth. Carefully constructed on the basis of thorough analysis, the schedule of characteristics developed in Stock Selection will provide a clear shopping list with which to identify potential assets for transaction.

Asset Identification: overview

Following completion of the Stock Selection Step, the REIT management team has a very clear understanding, based on rigorous analysis, of the profile of real estate asset which it is seeking to identify for transaction. Such clarity is essential for the fourth and final Step in the process of identifying potential assets for transaction which comprises Asset Identification. For the Asset Identification Step to be capable of implementation, Stock Selection needs to strike a fine balance between being prescriptive enough to preserve the integrity of REIT portfolio risk-return forecasts, while being flexible enough to permit multiple properties to fit within the Stock Selection criteria.

Through the Asset Identification Step, the REIT management team seeks to confirm that potential assets for acquisition meet the Stock Selection criteria and to determine those which have the potential for greater growth or lower risk contributing to the greatest propensity for mis-pricing. The extent of such mis-pricing is then considered in detail through the Advanced Financial Analysis Step in the Dealing Stage.

Accordingly, through the logical and sequential process of Strategic Asset Allocation, Tactical Asset Allocation, Stock Selection and Asset Identification, a REIT management team may construct a Property Portfolio Strategy that identifies assets for transaction which will contribute that level of performance which results in the REIT achieving its Goals and so attaining its Vision. Reflecting its grounding in the real estate market which is dynamic, formal review of the Property Portfolio Strategy by the Strategy Team and the Research Team should be undertaken annually with informal review quarterly or in the event of significant change in economic or real estate market conditions.

While the following sections consider Strategic Asset Allocation, Tactical Asset Allocation, Stock Selection and Asset Identification in the context of leading to property acquisition, the principles are equally applicable for leading to property disposal or another form of real estate transaction as considered in the Disposal Step and the Transformation Step, respectively, of the Optimising Stage below.

2.3 Strategic Asset Allocation

The first Step in a rational and logical approach to the process of gradually breaking down the entire real estate market into investable and non-investable sections, within which potential assets for acquisition by a REIT management team may be identified, comprises Strategic Asset Allocation. In the Strategic Asset Allocation Step, the entire real estate market is analysed through a range of risk-return lenses, including the different real estate sectors (such as office, retail, industrial, etc.) or different geographic areas (such as northern states, southern states, etc.), to identify the proportion of funds to be invested in each.

Spatial aggregation
Conventionally, Strategic Asset Allocation is considered in terms of sectors such as office, retail or industrial and geographic areas such as north or south. While such spatial aggregation is both familiar and convenient, there is evidence to suggest that other categorisation may be more appropriate (Hoesli and MacGregor, 2000). For example, economic base may provide a better descriptor as, while the office markets of Dallas and Denver are geographically separate; each is economically dependent on the oil industry for employment to drive office occupancy with a downturn in the oil industry potentially affecting each city despite their distance apart.

> Hoesli and MacGregor (2000) note that, while the conventional classification of the UK property market for portfolio construction is into three property types and eleven regions, plus various subdivisions of London depending on property type, the appropriate classification remains an unresolved issue.

Quantitative approaches
Strategic Asset Allocation draws heavily on modern portfolio theory and capital market theory together with applications of theory such as the Capital Asset Pricing Model. The following provides a broad introduction to each, for which a vast amount of research has been undertaken concerning the use in real estate that, for conciseness, will not be covered in detail here. Accordingly, readers are encouraged to refer to Brown and Matysiak (2000) for a detailed consideration of the theoretical aspects or to Geltner et al.

(2007) for a detailed consideration of the practical application in the context of real estate.

The application of modern portfolio theory, capital market theory and the Capital Asset Pricing Model also lend well to an approach based on a process of adopting a variety of iterations followed by reconciliation of outcomes, rather than reliance solely on a point estimate comprising a single set of variables. Depending on the circumstances, the use of fundamental analysis, scenario analysis and Monte Carlo simulation may also be considered useful.

Fundamental analysis relies heavily on the skill and judgment of the analyst, being subject to arbitrariness. Scenario analysis applies estimated probabilities to a variety of potential outcomes based on different combinations of input data, with the results then used to determine expected returns, standard deviation and correlation under the various envisaged scenarios. Monte Carlo analysis permits the variables comprising the scenarios to be selected randomly in a large number of combinations, so limiting the risk of bias (Pagliari, 1995).

From the range of alternatives for possible consideration, the use of scenario analysis provides useful insight into portfolio construction and asset pricing by highlighting the intricacies of relationships between the key variables. Based on such insight, the analyst is better placed to select the input data in order to narrow the projections of potential futures and so improve present decisions (Pagliari, 1995). A detailed consideration of the application of scenario analysis to real estate investment decision making may be found in Ratcliffe (2000).

It should be noted, however, that asset allocation and pricing are not static and may vary over time. The risk of each sector of the market may change over time and this will be reflected in changes in market risk, such that the volatility of portfolios relative to the market is not constant over time. Further, changes may occur to the risk free rate and the market premium leading to continual change in asset allocation and pricing. While such change may be continuous and relatively fast, it is unlikely that a REIT portfolio could be reshaped through acquisitions and disposals fast enough to benefit from every market shift. It is, therefore, appropriate to consider asset allocation and pricing in the context of the longer term with a focus only on major economic and market changes as the basis for amending asset allocation, changing pricing or portfolio reconfiguration (Brown and Matysiak, 2000).

Essentially, Strategic Asset Allocation considers the return and risk of different real estate sectors in different geographic locations and combines them through quantitative analysis into a portfolio forecast to achieve the highest level of return relative to risk. While used extensively in the equities fund management industry since inception in the 1950s, like the portfolio approach it did not start to be generally adopted in the real estate funds management industry until relatively recently and its use is still far from widespread. Accordingly, a substantial portion of the real estate funds management industry continues to adopt qualitative, implicit approaches to Strategic Asset Allocation based on naïve principles (Hudson-Wilson and Wurtzebach, 1994).

The adoption of quantitative approaches to Strategic Asset Allocation forms part of the move to a portfolio approach rather than a property by property approach to property portfolio management, as considered above. Consideration of real estate in the context of other asset classes, the capital markets and the wider economy has been driven by pressure from large, institutional investors and their advisers and the greater use and integration of real estate into mixed asset portfolios together with advances in research into Strategic Asset Allocation in a real estate context and the wider availability of data and software applications necessary to undertake the analysis (Hoesli and MacGregor, 2000).

Differences in terminology may be found between various texts in this area. Some authors use asset allocation as a term to refer to the proportion of funds to invest in real estate relative to other asset classes, such as equities or bonds, with sector allocation used as the term to refer to the proportion to be invested in each real estate sector (Brown, 1991). For the purposes of this text, however, Strategic Asset Allocation will be used as the term to cover the proportion of funds to be invested in different sectors and geographic areas within the real estate asset class for the medium to long term and Tactical Asset Allocation will be used as the term to cover an over weight or under weight investment in a particular sector or geographic area for the short to medium term.

It is proposed to consider Strategic Asset Allocation in the context of the application of the Capital Asset Pricing Model. In order to be aware of the limitations of the application of the Capital Asset Pricing Model to real estate, it is informative to understand the principles of modern portfolio theory and capital market theory which are considered briefly further below.

2.3.1 Modern portfolio theory

While variously defined, modern portfolio theory may be considered to collectively comprise a range of key portfolio management concepts including mean variance efficiency, diversification, efficient frontiers and optimal portfolios (Pagliari, 1995).

Seminal research by Markowitz (1952) into portfolio construction demonstrated that maximising expected return was not sufficient and that it was necessary to also consider the returns and variances of assets in combination within a portfolio. Further, to be efficient, a portfolio was not dependent upon simply comprising a large number of assets but should comprise those assets which provide the least risk or variance for a given level of return or the highest return for a given level of risk or variance (Pagliari, 1995).

Hence, an efficient or optimal portfolio is dependent upon the returns and variance of returns of the assets within the portfolio as well as the covariance between such assets. The principles of portfolio diversification may be applied to sector or geographic allocation as well as to assets, data permitting, being capable of use to determine the appropriate allocation to office, retail or industrial in north, south, east or west to derive an efficient or optimal portfolio.

Expected portfolio return may be expressed as a simple, weighted return of each asset's expected return multiplied by its weighting in the portfolio:

$$E(R_p) = \sum_{i=1}^{I} x_i * E(R_i) \qquad \text{[Equation 2.1]}$$

where:

$E(R_p)$ is the expected return on the multiple asset portfolio

x_i is the percentage of the portfolio invested in the ith asset

$E(R_i)$ is the expected return on the ith asset   (Pagliari, 1995)

However, the portfolio risk or variance is a combination of the different assets' variances, their weighting in the portfolio and the correlation of one asset's variance with that of another:

$$E(\sigma^2_p) = \sum_{i=1}^{I} x^2_i \, E(\sigma^2_i) + \sum_{i=1}^{I} \sum_{j=1}^{I} x_i \, x_j \, E(\sigma_{i,j}) \qquad \text{[Equation 2.2]}$$
$$\scriptstyle i \neq j$$

where:

$E(\sigma^2_p)$ is the expected variance of the multiple asset portfolio

$E(\sigma^2_i)$ is the percentage variance of the ith asset

$E(\sigma_{i,j})$ is the expected covariance between the ith and the jth asset $= \rho_{0,j}\sigma_i \sigma_j$

(Pagliari, 1995)

Significantly, for all correlation coefficients less than 1.0, the portfolios variance will be a non-linear combination of asset variances, their weightings and their correlation.

Following the example in Pagliari (1995), if a REIT management team was contemplating a portfolio of two equal value assets, this may comprise a combination of an industrial property with a forecast return of 12% and variance (as measured by standard deviation) of 15% together with a retail property with a forecast return of 8% and variance of 10%.

Using Equation 2.1 above, the portfolio return comprises the linear combination of the sectors' returns and their weights with a portfolio comprising 50% industrial and 50% retail having a return of 10%:

$$E(R_p) = x_A\ E(R_A) + x_B\ E(R_B) \qquad \text{[Equation 2.3]}$$
$$= 0.5(0.12) + 0.5(0.08)$$
$$= 0.10$$

Impact of perfect correlation

For a two asset portfolio, the equation for the portfolio variance may be stated as:

$$E(\sigma^2_p) = x^2_A E(\sigma^2_A) + x^2_B E(\sigma^2_B) + 2\rho x_A x_B \sigma_A \sigma_B \qquad \text{[Equation 2.4]}$$

(Pagliari, 1995)

The portfolio variance is dependent on the covariance between the sectors. If the returns of the industrial and retail sectors were perfectly correlated (being where $\rho_{A,B} = 1$), the portfolio variance would be a linear combination of the sectors' variances weighted by their respective portfolio allocations or 12.5% (being 0.5(0.15) + 0.5(0.10)).

Impact of imperfect correlation

In all other cases, the portfolio's variance will be less than the weighted sum of the individual sector's variances. Following the example in Pagliari (1995), if the correlation between the industrial and retail sectors was 0.5, then the portfolio variance would reduce by around 150 basis points compared to that for perfect correlation between the respective sectors.

Such risk reduction comprises the fundamental benefit of combining imperfectly correlated sectors, geographies or assets in a portfolio, being the essence of the concept of diversification. Through the use of efficient frontiers, the optimal combination of sectors, geographics or assets in a portfolio to provide the highest level of return for a given level of risk or the lowest level of risk for a given level of return may be derived.

Accordingly, for a given target level of return, the efficient frontier may be used to indicate the optimal combination of industrial and retail real estate to provide a portfolio with the lowest level of risk. Similarly, for a given target level of risk, the efficient frontier may be used to indicate the optimal combination of industrial and retail real estate to provide a portfolio with the highest level of return.

Importance of robust data

The principles outlined above may be applied to sectors of the real estate market, such as office, retail or industrial, as well as to geographic areas, such as north or south, or to individual assets. The critical issue in the application of modern portfolio theory to real estate is the availability of robust data, both historic time series data and forecasts for application based on future expectations over a specified time horizon (Brown, 1991).

Such historical time series data is founded upon the validity of real estate return data from which risk is measured as the volatility or variance in returns, with the covariance of returns then used to measure the way in which the total variance of two or more assets is altered when such assets are held together in the same portfolio. To derive an efficient frontier, estimates are required for expected return, expected standard deviation and the expected correlation of returns over a specified time period (Pagliari, 1995).

To apply the principles of modern portfolio theory to construct a real estate portfolio from four sectors of the real estate market in four geographic areas requires 16 risk and return estimates and 120 pairwise correlation estimates that are robustly based, rigorous and reliable. Given the constraints associated with real estate data and the often subjective and qualitative basis of forecasts, this is a significant quantity of data required at a quality level that may be challenging to source for many Research Teams, so contributing to an ongoing reluctance to fully implement modern portfolio theory (Geltner et al., 2007).

Accordingly, all of the limitations of real estate data need to be borne in mind when considering the results of the statistical analyses inherent in the application of modern portfolio theory. The absence of daily or monthly data points, the limitations of appraisal based capital return data and the low apparent volatility of real estate returns, which may be considered to be a flawed representation of real estate risk as it disguises the illiquidity of real estate and reflects a smoothing and lagging effect due to the infrequency of capital appraisals, are among the limitations impacting the efficacy of real estate data used in the application of modern portfolio theory (Pagliari, 1995; Baum, 2002).

A key aspect influencing diversification is the correlation structure between individual sectors, geographic areas or assets. Ideally, sectors, geographies or assets with negative correlations would be optimal to increase diversification benefits. At one level, it is unusual to find high negative correlations as there are usually systemic factors that cause returns to be positively correlated to some degree. Conversely, the correlation between individual properties may be low reflecting idiosyncratic factors specific to each property such as the location, building or tenancy.

Accordingly, while it may appear counter intuitive, a property which is considered high risk in its own right, such as a hotel, may significantly reduce risk in a portfolio if combined with an asset with which it has a low or negative correlation such as a warehouse. This aspect serves to focus attention on the risk of an individual asset in a portfolio context, with potentially less concern about the risk of the asset itself than that risk which the asset contributes to the portfolio (Wurtzebach et al., 1994; Brown and Matysiak, 2000).

2.3.2 Capital market theory and the Capital Asset Pricing Model

Capital market theory is variously defined but may be considered to comprise the link between modern portfolio theory and asset pricing, being a general theory of asset pricing based on the work of Sharpe (1964), Lintner (1965) and Mossin (1966). Following research into the capital market line and the security market line, Sharpe (1964) developed a model for stock portfolios that related security returns to the performance of an index of business activity and an error term. Further, for the pricing of assets, capital market theory asserts that it is not the total risk that is important but the level of risk that cannot be diversified away through combining assets within a portfolio, with investors not being willing to pay a premium for bearing risk that can be diversified away.

Capital Asset Pricing Model
The evolution of capital market theory led to the development of the Capital Asset Pricing Model which asserts that the return on any risky asset equals the linear combination of the risk free rate plus the sensitivity of the asset's non-diversifiable or systematic risk to the market portfolio's risk, expressed as beta (Pagliari, 1995).

The Capital Asset Pricing Model is most commonly expressed as:

$$E(R_i) = R_f + [E(R_m) - R_f] \, \beta_i \qquad \text{[Equation 2.5]}$$

where:
  $E(R_i)$ is the expected return on an investment
  R_f is the risk free rate
  $E(R_m)$ is the expected return on the market portfolio
  β_i is the beta, an expression of the relative volatility of the investment to the market

Central to the Capital Asset Pricing Model are the risk free rate, the expected market return, beta and the notion that risk can be split into sub-groups for which only non-diversifiable risk is rewarded. The risk free rate is generally proxied by a central government long term bond rate with the expected market return generally proxied by that for the stock market, though it should more correctly be the return on the universe of investable assets from equities to antiques though this presents some challenges in measurement.

Beta represents the systematic risk of an investment and provides a measure of the correlation of an investment with the market (Hoesli and MacGregor, 2000). Effectively, the Capital Asset Pricing Model states that an asset's expected risk premium is directly proportional to its beta, with the asset's risk premium being equal to its beta times the market price of risk (Geltner et al., 2007).

The concept of non-diversifiable risk is central to the Capital Asset Pricing Model and considers the risk inherent within an asset to comprise a combination of systematic risk, unsystematic risk and idiosyncratic risk. Systematic risk comprises those risks endemic to the system, being generally considered to be economic risks such as inflation, which cannot be diversified away. Unsystematic risks comprise those risks that are common to an asset class or sub-set of an asset class, such as regulatory planning risk, with idiosyncratic risks comprising those risks that are specific to an individual asset such as location, building or tenant. By combining properties within a portfolio, the impact of unsystematic and idiosyncratic risks may be significantly reduced through diversification in theory, though the significance of unsystematic and idiosyncratic risk in practice for real estate renders this challenging.

Assumptions underlying the Capital Asset Pricing Model
The Capital Asset Pricing Model is premised on a series of assumptions which may create limitations in application to real estate, including that:

- investors are **risk averse** and maximise their expected rate of return over a single period, which is limiting for real estate that is usually considered to be a multi-period investment medium;
- investors make their decisions solely on the **expected return** and **standard deviation** of portfolios, which is limiting for real estate where other, less rational considerations may be significant;
- expected return and standard deviation of such portfolios **exist**, which is limiting for real estate where data is imperfect;
- all capital assets are **infinitely divisible** so that parts of an asset can be bought, which is limiting for real estate as a relatively indivisible asset class with large lot sizes;
- investors are **price takers**, so no individual can affect the market by buying and selling, which is limiting for real estate in certain economic and real estate market conditions;
- there are **no taxes or transaction costs**, which is limiting for real estate where taxes may be significant and transaction costs high;
- there exists a **risk free asset** in which there can be unlimited investment or borrowing at the same rate and within which inflation is fully anticipated;

- all assets, including human capital, are **marketable**, which is potentially limiting for real estate if non-marketable assets are excluded;
- all **information is free** and simultaneously available to all investors, which is challenging for real estate where information is often proprietorial and closely guarded; and
- all investors agree on the period under consideration and have **identical expectations about risk**, which may be limiting in the context of real estate where time periods and risk expectations may differ between participants.

An investor who conforms to the first four conditions would choose a portfolio on the efficient frontier under modern portfolio theory, with the other assumptions requiring to be built in to the Capital Asset Pricing Model and the interpretation of its results (Hoesli and MacGregor, 2000).

Despite the limitations and the constraints applicable to the use of the Capital Asset Pricing Model in real estate, it appears to be gaining popularity as a pricing model for specific real estate investments. If the beta and the expected market return are known, then the expected return on a prospective real estate investment can be calculated and compared against the return which the asset is priced to deliver, as considered further in Chapter 3 (Hoesli and MacGregor, 2000).

An alternative to the Capital Asset Pricing Model

Reflecting the limitations and constraints arising from the application of capital market theory, an alternative to the Capital Asset Pricing Model is Arbitrage Pricing Theory which contends that there is not just one market risk factor, but a series of identifiable systematic risk factors together with an error term representing unsystematic and idiosyncratic risk for which investors are rewarded (Wurtzebach et al., 1994).

While the practical application of Arbitrage Pricing Theory to real estate has not yet been subject to the detailed academic research that precedes adoption by the real estate funds management industry, it has intuitive appeal for an asset class with the characteristics of real estate.

Use of modern portfolio theory in practice

While the use of modern portfolio theory in real estate funds management is suspected to be increasingly common, there is little research to determine the current extent of such use.

Research by Worzala and Bajtelsmit (1997) found less than 25% of US pension funds used modern portfolio theory, concluding that real estate investment managers are reluctant to adopt newer financial techniques that are being used in other asset classes. This may have been justified in part, as Brown and Matysiak (2000) note, by portfolios of less than 50 properties being unlikely to benefit from specific regional allocations with most of the performance coming from idiosyncratic risk within individual properties. Accordingly, while a broad indication of allocation to sectors may be useful in terms of identifying a general risk class, the critical decisions are made at the individual property level. While this may suggest a focus on individual properties rather than regional allocations, Brown and Matysiak (2000) caution that as portfolios get larger, greater attention will be required to regional allocations. Accordingly, if Strategic Asset Allocation is not yet dominant in real estate funds management, it is only a matter of time and growth in portfolio sizes before it becomes so.

Interestingly, Webb and McIntosh (1986) surveyed US REITs and found 47% diversified by property type while 63.8% diversified by geographic location. Research by Louargand (1992) found the dominant explicit criteria used for diversification in those equity real estate portfolios surveyed were property type (89%), geographic region (72%), property size (50%), economic location (41%) and metropolitan area (39%). The findings supported those of Webb (1984) who found US life insurance companies and pension funds diversified principally by property type (61%) and geographic region (62%). Accordingly, current growth in the use of modern portfolio theory may be founded in long adopted principles of diversification.

However, asset allocation and pricing models are, by their nature, limited in their application by real world conditions. Such models are based on retrospective judgments of performance and risk but decisions are made relative to current expectations of the future and current business constraints. While a decision maker may believe in the required optimum exposure levels indicated by an asset allocation model, the final decision may be influenced by factors outside the parameters of model. Similarly, the asset allocation model fails to encompass an investor's current perceptions of the relative merits of each asset class and is also subject to cognitive limitations and biases in the decision maker (French and French, 1997).

Accordingly, the allocation ranges for sectoral or geographic investment suggested by the application of modern portfolio theory should be considered to be guide posts for the Portfolio Management, Strategy and Research Team to use when making individual property investment level decisions. While this allows some latitude in implementation, such latitude should be considered limited if the diversification benefits of the asset allocation ranges are to be realised (Pagliari, 1995).

2.3.3 Strategic Asset Allocation

Strategic Asset Allocation comprises the first of four Steps in a rational and logical process of gradually breaking down the entire real estate market into investable and non-investable sections, within which potential assets for acquisition by a REIT management team may be identified.

The entire real estate market may be analysed through a range of risk-return lenses, including different real estate sectors (such as office, retail, industrial, etc.) or different geographic areas (such as northern states, southern states, etc.).

Strategic Asset Allocation draws heavily on modern portfolio theory and capital market theory together with applications of theory such as the Capital Asset Pricing Model. Through such approaches, Strategic Asset Allocation considers the risk and return of different real estate sectors in different geographic locations and combines these through quantitative analysis into a portfolio forecast to achieve either the highest level of return relative to risk or the lowest level of risk relative to return. However, in the adoption and implementation of such approaches, explicit regard should be had to the limitations and constraints of real estate data.

2.4 Tactical Asset Allocation

For the purposes of this book, Strategic Asset Allocation will be used as the term to cover the proportion of funds to be invested in different sectors and geographic areas within the real estate asset class and Tactical Asset Allocation will be used as the term to cover an overweight or underweight investment in a particular sector or geographic area for a limited time period. Through Strategic Asset Allocation, the REIT management team determined an optimal combination of real estate sectors and geographic areas for the purposes of portfolio construction.

While more a side Step, rather than the second of four sequential Steps, in the asset allocation process, Tactical Asset Allocation seeks to determine if any of the target markets considered offer sufficient potential outperformance to warrant a Tactical Asset Allocation, being an increased level of investment for a limited time period. Accordingly, in many circumstances, REIT real estate investment decision making may progress directly from Strategic Asset Allocation to Stock Selection with only limited consideration of Tactical Asset Allocation.

Characteristics of Tactical Asset Allocation
Given the nature of Tactical Asset Allocation, those target markets offering sufficient potential outperformance to warrant a Tactical Asset Allocation are likely to be tightly defined. For example, in the office sector, such a target market may be a particular city to reflect underlying market characteristics in that city which drive mis-pricing whereas, in the retail sector, such a target market may be geographic (such as shopping centres in a particular state being mis-priced relative to other states) or sub-sectoral (such as community centres being mis-priced relative to sub-regional shopping centres). In each case, such mis-pricing may be expected to be

corrected by the market in the medium term, providing an opportunity for outperformance for a definable upcoming period.

Tactical Asset Allocation may be considered to be tactical relative to the dominant pattern of diversification grouping adopted for the purposes of Strategic Asset Allocation. The dominant pattern may be sectoral, geographic or another basis with Tactical Asset Allocation then often made relative to that pattern. For example, where Strategic Asset Allocation is on a sectoral basis, this may be complemented by Tactical Asset Allocation on a sectoral basis (Hoesli and MacGregor, 2000). There are, however, a range of approaches to Tactical Asset Allocation which are considered further below.

Usually, a Tactical Asset Allocation is a small or moderate shift from the Strategic Asset Allocation of the order of a maximum of 2–5% of portfolio value, being for a short term only. A larger allocation or a longer time period may represent an unacceptable level of risk to the REIT portfolio through the introduction of significantly higher levels of idiosyncratic and unsystematic risk into the portfolio. Effectively, Tactical Asset Allocation is counter to the diversification sought through Strategic Asset Allocation and so should be used very sparingly in portfolio management.

Heavily premised on market timing and information processing, Tactical Asset Allocation can be devastating for portfolio risk and return if the timing turns out to be sub-optimal or the analysis and forecasts turn out to be incorrect. Great care is, therefore, required in the decision making process leading to a Tactical Asset Allocation investment as excessive trading will expose the portfolio to substantial transaction costs, further compounding the gap between a REIT's performance and that of its competitors (Hoesli and MacGregor, 2000).

By completion of the Tactical Asset Allocation Step, a REIT should have identified sectors and/or geographies and/or cities that may be likely to be sources of short term outperformance together with a clear understanding of the likely timeframe for such outperformance.

There are various approaches to endeavouring to identify markets likely to offer short term outperformance, with limitations of space precluding coverage of each. Accordingly, the principal approaches of:

- spatial based approaches including:
  - sector strategies;
  - geographic strategies;
  - economic base strategies; and
- style based approaches including:
  - core portfolio;
  - value added approaches;
  - opportunistic approaches; and

- other approaches including:
  - asset strategies;
  - lease structure strategies;
  - lifecycle strategies;
  - rotational strategies;
  - replacement cost; and
  - specialised strategies,

will be briefly considered below, but this is not to say that other approaches do not also have merit. Indeed, some REITs have enjoyed considerable outperformance from successful Tactical Asset Allocation through adoption of an unconventional or unexpected approach, but have yet to prove their ability to do so consistently.

2.4.1 Spatial based approaches

Subject to the level of discretion permitted within the REIT governing documents, a REIT manager may adopt an approach to Tactical Asset Allocation based on a short term under or overweight position to a particular sector of the real estate market or geographic area.

Sector strategies
Seeking outperformance through Tactical Asset Allocation to a particular sector, such as office, retail or industrial real estate, may be driven by a view on the relativity of such sectors to each other, between geographic locations or in response to economic changes. For example, prevailing pricing of office relative to retail may offer the opportunity for potential outperformance through Tactical Asset Allocation as may the prevailing pricing of office in one city relative to office in another city. Similarly, economic changes impacting the financial services sector may benefit the office property sector or economic changes in manufacturing may benefit the industrial property sector offering potential outperformance that may be captured through Tactical Asset Allocation (Pagliari, 1995).

Geographic strategies
Tactical Asset Allocation on a geographic basis may be based on the conventional division of a national real estate market (such as north, south, east or west) or on geo-political, geo-economic, geo-social or other bases as a potential source of outperformance through Tactical Asset Allocation.
   Geo-political divisions include by state, county, city and so forth with geo-economic divisions including the rust belt, energy belt, food belt and so forth. Geo-social divisions may comprise census zones, classifications by age or by family structure and other bases may include climate divisions

(such as the sun belt, frost belt or hurricane zones), topographic or geologic zones (such as Pearl River Delta or Rocky Mountains) or time zones (Pagliari, 1995).

Economic base strategies
An increasingly popular basis for Tactical Asset Allocation comprises a focus on economic base, where the search for outperformance is based on the dominant underlying industry employment type of an area. The underlying industry is that which exports goods from the local economy, thus bringing money into the local economy and being the engine for growth in real estate demand in that area. Following a landmark study by Hartzell et al. (1987), approaches based on economic location have gained greater prominence in both Strategic and Tactical Asset Allocation.

2.4.2 Style based approaches

Subject to the level of discretion permitted within the REIT governing documents, a REIT manager may adopt an approach to Tactical Asset Allocation based on the REITs adopted investment management Style.

Core portfolio approach
Whereas an index portfolio seeks to replicate a market, a core portfolio seeks to provide a risk adjusted return that is approximately equal to the market but through the holding of only a small portfolio of properties. Tactical Asset Allocation to generate outperformance may be adopted within core portfolios through the acquisition of individual assets with high risk adjusted returns but low correlation with other assets in the portfolio (Pagliari, 1995).

Value added approach
Sometimes also referred to as the core plus approach, the value added approach seeks to achieve outperformance through Tactical Asset Allocation by identifying opportunities to add value. This may include selecting markets where development to address undersupply may generate outperformance or individual assets where refurbishment, remodelling or focused, active asset management may generate outperformance (Pagliari, 1995).

Opportunistic approach
The opportunistic approach to generating outperformance through Tactical Asset Allocation includes a wide spectrum of higher risk approaches. These may range from identifying opportunities arising from the prospect of reletting partial vacancy in a building to a contrarian approach of acquiring empty buildings in temporarily over-supplied markets where confident of long term economic growth (Pagliari, 1995).

2.4.3 *Other approaches*

Subject to the level of discretion permitted within the REIT governing documents, in addition to spatial based approaches and style based approaches, a range of other approaches to Tactical Asset Allocation, tending towards asset specific, are available to a REIT manager.

Asset strategies
An asset strategy focuses on the distinguishing features of a particular asset as a source of potential outperformance through Tactical Asset Allocation. Reflecting the idiosyncratic nature of individual properties with differing characteristics of cash flow and sale liquidity and with investment grade real estate being a very small sub-set of the whole real estate market, the scope for asset strategies is potentially considerable (Pagliari, 1995).

Lease structure strategies
The ability to generate outperformance from a Tactical Asset Allocation based on lease structures is usually a result of the tenant's credit rating, the lease length or the rent review structure. Tenants with temporary or short term balance sheet or business cash flow problems may attract temporary credit rating downgrades taking them out of the investable universe for some other investors and so offering a potential outperformance opportunity. Similarly, properties with unusually short or long lease terms, unusual rent review patterns or rent reviews offering exposure to a strongly rising market may offer the potential for outperformance (Pagliari, 1995).

Lifecycle strategies
Tactical Asset Allocation based on the real estate lifecycle seeks to identify opportunities for potential outperformance arising from the risk-return changes as a property moves through the various phases of the investment holding period cycle (Pagliari, 1995).

Rotational strategies
Within the equities market, portfolio managers may follow a rotational strategy to respond to fundamental economic conditions. At the beginning of an economic expansion phase, investors may focus on consumer durables or discretionary spending products, rotating to focus on capital goods companies that will benefit from the need to grow productive capacity as the economy moves into expansion phase and then rotating into companies offering consumer non-durables/non-discretionary spending products as the economic expansion matures.

The same principles are capable of application to rotational strategies in real estate portfolio management through different sector or geographic market cycles as the economy moves through expansion to maturity. It is relevant to think in terms of rotational strategies at a macro rather than individual real estate level. For example, principally income or rent driven rotational strategies are based on differing occupier space supply/demand conditions at a local market level. However, principally capital appreciation driven rotational strategies are based on capital market conditions such as the expectation of capitalisation rate changes due to changes in the bond rate or inflation expectations (Pagliari, 1995).

Replacement cost
Due to a variety of possible factors, properties within various markets may fall in value to a level below replacement cost. Accordingly, this serves to limit the prospect of new development within that market until value levels generally rise above replacement cost to a margin sufficient to make such new development attractive. Therefore, an approach to sourcing outperformance through Tactical Asset Allocation may be to target markets where value levels have fallen below replacement cost but where market fundamentals will drive short to medium term value increases to generate outperformance (Pagliari, 1995).

Specialised strategies
While there is a danger that almost any form of Tactical Asset Allocation could be argued to be a specialised strategy if it does not easily sit within one of the other categories considered above, some alternative forms of Tactical Asset Allocation may be legitimately considered as specialised strategies.

For example, outperformance may be achieved through Tactical Asset Allocation using a duration strategy, where a real estate asset is acquired for the short term to provide a period of strong cash flow to match and offset the duration of a short period of weak cash flow in another, long term real estate asset holding. Alternatively, outperformance may be achieved based on a Tactical Asset Allocation to a bulk purchase strategy, where a job lot of properties is acquired of differing qualities with a view to retaining some assets and trading the balance. Clearly, if undertaken on a large scale or with regularity, a bulk purchase strategy could fundamentally change the nature of a REIT and so stretch the proposition of a bulk purchase strategy being a specialised strategy within Tactical Asset Allocation (Pagliari, 1995).

In one widely publicised specialised Tactical Asset Allocation, the Sydney based REIT, Schroders Property Fund, took a significant overweight position in sub-regional shopping centres which were trading at initial yields of around 14% following the real estate market downturn of the early 1990s.

While the strategy was highly successful, with such centres trading at capitalisation rates of around 9% within a few years thereafter, such Tactical Asset Allocation success was not repeated consistently.

2.4.4 *Tactical Asset Allocation*

While more a side Step rather than a sequential Step in the asset allocation process, Tactical Asset Allocation seeks to determine if any of the target markets considered offer sufficient potential outperformance to warrant an increased level of investment for a limited time period.

Tactical Asset Allocation may be considered through a range of approaches; including sectoral, geographic and economic base approaches; Style based approaches including core, value added and opportunistic; and other approaches such as asset, lease structure, lifecycle, rotational and replacement cost strategies. Significantly, each approach is premised on principles opposite to those embraced in diversification through Strategic Asset Allocation. Through Tactical Asset Allocation, a REIT is intentionally taking on idiosyncratic and unsystematic risk which must be reflected in the risk adjusted forecast return to justify the proposed Tactical Asset Allocation.

By completion of the Tactical Asset Allocation Step, a REIT should have identified sectors and/or geographies and/or cities that may be likely to be sources of short term outperformance together with a clear understanding of the likely timeframe for such outperformance.

Following completion of the Tactical Asset Allocation Step, the REIT management team may embark upon the Stock Selection Step to determine the characteristics of a property asset for acquisition, before then seeking to find such an asset through the Asset Identification Step, each of which are considered further below.

2.5 Stock Selection

Having completed a rigorous analysis to determine Strategic Asset Allocation and Tactical Asset Allocation, Stock Selection comprises the third of the four Steps in the process of identifying potential assets for acquisition, with the purpose of Stock Selection being to determine those criteria that may make assets suitable for acquisition by the REIT for inclusion in the portfolio.

Some criteria will be determined by the requirements of the portfolio as a whole following the Strategic Asset Allocation process, such as return expectation, risk tolerance and potential lot size. Such criteria may be considered generic to the portfolio rather than specific to the asset.

Other criteria will be determined by aspects of the sector of the real estate market in which the asset sits. Such criteria as preferred location, asset age, tenant profile and so forth will vary between the office, retail and industrial sectors of the real estate market. For example, that which comprises a preferred location for an office asset may differ significantly from that for a retail asset, with each differing from that for an industrial asset. Accordingly, such criteria may be considered specific to the asset rather than generic to the portfolio.

While Stock Selection identifies the types of assets that would be suitable for acquisition by a REIT for the portfolio, it does not identify a specific building for acquisition. Such specific building identification is undertaken in the fourth and final Step in the process, being the Asset Identification Step (Hoesli and MacGregor, 2000).

2.5.1 Generic criteria

Central to the Strategic Asset Allocation and Tactical Asset Allocation Steps of the Planning Stage was the enunciation of a target rate of return and risk profile for the REIT portfolio to which Stock Selection needs to have regard.

Stock Selection should, therefore, generally only consider assets offering target return and risk, higher return with target risk or lower risk with target return. However, Stock Selection based on the risk adjusted return should still be considered for assets offering higher return with higher risk than target or lower return with lower risk than target subject to detailed analysis and careful consideration of the impact of such assets on the portfolio.

Lot size

The number of properties to be held in a REIT portfolio to optimise the benefits of diversification provides the fundamental determinant of the target lot size for Stock Selection. In general terms, smaller REITs having fewer properties will display greater levels of idiosyncratic risk than larger REITs with more properties, thus increasing the importance of the specific criteria of Stock Selection for smaller REITs (Hoesli and MacGregor, 2000).

As the number of assets in the REIT portfolio increases, portfolio variance gradually decreases until it reaches the average covariance between all assets, effectively being the systematic risk level where the return follows that of the market. While a significant reduction in risk occurs when a second asset is added to a portfolio (assuming it is not replicative of the initial asset), research by Brown and Matysiak (2000) suggests that most of the reduction in risk occurs within the range of ten to twenty properties, after which the rate of risk reduction slows dramatically as shown in Figure 2.2.

For a larger mixed asset portfolio, Brown (1991) suggests that a portfolio comprising between twenty to thirty properties is approaching its systematic risk level where further diversification is unlikely to contribute significantly to portfolio risk reduction. Further, research by Brown and Matysiak (2000) suggests that for a portfolio of around thirty properties, equally weighted, it should

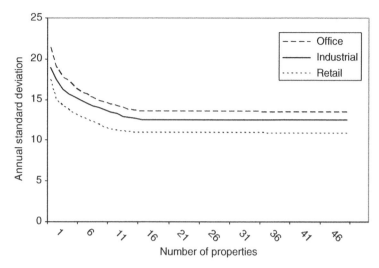

Figure 2.2 Risk reduction and portfolio size annual returns – December 1987 to December 1996. From the Author and Brown and Matysiak (2000). *Real Estate Investment: A Capital Market Approach* (Figure 11.2, p.330). © 2000 Financial Times/Prentice Hall, Pearson companies. Reproduced by permission.

be possible to obtain a level of risk reduction in the order of 65% compared to a single real estate asset portfolio and for the market to then explain about 75% of the variation in portfolio returns. However, the authors note that such a portfolio would still exhibit a high level of idiosyncratic risk such that two similarly weighted portfolios could still have considerably different returns on a period by period basis reflecting differences in idiosyncratic risk.

Accordingly, as a starting point for Stock Selection for a larger mixed asset portfolio, an assumption that each asset will comprise between 5–10% of the portfolio provides an initial guide for lot size with a longer term target of each asset comprising between 3–5% of the portfolio. However, this is significantly influenced by the level of idiosyncratic risk in the portfolio arising from the specific criteria of those individual real estate assets comprising the portfolio. Further, for smaller portfolios, the lumpy nature of real estate investments may result in each asset comprising a larger portion of the portfolio initially but decreasing as the portfolio grows.

2.5.2 *Specific criteria*

While generic criteria such as return expectation, risk tolerance and potential lot size are determined by the requirements of the portfolio as a whole following the Strategic Asset Allocation process, other criteria are determined by aspects of the sector of the real estate market in which the asset is situated and the individual asset itself.

Such specific criteria may be considered to comprise the traditional real estate market concept of the investment quality of an asset while, in capital market terms, are also the principal contributors of idiosyncratic risk for that asset. Having regard to the impact of idiosyncratic risk on property portfolio diversification, referred to above, it is preferable to include assets within the portfolio for which the specific criteria exhibit the greatest difference or diversity.

Specific criteria may further be considered to comprise, currently or in the foreseeable future, either contributors to potential growth or contributors to potential risk. Clearly, it is preferable to select assets whose specific criteria contribute to the growth profile while being cogniscent of and managing any specific criteria contributing risk.

There is a wide range of specific criteria of real estate that could be considered but, for the purposes of conciseness only, four groups will be considered below being legal, location, building and tenancy criteria. This is not to say that other specific criteria are unimportant and all should be considered during Stock Selection.

Legal criteria
The real estate asset class is affected by the law to an extent not found in other asset classes, with both statute and common law contributing to the legal framework within which real estate is situated.

Indefeasibility of title is, of course, paramount to real estate ownership and key to the right to use land for the purposes of generating income. Title may be freehold or leasehold with some REITs adopting a Stock Selection criterion of only investing in freehold real estate. While freehold title confers the right to generate income in perpetuity, leasehold title provides the right to generate income for a fixed period which may be considered to be both a growth and risk characteristic.

Consistent with the concept of real estate as a bundle of rights, any aspect of title that limits such rights may be considered a risk characteristic. Defects in title, easements or other limitations of property rights, such as water rights or air rights, may constrain growth and increase risk such that a Stock Selection criterion may be unencumbered title.

A broader aspect of legal risk is the possibility that government may alter the laws that affect real estate investment. Such laws may include taxation, planning or heritage or the prospect of intervention by government to protect some aspect of public interest. Those real estate assets exhibiting operating business criteria, such as shopping centres, may be most vulnerable to changes in the law or government intervention, particularly concerning politically sensitive issues, requiring consideration by a REIT when determining Stock Selection criteria.

Location criteria

Location within an established area for the type of use may be a key Stock Selection criterion for all types of real estate asset. Thereafter, the selection criteria concerning location may be expected to vary significantly between office, retail and industrial real estate assets.

Office assets may be located within a downtown precinct, suburban area or office park with the locational criteria of each differing. Downtown locations are generally ranked in quality by street name, with certain streets or sections of downtown synonymous with certain office uses such as banking, insurance or advertising. With many cities seeking to decrease downtown car use, proximity to public transport and commuter retailing may be part of the selection criteria. For suburban and office park locations, access to car parking as well as public transport with an enhanced retail offer to include facilities such as child care or a gym or fitness centre may be included in the selection criteria.

Retail assets may have selection criteria based on competition from other existing or proposed centres and proximity to other major retailers, often expressed as a minimum distance from another centre or retailer outlet or a minimum trade area population. Similarly, adequate road access for shoppers from surrounding suburbs supported by a public transport network may be included as selection criteria.

For industrial real estate, location may be considered in terms of proximity to an airport or sea port or in terms of the quality of access to the freeway system with selection criteria expressed as a minimum distance to port or to a freeway of a minimum specified number of traffic lanes.

Building criteria

Relevant building criteria may vary considerably between office, retail and industrial real estate with Stock Selection criteria often being expressed very specifically for different asset types. For example, door and eaves heights may be important selection criteria for industrial real estate whereas high rise or foyer quality may be important selection criteria for office real estate.

For most office, retail and industrial real estate assets, Stock Selection criteria may include structural aspects such as cladding, elevation, orientation, views, appearance, finishes, technology and services, with the required standard changing continuously over time. Similarly, age, physical condition, requirement for maintenance and capital expenditure, flexibility of design and prospects of functional or technical obsolescence may be key selection criteria impacting on potential growth or risk for office, retail and industrial assets.

Tenancy criteria

Greater consistency may be expected between the tenancy selection criteria for office, retail and industrial real estate as, in each case, the tenancy is the fundamental source of cash flow for the investment. Accordingly, it is not uncommon for the tenancy selection criteria to be framed with regard to the financial substance of the tenant, for which credit worthiness is often a proxy, having a requirement for either a government backed cash flow or a minimum specified credit agency rating.

A preferred lease structure may also be specified within tenancy selection criteria. A minimum unexpired lease term may be specified, in order to enhance or at least maintain the REIT's portfolio weighted average lease expiry profile. Similarly, a rent review basis may be specified, such as minimum annual fixed increases with periodic reviews to open market rental value, in order to ensure that the REIT's revenue increases progressively.

In order to protect the cash flow for the duration of the lease, tenancy selection criteria may include strict requirements surrounding lease alienation. Constraints on assignment and sub-letting are common selection criteria to maintain the obligation of the current tenant to underwrite cash flow even if the lease is transferred to another party in future years.

2.5.3 Stock Selection

By the completion of the Stock Selection Step, a REIT should have a very clear specification for the criteria of assets which are suitable for inclusion in the portfolio. Such criteria will include those generic to all assets such as return expectation, risk tolerance and potential lot size, as well as those specific to individual assets such as legal, location, building and tenancy criteria.

Having carefully constructed such a clear shopping list with which to identify potential assets for acquisition, a REIT is now in a position to undertake the final Step of identifying potential assets for acquisition.

2.6 Asset Identification

While Stock Selection identifies the types of assets that would be suitable for acquisition by a REIT for inclusion in the portfolio, it does not identify specific buildings for acquisition. Such identification is undertaken in the fourth and final Step in the Planning Stage, being Asset Identification (Hoesli and MacGregor, 2000).

However, a fine balance needs to be struck in the principles of Stock Selection between being prescriptive enough to preserve the integrity of REIT portfolio risk-return forecasts, while being flexible enough to permit multiple properties to fit within the Stock Selection criteria given that, at any point in time, only a subset of that sample may be available for consideration in the Asset Identification Step. Therefore, if the Stock Selection criteria are defined too prescriptively, the number of properties available for potential acquisition through Asset Identification may, at best, be one or two or, at worst, be zero.

Asset Identification comprises the process of developing a target list of assets that meet the Stock Selection criteria, prior to determining how much the REIT should pay for such assets in the Dealing Stage. Accordingly, it is necessary to have regard to concepts that are particularly relevant in determining how much to pay for an asset, being the pricing process, during the Asset Identification step.

The pricing process requires an understanding of the concepts of price, worth and value (considered further in Chapter 3), which are built upon concepts of market efficiency and information processing that are considered below. Starting with the Asset Identification Step and continuing through the Dealing Stage, information is collected and considered in the context of pricing in order to endeavour to find assets that are incorrectly priced by the market.

This is the process of impounding information into pricing, whereby the Portfolio Management Team seeks to collate and analyse information concerning various aspects of Stock Selection in the context of the target list of potential assets for acquisition and then to impound this information into a pricing process to identify assets that are mis-priced, ideally those that are under priced in an economic sense.

Impounding information in a pricing process
Locating mis-priced assets in competitive real estate markets is extremely difficult and generally only achievable through luck, insider trading or the application of superior analytical and forecasting skills (Brown and Matysiak, 2000). The following outlines the general principles of market efficiency and information processing by which information is impounded in a pricing process. This is usually considered by the Portfolio Management, Strategy and Research Teams and forms an essential foundation for both the Preliminary Analysis and Advanced Financial Analysis Steps in the ensuing Dealing Stage.

2.6.1 Market efficiency

In order to understand the role of information in a pricing process, it is necessary to comprehend the implications of market efficiency. One of the key principles of modern finance theory is that prices reflect all knowable information, with rational market participants paying prices (or making pricing decisions) with regard to everything that they know about an asset.

Accordingly, knowing more or less about an asset may lead to a conscious decision to pay more or less for that asset. The critical variables are, therefore, the nature, quantity and quality of that information and the amount more or less that may be paid as a result of knowing that information.

Market efficiency concerns the extent to which, on average, the price at which assets trade reflects all known information, with most markets tending to be reasonably efficient. Accordingly, this may make it difficult to consistently discover assets for acquisition that are under priced relative to the risk of the asset (Brown and Matysiak, 2000).

Efficient Market Hypothesis
Under the Efficient Market Hypothesis, a market is efficient where prices respond to all knowable information. Consistently, if the real estate market was efficient then prices would change as the market responded to each piece of new information becoming known. Accordingly, if the real estate market was efficient, it would be impossible for real estate investors to earn abnormal returns from specialist market knowledge. However, if the real estate market was not completely efficient, real estate investors with specialist market knowledge may be able to identify under priced assets and so earn abnormal returns (Brown and Matysiak, 2000).

As markets move in and out of equilibrium, there may be periods when assets appear over or under priced and so present the opportunity to earn abnormal returns. This may occur most obviously in the real estate market during periods of boom or bust where there are rapid upward or downward price movements. Such periods present the potential for reduced market efficiency and an increased prospect of being able to identify under priced properties using specialist knowledge and so to earn abnormal returns. However, to do so consistently may be challenging.

In a perfect market, prices would fully and instantaneously reflect all available information creating optimal efficiency. However, a perfect market is also frictionless with costless and immediate information and is populated with rational investors who prefer more return to less for a given risk preference. A frictionless market involves no transaction costs or taxes, with all assets being perfectly divisible and marketable. It is evident that the real estate market is unlikely to be a perfect market, as it fails to meet the criteria for being frictionless and displays both high costs and long delays in the availability of information, so it may be likely that prices in the real estate market do not fully and instantaneously reflect all available information and so the real estate market does not exhibit optimal efficiency.

Forms of market efficiency
Seminal research by Fama (1970) proposed three levels or forms of market efficiency being:

- **weak form efficiency** – where prices reflect historic information, such as previous prices and sale dates, so that no investor can earn excess returns from trading rules based on a past series of prices;
- **semi strong form efficiency** – where prices reflect all publicly available information, such as a recent planning consent or new letting data, so that no investor can earn excess returns based on publicly available information; and
- **strong form efficiency** – where prices reflect all information including information only known to corporate insiders and specialists, such as insider information, so that no investor can earn excess returns from any information whether publicly available or not (Brown and Matysiak, 2000; Hoesli and MacGregor, 2000).

The real estate market is generally considered to be weak form efficient, with the use of a time series of returns or historic market trends being unlikely to, for example, generate abnormal returns. This implies that all historic information about location, building, tenant and so forth is already incorporated into prices and so cannot be exploited to earn abnormal returns (Brown, 1991).

Further, the real estate market is generally not considered to be semi-strong form efficient as prices may not reflect all publicly available information. Planning information, newspaper reports, published reports and so forth may all be publicly available information but it is not clear that all are fully reflected in prices. It may be that analysis of such publicly available information may provide the ability to identify assets where such information has not been reflected in prices and so an opportunity to earn abnormal returns exists. However, this leads to the question as to whether the cost of resources required for undertaking such analysis is likely to be adequately compensated by the potential abnormal returns earned.

Similarly, the real estate market is generally not considered to be strong form efficient with all private information, of the nature of insider information, not reflected in prices. The traditional example adopted is of a developer who is aware of a tenant requirement for a showroom on a highway junction and acquires a vacant block of land on a highway junction from an uninformed vendor, earning abnormal returns from the development and subsequent letting to the showroom tenant. Given the myriad of opportunities for private information in the real estate market, the prospects of achieving strong form efficiency would appear limited.

With the real estate market being weak form efficient, there would appear to be opportunities to earn abnormal returns through the identification and use of information currently available but not reflected in prices, though this may be costly in terms of search, analysis and transaction costs and time. Information currently available may include information about events that have been announced but have not yet occurred and information that can reasonably be inferred. As such, current information may be considered analogous to rational expectations (Hoesli and MacGregor, 2000).

However, there is also the opportunity to earn abnormal returns through the identification and use of information concerning the future that is not reflected in current prices and does not form part of current rational expectations. This may be achieved through the use of forecasting which is considered further in Chapter 3.

2.6.2 Information processing

The ability to identify mis-priced real estate depends entirely on how well information is processed. This has implications for not only the type of information that is collected but also the way in which and the extent to which it is processed. Given the extent of information sources available, the range of analytical techniques available and the number of expert analysts working in the area, the scope for information processing in REIT investment is potentially vast and the opportunities for identifying mis-pricing and, thus, potential outperformance should be considerable (Hoesli and MacGregor, 2000).

To be effective as an investment management Style, active management depends on some level of market inefficiency with some information on some aspect of a real estate investment somewhere not being reflected in price. Such information may be systematic to the sector or specific to the asset and may be transient or may last for a long time (Hoesli and MacGregor, 2000).

Accordingly, the potential extent of sources of information from which mis-pricing may be identified is very wide including such dimensions as the sector, the asset, the short term and the long term. It is therefore proposed, for convenience rather than seeking to limit the range, to consider some of such sources of information through the lenses of currently available information and forecast information.

Current information
Considering currently available information, the identification of assets for acquisition may be achieved through either the Capital Transactions Team being aware of or having being introduced to particular properties (externally introduced properties) or by the Portfolio Management, Strategy or Research Teams analysing currently available information on known properties within the target market (internally identified properties).

For both externally introduced and internally identified properties, the current information analysis process is common and provides an initial filter. For externally introduced properties, the information analysis process seeks to confirm that the identified assets meet the Stock Selection criteria.

For internally identified properties, the Stock Selection criteria are used in the information analysis to filter and identify potential properties.

Each requires the collection of all currently available information including historic information, publicly available information and, if possible, private or insider information. Such information not only verifies that the property accords with the Stock Selection criteria but may also assist in identifying aspects of the property that may positively or negatively affect the pricing of the property through being a source of growth or risk potential greater than that which the market may have priced in to the property. Effectively, this is part of the process of impounding information into pricing in search of a mis-priced asset that has the potential to deliver abnormal returns.

Specific characteristics
As with Stock Selection, at the individual property asset level there is a wide range of specific characteristics of real estate that could be considered for information processing purposes but, for conciseness, only four groups will be referred to below, being legal, location, building and tenancy characteristics. This is not to say that other specific characteristics are unimportant and all should be considered during information collection.

Concerning current legal information, the Stock Selection criteria may specify freehold title which is usually straightforward to confirm in principle for the purposes of the Asset Identification Step. Any unusual features of freehold title, such as covenants benefiting or burdening the title, should be considered in this Step in terms of their possible impact on growth or risk prospects and thus pricing. If the Stock Selection criteria were leasehold, information collection for Asset Identification may include details of lease length, rent review basis and frequency, limitations on transfer and so forth that may have a pricing impact.

Location is a critical property specific Stock Selection criterion for current information collection at the Asset Identification Step. Stock Selection criteria such as prime and downtown require interpretation in the context of a given city and may include not only properties facing principal thoroughfares but also a web of side streets and back streets. A Stock Selection criterion of prime may be likely to limit the interpretation to the principal thoroughfares only but information is then required concerning the implications on growth and risk of each of the principal thoroughfares, different positions along each of the principal thoroughfares, significance of corner locations, proximity to public transport and so forth. Information collection may verify previously held views on the relative quality of location and position of each of the potential properties for acquisition or may provide new information, such as a shift in tenant location preferences to a group of newer buildings away from the traditionally considered core area, which may have pricing implications.

A Stock Selection criterion for maximum building age requires careful consideration, particularly when combined with the location criteria such as downtown which tends towards the assets for identification being high rise. However, if market participants generally are focusing on high rise, current information collection may indicate growth or risk potential for mid-rise buildings that differs from expectations and so may have a pricing impact. While a mid-rise building may or may not meet the Stock Selection criterion for lot size, the example serves to illustrate the principle of Stock Selection striking a fine balance between being prescriptive enough to preserve the integrity of REIT portfolio return and risk forecasts, while being flexible enough to permit multiple properties to fit within the Stock Selection criteria.

Perhaps the Stock Selection criterion with the greatest requirement for current information collection at the Asset Identification Step is that for tenant profile, such as a specified criterion being principally leased to a corporate tenant. The nature of the lease and the nature of the tenant are each major sources of growth and risk for an investment property cash flow and so provide considerable scope for current information collection to determine if expectations are met or if there may be a positive or negative pricing impact arising. It should be noted that a selection criterion such as principally corporate may exclude government as a sole tenant, but may be interpreted to include government as one of a range of tenants in an investment property where corporates form the majority. Analysis of current or historic tenancy schedules will provide useful comparative data not only for the subject property but also relative to the REIT's existing portfolio.

At the Asset Identification Step, analysis is still at a relatively high level concerning tenant profile. The Portfolio Management Team will seek to understand the nature of the leases in terms of the duration of cash flows, weighted average lease expiry and rent review profile of the cash flow for comparative analysis of the potential properties under consideration and with the portfolio as a whole. For multi-let properties, the nature of the tenant profile may be determined by the risk weighted profile of the cash flow on the basis of tenant creditworthiness as determined by a credit rating agency.

For example, Table 2.2 describes the creditworthiness of four tenants occupying a property identified for potential acquisition. Adopting a simple risk weighting approach, the risk weighted average creditworthiness for the cash flow for the identified property may be determined to be Aa3, providing a point estimate for comparison with other identified properties and the portfolio average. Creditworthiness may also be used to weight the nature of leases providing, for example, a basis upon which to consider the extent to which open market rent reviews in the lease to Tenant D contribute greater risk weighted potential growth than open market rent reviews in the lease to Tenant C.

Table 2.2 Risk weighted tenant profile.

Tenant	% of gross income	Moody's credit rating
A	40%	Aaa
B	20%	Aa3
C	20%	A3
D	20%	Baa1

Source: Author (after Hoesli and MacGregor, 2000).

Having considered all current information concerning relevant aspects of the nature of the lease and the nature of the tenants as sources of growth and risk in the cash flow for those properties identified, the Portfolio Management Team are well placed to form a view on whether expectations vary from actuality and the impact that this may have on pricing.

Impact on property level cash flow
While collecting and analysing current information on the building and the tenant, the Portfolio Management Team may also form views on operational aspects of the respective properties identified. In addition to scope for reducing costs identified during the building information analysis or scope for increasing revenue identified during the tenant information analysis, the Portfolio Management Team may identify other areas where better operational performance at the property level may be achievable leading to potential higher growth or lower risk and so contributing to mis-pricing of the asset identified. For example, better operational performance may result from the application of economies of scale by a particular REIT manager, potentially providing a pricing advantage.

Having collected and analysed all currently available information, the Portfolio Management Team are in a position to verify the extent to which identified properties accord with the Stock Selection criteria and to identify aspects of each property that may positively or negatively affect the pricing of the property, through being a source of growth or risk potential greater than the market may have priced in for the property. There is a very fine balance between undertaking such data collection and analysis in sufficient depth to identify scope for mis-pricing but not in so much depth that the costs of data collection and analysis erode the gains from potential abnormal returns (Brown and Matysiak, 2000).

Having analysed identified properties through the lens of current information, a target list of assets for potential acquisition may be prepared. Though considered in greater detail in the Advanced Financial Analysis Step of the Dealing Stage, outlined in the next chapter, identified assets may also be analysed through the lens of forecast information concerning future performance by the Portfolio Management, Strategy and Research Teams.

Forecast information

The use of forecasts as a source of information to identify mis-pricing by the market presents probably the greatest scope for contribution by the Portfolio Management, Strategy and Research Teams to generating outperformance by a REIT. Forecast data may be bought from a data provider or developed by the Research Team, with both sources requiring analysis and interpretation by the Research Team (Baum, 2002).

The effective implementation of an active investment management Style is dependent on forecasting ability. Strong forecasting abilities are likely to generate abnormal returns through an active investment management Style with those REITs lacking strong forecasting abilities unlikely to generate abnormal returns and so more suited to adopting a passive investment management Style (Brown and Matysiak, 2000).

The development of both a rigorously grounded forecasting process and an interpretation process that is proven to be effective over time provides not only an unassailable raison d'être for the Portfolio Management, Strategy and Research Teams but also a strong competitive advantage for the REIT itself with proprietorial research jealously guarded and never shared (Hoesli and MacGregor, 2000).

The Research Team will generally focus on two principal areas for forecasting purposes, being the rental growth outlook and the outlook for movements in capitalisation or discount rates. Importantly, forecasts of rental growth and capitalisation or discount rate movement should not be prepared in isolation, as each is inextricably linked to the other (Hudson-Wilson and Wurztebach, 1994).

In initial overview of data for the prevailing level of rental and capitalisation or discount rates may indicate apparent anomalies for further attention. For example, rents for a given property may '*look low*' relative to others or the capitalisation rate may '*look high*' relative to others, prompting closer analysis. Alternatively, relatively low rents or high capitalisation rates currently may only become apparent after detailed forecasting has been undertaken.

Similarly, in periods of rapid upward or downward rent or capitalisation or discount rate movement, an initial overview may provide greater guidance to the direction and level of movement than that derived from detailed forecasting, given the volatility of inputs to the forecasting process. Accordingly, insightful overview should not necessarily be discarded as irrelevant with sole reliance on econometric forecasting, but a balance struck between the adoption of each as market circumstances dictate (Baum, 2002).

Econometric modelling

Econometric models developed for the purposes of forecasting rental growth and capitalisation or discount rate movements generally focus on a series of variables considered to be drivers, with the identification of variables and the specification of the relationship between them comprising the key intellectual property that distinguishes the success of one REIT Research Team's models from another. Accordingly, the design and specification of such forecasting models are generally jealously guarded secrets.

The conceptualisation of econometric models is based on the current understanding of relevant economic theory concerning the operation of the real estate market, with such theory in a constant state of evolution as academics and researchers add to the body of knowledge. While it is tempting to include a wide range of variables in a model that economic theory suggests may have some relevance to rental value or capitalisation or discount rate movements, identification of relevant variables and those for which measurement by reliable data, either directly or by proxy, is possible is a major challenge. The key issue is practicability which may be succinctly summarised as:

> *'In property market model building, plausibility usually goes hand in hand with parsimony and elegance.'* (Hoesli and MacGregor, 2000)

Essentially, there are two principal approaches to econometric model building for real estate forecasting being to either start with a wide range of variables and then progressively remove those that do not add sufficiently to forecasting power or to start with one variable and progressively add those that contribute sufficiently to forecasting power.

For real estate forecasting, the number of informative variables for econometric models is generally found to be relatively small with around five variables often found to be sufficient. Real estate market modelling, as with modelling generally, raises a wide range of issues around statistical and econometric validity which require the skills of an expert statistician or econometrician to consider. Accordingly, REIT Research Teams often include qualified and experienced statisticians and econometricians to manage such issues and reliance on models developed by those without such skills may be considered to comprise an unacceptable REIT governance risk (Hoesli and MacGregor, 2000).

Modelling rentals
Rental growth forecasting models will generally include variables for supply and demand. For example, in an office market, supply variables may include the amount and type of vacant space, the level of new development underway, the level of new development for which planning consent has been granted but construction not yet commenced together with an assessment of probability of construction and so forth. Demand variables may include white collar employment trends by economic sector, average space per employee trends, expectations for changes in taste concerning different locations or positions and so forth.

The supply and demand variables will then be combined in an econometric model to forecast trends in rentals which may be undertaken at the level of the sector (for example, the entire office market or the office market of a given city), the sub-sector (for example, the office market for a downtown area), a distinct grouping within a sub-sector (for example, the banking precinct within a downtown sub-sector) or the asset level (for example, a specific building). In each case, care is required with the quality of data used in the model given that, as the level of granularity increases, the availability of data generally decreases. For example, models at a national level may efficaciously link rental growth to key economic and real estate market variables but this may be more challenging at a regional or city level (Baum, 2002).

Modelling capitalisation or discount rates

Forecasts of rental growth are then central to forecasts of capitalisation or discount rate movement, with the rigour, robustness and reliability of the econometric model developed to forecast capitalisation or discount rate movements being heavily dependent upon the rigour, robustness and reliability of the econometric model developed to forecast rental growth. Econometric models developed to forecast capitalisation or discount rates will generally include a range of economic and capital markets variables such as inflation expectations, risk free rate or central government bond rate expectations and some measure of risk premium expectations which may incorporate or act as a measure of sentiment.

The final step in the forecasting process is then to combine the forecasts for rental growth with those for capitalisation or discount rate movements to provide a forecast of total return expectation. Depending on the level at which the forecasts were prepared, adaptation may be required for application at the individual asset level. Having regard to such forecasts, the Portfolio Management, Strategy and Research Teams may then identify and focus on those aspects of identified property assets that may contribute to higher growth or lower risk than forecast and so may influence pricing. The use of forecast information may then assist in providing a preference ranking for identified property assets, building on the analysis of current information previously undertaken.

Information processing

Through the lenses of current information and forecast information, the wide range of sources of information concerning alternative assets may be narrowed and then processed in a logical and rational manner. The purpose of such information processing is to ensure adherence with Stock Selection criteria, to develop a target list of potential properties for acquisition, to seek to identify the potential for mis-pricing and so to identify potential opportunities for abnormal returns.

Having identified properties that have the greatest propensity for mis-pricing, it is now necessary to impound the information collated into pricing in order to establish whether such assets are mis-priced and so may offer a source of abnormal return which is considered further in the next chapter.

2.6.3 Asset Identification

Following completion of the Asset Identification Step, a REIT should have applied the filter of current and forecast information to identify a target list of potential assets for acquisition that meet the Stock Selection criteria and have the highest potential for greater growth or lower risk contributing to the greatest propensity for mis-pricing. The Asset Identification Step may overlap with the Preliminary Negotiation Step of the Dealing Stage, with the application of forecast information in the assessment of whether a potential acquisition is mis-priced being undertaken in the Advanced Financial Analysis Step of the Dealing Stage.

2.7 Super REIT

Having completed the Envisioning Stage, Super REIT has developed a Vision to be the premier diversified REIT on the stock exchange, interdependent with its adopted generic and specific investment management Style which is active, top down, growth and value added, respectively. To attain this Vision, Super REIT has identified four Goals including to be within the top quartile return performance with lowest quartile tracking error of the stock exchange REIT index every year. Consistently, Super REIT's Strategic Plan focuses on return optimisation at the REIT, portfolio and property level together with effective risk management, supported by a large number of specified Objectives encompassing all REIT management executives in the respective Teams and so aligning the motivations and actions of all REIT management executives with the attainment of Super REIT's Vision.

Accordingly, Super REIT now seeks to develop a Property Portfolio Strategy which will contribute that level of performance which results in the target quartile ranking within the stock exchange REIT index. An approach to and issues associated with targeting top quartile rankings were considered above. Such an approach may provide the REIT management team with an indication of the potential range or goal posts within which the target quartile performance of the stock exchange REIT index may lie.

Following completion of the Strategic Asset Allocation Step, Super REIT may determine to invest 50% of funds in the retail sector, 40% in the office sector and 10% in the industrial sector with 60% of funds to be invested in northern states and 40% in southern states. Comparison of the determined Strategic Asset Allocation to the current composition of the REIT portfolio may indicate the need for limited portfolio rebalancing which, while considered further in Chapter 6, is assumed to not be required for Super REIT at this time.

Following completion of the Tactical Asset Allocation Step, Super REIT may determine to make a Tactical Asset Allocation of 2.5% to Metropolis, a minor city in a northern state, for a period of two years. Metropolis is identified to currently have an undersupply of office accommodation and to be facing increased forecast demand for office space due to a recent increase in local economic activity. Analysis indicates that it will take three years for new office supply to be developed and in the interim there is likely to be significant rental growth as various occupiers compete for a limited amount of vacant office accommodation.

Effectively, Super REIT is overweighting its portfolio to office in a nominated city in a northern state in order to benefit from forecast short term outperformance, with a two year holding period horizon anticipating benefit from rising rental levels with sale before new office buildings are completed and the accommodation supply increases. Comparison of the existing portfolio composition with the Tactical Asset Allocation may identify the requirement to increase the exposure to the office sector in Metropolis through acquisition.

Following completion of the Stock Selection Step, Super REIT may identify that the target lot size should be around $375 million each, or 2.5% of the REIT total portfolio. Further, this should be invested in properties with freehold title in order to avoid any of the problems associated with diminishing leasehold title and onerous obligations. Office stock should be located in prime office locations within the downtown precincts of specified cities, rather than near city or suburban locations. Additionally, stock should comprise A grade, high rise, modern office towers being less than ten years old, rather than B grade, low rise office properties being more than ten years old and principally leased to corporate tenants (being of greater credit worthiness than professional services firms) rather than government tenants (who may be more unwilling to pay higher rents than corporate tenants).

With a requirement for office property in Metropolis and with defined Stock Selection criteria, the Portfolio Management, Strategy, Research and Capital Transactions Teams now need to identify a target list of office properties that are around $375 million with freehold title in prime office locations within the downtown precinct of Metropolis and which are A grade, high rise, modern office towers less than ten years old and principally leased to corporate tenants.

Based on existing market knowledge, the Capital Transactions, Portfolio Management, Strategy and Research Teams identify three potential properties for acquisition in Metropolis and a further property is externally introduced to the Capital Transactions Team through their extensive network of real estate market contacts.

The Asset Identification Step overlaps with Steps in the Dealing Stage as some properties may be already known to the Portfolio Management, Strategy and Research Teams, some may already be known to the Capital Transactions Team and some may surface as a result of this particular acquisition requirement.

Having undertaken the Property Portfolio Strategy, Strategic Asset Allocation, Tactical Asset Allocation, Stock Selection and Asset Identification Steps, Super REIT has now completed the Planning Stage which may result in Super REIT having identified a target list of specific assets for acquisition. This now leads into the Dealing Stage of the REIT real estate investment decision making process where Super REIT may convert the target list into an in-principle transaction for the acquisition of a nominated asset. Further, Super REIT has now completed the Preparing Phase, comprising the Envisioning and Planning Stages, being now ready to move into the second Phase being the Transacting Phase.

2.8 Preparing Phase

Completion of the Envisioning Stage and Planning Stage finalise the Preparing Phase of the REIT real estate investment decision making process. Essentially, the REIT has articulated where it is going and how it is going to get there, providing unitholders with a clear understanding of the risk-return profile to expect from the managers investment of their funds.

Having completed the Preparing Phase, the REIT now moves into the Transacting Phase comprising the Dealing Stage and Executing Stage, where the REIT manager seeks to implement the outcomes of the Preparing Phase through the creation of a tangible real estate portfolio. Completion of the Transacting Phase then gives way to the Observing Phase, comprising the Watching and Optimising Stages, of the REIT real estate investment decision making process.

2.9 Summary

The first Phase of the REIT real estate investment decision making process, the Preparing Phase, comprised the Envisioning Stage (considered in Chapter 1) and the Planning Stage (considered in this Chapter). The Planning Stage comprises the Steps of development of the Property Portfolio Strategy, Strategic Asset Allocation, Tactical Asset Allocation, Stock Selection and Asset Identification.

The Planning Stage comprises a rational and logical process, which gradually breaks down the entire real estate market to identify sectors, geographies and the profile of individual assets for potential acquisition, together with an appreciation of those aspects that may be mis-priced and so contribute outperformance. As such, the Planning Stage may combine the use of sophisticated quantitative analysis, such as modern portfolio theory and the Capital Asset Pricing Model, as well as qualitative, judgmental approaches based on knowledge and experience. Adherence to the enunciated process of the Planning Stage, through each of the Steps of Strategic Asset Allocation, Tactical Asset Allocation, Stock Selection and Asset Identification, provides the levels of transparency and clarity that are consistent with the role of the REIT as a fiduciary.

Strategic Asset Allocation, through the use of modern portfolio theory and the Capital Asset Pricing Model, promises much for the improvement of real estate investment decision making. However, while the situation is continually improving, current shortcomings in the quality and availability of real estate data significantly limit the benefits from application.

While Tactical Asset Allocation offers the opportunity to achieve outperformance through the adoption of a wide range of strategies within sectoral, geographic, style based and other approaches, such strategies are counter to the principles of diversification. Through Tactical Asset Allocation, a REIT is intentionally taking on idiosyncratic and unsystematic risk which must be reflected in the risk adjusted forecast return to justify the proposed acquisition.

A key aspect of the application of knowledge and experience is the achievement of an implementable balance between the asset profile indicated during Strategic Asset Allocation, Tactical Asset Allocation and Stock Selection using quantitative approaches and the heterogeneous nature of the real estate market. Such a balance should be prescriptive enough to preserve the integrity of REIT portfolio risk-return forecasts, but also flexible enough to permit multiple properties to fit within the Stock Selection criteria. If too narrow, then no properties will be sourced and if too wide, then too many properties will be sourced, with both alternatives consuming significant time and resources during which months the real estate market will have moved on, such that the whole process will require repeating. Meanwhile, valuable time in generating incremental, accretive returns has been irretrievably lost.

It is, however, such an heterogeneous nature that provides the basis for many of the limitations of market efficiency in the real estate market that provide sources for potential mis-pricing. An appreciation of the concepts of market efficiency, information processing and the contributors to mis-pricing in the context of Stock Selection and Asset Identification provide the building blocks for the identification of accretive real estate acquisition opportunities.

Completion of the Planning Stage may result in the conversion of the REIT's Vision into the identification of a target list of specific real estate assets for potential acquisition that meet the Stock Selection criteria and may be mis-priced, leading into the Dealing Stage of the REIT real estate investment decision making process, which is considered in the next chapter.

Completion of the Envisioning Stage and the Planning Stage mark completion of the first of the three Phases, the Preparing Phase, wherein the REIT articulates where it is going and how it is going to get there, providing unitholders with a clear understanding of the risk-return profile to expect from the manager's investment of their funds.

This leads to the second Phase of the REIT real estate investment decision making process, the Transacting Phase, completion of which then leads to the third and final phase, the Observing Phase.

2.10 Key points

- The **Planning Stage** is the second and final Stage in the Preparing Phase, being the first of three Phases preceding the Transacting Phase and the Optimising Phase.
- The Planning Stage is an **iterative process** comprising the Strategic Asset Allocation, Tactical Asset Allocation, Stock Selection and Asset Identification Steps.
- **Principal participants** in the Planning Stage are the Portfolio Management, Strategy and Research Teams.
- **Property Portfolio Strategy** provides the route map linking a REIT's Vision to an operational real estate portfolio.
- Property Portfolio Strategy emphasises the predominant **role of the portfolio** over the specific asset, where the impact of an asset on the portfolio is of greater consequence than the acquisition as an independent transaction.
- The real estate portfolio will be likely to be in a **constant state of imperfection**, whereby exact target allocations are rarely, if ever, achieved and the performance of the REIT portfolio at best approximates the target risk-return forecasts.
- **Strategic Asset Allocation** comprises the analysis of the entire real estate market through a range of lenses, such as sectoral or geographic, using quantitative analysis to identify investable and non-investable sections and the optimal allocation to each to achieve the target risk-return forecasts.

- Allocation ranges derived from Strategic Asset Allocation should be considered as **guide posts** for the Portfolio Management, Strategy and Research Teams to use when making individual property level decisions.
- **Tactical Asset Allocation** offers the opportunity to achieve outperformance through an overweight or underweight exposure in the REIT portfolio in the short term. It is, however, counter to the principles of diversification through the intentional acceptance of idiosyncratic and unsystematic risk and so must be justified by an appropriate forecast risk adjusted return.
- **Stock Selection** comprises the process of determining those criteria that may make assets suitable for acquisition by a REIT including generic criteria (such as return and risk expectation or lot size) and specific criteria (such as legal, location, building or tenancy criteria), being a balance between being flexible enough to permit implementation but constrained enough to preserve the integrity of REIT portfolio risk-return forecasts.
- **Asset Identification** comprises the process of identifying potential assets for acquisition that meet the Stock Selection criteria and indicate potential for greater growth or lower risk and the propensity for mis-pricing.
- Completion of the Planning Stage may result in the conversion of the REIT's Vision into an **identified target list of specific real estate assets** for potential acquisition that meet the Stock Selection criteria and may be mis-priced.
- Completion of the Envisioning Stage and the Planning Stage mark completion of the first Phase, the Preparing Phase, wherein the REIT articulates where it is going and how it is going to get there, providing unitholders with a **clear understanding of the risk-return profile** to expect from the manager's investment of their funds, positioning the REIT to then enter the second phase, the Transacting Phase.

References

Further information concerning issues considered in this chapter may be found in the following texts:

Baum, A.E. (2002) *Commercial Real Estate Investment*, Estates Gazette, London.
Brown, G.R. (1991) *Property Investment and the Capital Markets*, E&FN Spon, London.
Brown, G.R. and Matysiak, G.A. (2000) *Real Estate Investment: A Capital Market Approach*, Financial Times Prentice Hall, Harlow.
Fama, E.F. (1970) Efficient Capital Markets: A Review of Theory and Empirical Work, *Journal of Finance*, **XXV**(2), p.383.

Geltner, D.M., Miller, N.G., Clayton, J. and Eichholtz, P. (2007) *Commercial Real Estate Analysis and Investment*, Thomson South-Western, Mason.

Hartzell, D., Schulman, D. and Wurtzebach, C. (1987) Refining the Analysis of Regional Diversification for Income Producing Real Estate, *Journal of Real Estate Research*, **2**(2), p.85.

Hoesli, M. and MacGregor, B. (2000) *Property Investment – Principles and Practice of Portfolio Management*, Longman, Harlow.

Hudson-Wilson, S. and Wurztebach, C. (1994) *Managing Real Estate Portfolios*, Irwin, Burr Ridge.

Lintner, J. (1965) Security Prices, Risk and Maximal Gains From Diversification, *Journal of Finance*, **20**(4), p.587.

Louargand, M.A. (1992) A Survey of Pension Fund Real Estate Portfolio Risk Management Practices, *Journal of Real Estate Research*, **7**(4), p.361.

Markowitz, H.M. (1952) Portfolio Selection, *Journal of Finance*, **7**(1), p.77.

Mossin, J. (1966) Equilibrium in a Capital Asset Market, *Econometrica*, **34**(4), p.768.

Pagliari, J.L. (ed.) (1995) *The Handbook of Real Estate Portfolio Management*, Irwin, Chicago.

Ratcliffe, J. (2000) Scenario Building: A Suitable Method for Strategic Property Planning? *Property Management*, **18**(2), p.127.

Sharpe, W.F. (1964) Capital Asset Prices: A Theory of Market Equilibrium Under Conditions of Risk, *Journal of Finance*, **XIX**(3), p.425.

Webb, J. (1984) Real Estate Investment Acquisition Rules for Life Insurance Companies and Pension Funds: A Survey, *AREUEA Journal*, **12**(4), p.495.

Webb, J. and McIntosh, W. (1986) Real Estate Acquisition Rules for REITs: A Survey, *Journal of Real Estate Research*, **1**(1), p.67.

Worzala, E.M. and Bajtelsmit, V.L. (1997) Real Estate Asset Allocation and the Decisionmaking Framework Used by Pension Fund Managers, *Journal of Real Estate Portfolio Management*, **3**(1), p.47.

Wurtzebach, C.H., Miles, M.E. and Cannon, S.E. (1994) *Modern Real Estate*, John Wiley & Sons, Inc., New York.

3

Dealing

Chapter 1 outlined the Envisioning Stage of the REIT real estate investment decision making process comprising the Steps of development of a Vision, Goals, Style, Strategic Plan and Objectives for the REIT. On completion of this Stage, the REIT should have a clearly articulated destination together with a high order route map by which to get to the destination and some measurable outcomes to determine whether or not the REIT has arrived at the destination.

Having completed the Envisioning Stage, Super REIT has developed a Vision to be the premier diversified REIT on the stock exchange, interdependent with its adopted generic and specific investment management Style which is active, top down, growth and value added, respectively. To attain this Vision, Super REIT has identified four Goals including to be within the top quartile return performance with lowest quartile tracking error of the stock exchange REIT index every year. Consistently, Super REIT's Strategic Plan focuses on return optimisation at the REIT, portfolio and property level together with effective risk management, supported by a large number of specified Objectives encompassing all REIT management executives in the respective teams and so aligning the motivations and actions of all REIT management executives with the attainment of Super REIT's Vision.

Chapter 2 then outlined the Planning Stage of the REIT real estate investment decision making process comprising the Steps of development of the Property Portfolio Strategy, Strategic Asset Allocation, Tactical Asset Allocation, Stock Selection and Asset Identification. On completion of this Stage, the REIT should have converted its Vision into an identified target list of specific property assets for potential acquisition that meet the Stock Selection criteria and may be mis-priced.

Global Real Estate Investment Trusts: People, Process and Management,
First Edition. David Parker.
© 2011 David Parker. Published 2011 by Blackwell Publishing Ltd.

On completion of the Planning Stage, Super REIT has developed a Property Portfolio Strategy with a Strategic Asset Allocation comprising a sectoral allocation (50% retail, 40% office, 10% industrial) and geographic allocation (60% northern, 40% southern states), enhanced by a Tactical Asset Allocation of 2.5% to the office sector in the northern city of Metropolis for a period of two years reflecting a forecast undersupply of office accommodation. Within the allocation to the office sector, Super REIT has developed Stock Selection criteria specifying lots of around $375 million each, being freehold title in prime office locations within the downtown precincts of specified cities and A grade, high rise, modern office towers that are less than ten years old, being principally leased to corporate tenants.

Completion of the Envisioning Stage and the Planning Stage mark the completion of the first of the three Phases, the Preparing Phase, wherein the REIT articulates where it is going and how it is going to get there, providing unitholders with a clear understanding of the risk-return profile to expect from the managers investment of their funds.

Having completed the Preparing Phase, the REIT then moves into the second of the three phases, the Transacting Phase, comprising the Dealing Stage (considered in this chapter) and the Executing Stage (considered in Chapter 4), wherein the REIT manager seeks to implement the outcomes of the Preparing Phase through the creation of a tangible property portfolio leading to the third and final phase, the Observing Phase, of the real estate investment decision making process which comprises the Stages of Watching and Optimising.

The REIT now enters the Dealing Stage of the REIT real estate investment decision making process which is the subject of this chapter. The Dealing Stage comprises the Steps of Preliminary Negotiation, Preliminary Analysis, Structuring, Advanced Financial Analysis and Portfolio Impact Assessment.

Completion of the Dealing Stage may result in the REIT having converted a target list of specific real estate assets for potential acquisition into an in-principle transaction for the acquisition of a nominated asset, leading into the Executing Stage which is considered in the next chapter.

It should be noted that the Dealing and Executing Stages may be commonly applied to real estate acquisitions, real estate disposals and other real estate transactions. For the sake of simplicity, this and the following chapter consider the Dealing and Executing Stages in the context of a real estate acquisition. Arguably, given not only the financial costs of disposal but also the loss of sunk costs of considerable intellectual capital from past management of the real estate asset, disposal requires as much if not more careful analysis and consideration than acquisition.

Accordingly, by the end of this chapter, the reader should understand:

- the importance of maintaining a wide **network of contacts** in the real estate market and of the Portfolio Management, Strategy, Research and

Capital Transactions Teams working closely together through the lengthy, iterative and repetitive Dealing Stage;

- the **challenging balance**, between theoretical principles and practical real estate market limitations, required for the effective implementation of Property Portfolio Strategy;
- the role of **market efficiency and information processing**, by impounding information into prices through the use of a pricing model, in the determination of mis-pricing;
- the role and management of risk within a pricing model together with the role of **explicit risk analysis**;
- the relationship between a REIT's **weighted average cost of capital and target return** and issues associated with and the suitability of commonly used decision rules such as **NPV** and **IRR**; and
- the distinction between **price, value and worth**, in the context of real estate investment, and their relationship with mis-pricing.

3.1 People

While the steps comprising the Planning Stage principally involved the Portfolio Management Team with support from the Strategy Team and Research Team, the transition into the Dealing Stage involves further support from the Capital Transactions Team.

The iterative process of the evolving Asset Identification Step that continues into the Preliminary Negotiation Step of the Dealing Stage requires the combined contribution of the Portfolio Management, Strategy, Research and Capital Transactions Teams working as an interactive group. While the Capital Transactions Team may be likely to contribute to the Asset Identification Step of the Planning Stage, their principal involvement may be likely to flow from the Preliminary Negotiation Step of the Dealing Stage through to the Settlement Step of the Watching Stage.

3.1.1 Capital Transactions Team

The role of the Capital Transactions Team is to acquire and dispose of real estate assets, with the principal purpose of the role being to provide the interface between the REIT and transacting participants within the real estate market and the scope of the role including all portfolios within the REIT.

The Capital Transactions Team usually reports to the Portfolio Management Team, without any direct reports but usually responsible for managing a wide range of external leasing and sales agency, marketing and other service providers.

The principal contribution of the Capital Transactions Team is to facilitate the addition or deletion of assets to or from portfolios, with the functions of the role including:

- **sourcing vendors** with assets for acquisition that accord with Stock Selection criteria;
- **sourcing purchasers** of assets for disposal;
- negotiating **heads of terms** for acquisition or disposal of assets;
- continuing **focus on market activity**, transacting participants, rental value and capital value trends; and
- maintaining an **extensive contact network** of market participants and influencers.

Depending on the size of the REIT, the Capital Transactions Team may be arranged as generalists dealing with all types of real estate nationally or as sectoral and/or geographic specialists. If the Strategic Plan of the REIT involves international investment, consideration will need to be given to offshore strategy, research and capital transactions capacity in key countries, regions or cities depending on the nature of the REIT's broker relationships and adoption or otherwise of a local joint venture partner business model.

3.2 Preliminary Negotiation

The search for potential acquisition properties is an iterative process that commences in the Asset Identification Step with those properties already known to the Portfolio Management, Strategy, Research or Capital Transactions Teams analysed through the filter of current available information to identify those that may appear likely to be mis-priced.

The Dealing Phase commences with the Capital Transactions Team undertaking a co-ordinated search of the target market to identify assets that fit the Stock Selection criteria but are not already known to the Portfolio Management, Strategy, Research or Capital Transactions Teams. The formalisation of the search through the announcement of a specific require-ment may lead to externally introduced properties, being those where vendors or brokers contact the Capital Transactions Team to offer a property, as well as legitimising the cold-call approach by the Capital Transactions Team to real estate owners to gauge an interest in sale. Retention of a bro-kerage firm may also assist the Capital Transactions Team in accessing a deeper pool of opportunities.

The Capital Transactions Team function of maintaining an extensive contact network of market participants and influencers cannot be underes-timated given the decentralised and inefficient nature of the real estate market. As Baum (2002) succinctly observes, when *'operating in the complex market web of telephone, email and socializing'*, interpersonal skills are essential with the contact network fundamental to access an appropriate quantity and quality of potential transactions. Given the high level of competition, such close relationships provide early knowledge of product availability offering a competitive advantage. Consistent with the importance of such contact information, research by Gallimore et al. (2000) found that personal contacts and information gained outside of the public domain was weighted more highly by market participants than data accessible to everybody.

Original research by Gallimore et al. (2000) found that 62% of investors stated individuals or market contacts to be an important data source in the UK property investment business.

The authors suggest that the reliance of UK property investors on contact information makes property investment one of the last remaining '*coffee house*' businesses in the UK.

However, given the level of interaction that should be ongoing between the Capital Transactions Team and other real estate market participants, it is likely that their awareness of potential properties for sale would be extensive such that those arising from the formalisation of the search may be few.

The process of Asset Identification is, however, iterative being a repetitive cycle of search, suggestions and filtering through current available information from which a target list of specific assets for acquisition gradually distils that generally meet the Stock Selection criteria and indicate potential for greater growth or lower risk so increasing the propensity for mis-pricing.

As previously noted, the principles of Stock Selection require a fine balance to be struck between being prescriptive enough to preserve the integrity of REIT portfolio risk-return forecasts while being flexible enough to permit multiple properties to fit within the Stock Selection criteria given that, at any point in time, only a subset of that sample may be available for consideration. Therefore, if the Stock Selection criteria are defined too prescriptively, the number of properties available for potential acquisition through Asset Identification may, at best, be one or two or, at worst, be zero.

If, for example, the Stock Selection criteria broadly encompassed eight properties within a given market, it may be possible that less than four may be available for sale at a given time. Further competition from other investors may result in the number of properties available for sale being fewer or the prices being higher, reducing the prospect of securing a mis-priced property and so earning abnormal returns. This serves to reinforce the importance of the original, proprietorial research undertaken by the Strategy and Research Teams in identifying markets for potential outperformance ahead of other market participants and the unassailable advantage that an effective Strategy Team and Research Team can therefore provide to a REIT.

It may be assumed, for the purposes of this example, that three of the four available properties were internally identified and one was externally introduced in the Asset Identification Step. During the Preliminary Negotiation Step, the Capital Transactions Team will undertake initial discussions with the owners of the four identified properties to establish whether or not there is a willingness to sell and, if so, the nature of the terms upon which such a transaction may take place. The Capital Transactions Team may also attempt to obtain further information from the owners of the four identified properties for use in the next Step, Preliminary Analysis.

Given that three of the four potential acquisition properties on the target list were internally identified, it is possible that the owners are not willing to consider sale at the given time. Following Preliminary Negotiation, the Capital Transactions Team may ascertain that two of the four owners are unwilling to consider sale at the given time, resulting in Preliminary Negotiation reducing the target list of potential properties for acquisition to two properties.

As is often the case, neither of the two properties on the target list of potential properties for acquisition may exactly match the Stock Selection criteria, though both are close to the Stock Selection criteria but each display some positive and some negative characteristics (or growth characteristics and risk characteristics) relative to the Stock Selection criteria. Accordingly, Preliminary Analysis is required to seek to determine which of the potential acquisition properties may be preferable.

3.3 Preliminary Analysis

Preliminary Analysis is effectively undertaken on an ongoing basis by those involved in the REIT real estate investment decision making process, without necessarily realising that they are doing so, to provide a quick snapshot of the characteristics of the transaction under consideration. The simplistic, single period analyses that comprise Preliminary Analysis also provide the short form currency of discussion on relativity within the REIT industry.

The most typical and regularly used form of single period analysis comprises some form of net income to capital relativity expression, such as the capitalisation rate, which may be quoted on an unqualified basis for properties offered for sale, bids made or sales completed to provide an instant measure of relativity against a previously quoted capitalisation rate or expression for other transactions. Regardless of the pinpoint accuracy or otherwise of the capitalisation rate or expression quoted, its appeal lies in its apparent simplicity.

In addition to a wide range of quantitative Preliminary Analysis techniques, the REIT investment decision making process also incorporates complementary qualitative Preliminary Analysis techniques.

3.3.1 Qualitative Preliminary Analysis

Qualitative Preliminary Analysis may be summed up by the notion of *'feel'* or *'gut feel'* for a specific potential real estate acquisition, being a qualitative screening process undertaken intuitively or instinctively by a REIT management executive based on past experience and grounded in prior knowledge, being often summarised in a simple tick/cross table to develop a *'feel'* for alternative properties.

The process may include regard to such qualitative screening factors as prior knowledge of an area or experience with a property type, the perceived opportunity to add value or acquire the property at a discount, various portfolio considerations, the availability of finance and so forth (Gallimore et al., 2000). Further, perception and subsequent behaviour are largely influenced by the most immediate past experience (Roulac, 2001) such that a recent successful transaction in a particular real estate sector may lead to a potentially unfounded confidence in the ability to pick the next successful transaction.

The role of Qualitative Preliminary Analysis should not be underestimated and requires careful management. While aspects of a property may change over time, such as the tenancy profile, following the addition of further tenants of increased creditworthiness, or building profile, following a major air conditioning upgrade, if the recollection of the head of the Capital Transactions Team is of the property prior to such changes, the property may be deleted from the target list based solely on Qualitative Preliminary Analysis. In such a situation, reflecting the dynamics of team interaction, it will require considerable fortitude on the part of other team members, supported by the results of Quantitative Preliminary Analysis, to return such a property to the target list.

3.3.2 Quantitative Preliminary Analysis

As referred to above, the simplistic, single period analyses that comprise Quantitative Preliminary Analysis also provide the short form currency of discussion on relativity within the REIT industry. As such, the measures

Table 3.1 Quantitative preliminary analysis: common US heuristics.

Method	Form	Heuristic
Payback methods	Multipliers	Gross income multiplier
		Net income multiplier
		Before tax cash flow multiplier
		After tax cash flow multiplier
	Rates of return	Overall capitalisation rate (most commonly used)
		Equity dividend rate
		After tax return
Average rates of return		Average return on net operating income
		Average return on before tax cash flow
		Average return on after tax cash flow

From Jaffe and Sirmans (2001). *Fundamentals of Real Estate Investments*, 3E. © 1995 Delmar Learning, a part of Cengage Learning, Inc. Reproduced by permission. www.cengage.com/permissions.

commonly used vary between countries though the most common, being some form of net income to capital relativity expression such as the capitalisation rate, is adopted in some form in most countries with an active REIT market.

Such derivations of the capitalisation rate or other expression of some form of income relative to some form of capital value, may be calculated based on the limited amount of information available on a potential real estate acquisition at the point of Preliminary Analysis. In each case, Quantitative Preliminary Analysis comprises heuristics, being simple, single period expressions that omit more information about the potential real estate acquisition than they contain, but offer a *'quick and dirty'* approximation of more rigorous analysis and provide an instant impression of relativity upon which to form an initial opinion. Accordingly, it is common to consider several forms of Quantitative Preliminary Analysis measures as individual measures considered in isolation may provide an inappropriate impression of the potential real estate acquisition.

Drawing heavily on the work of Jaffe and Sirmans (2001), to which the reader is directed for more detailed consideration, measures of Quantitative Preliminary Analysis may be grouped into three types being heuristics (rules of thumb), ratio analysis and appraisal techniques.

Heuristics
Such measures generally comprise some form of payback method or reciprocal rate of return and average rate of return measures, including those heuristics summarised in Table 3.1. Focus on before/after tax and equity based measures may be less common outside the US, but the basic principles of simple dual variable expressions and averaging are common in many

Table 3.2   Ratio analysis: common US ratios.

Form	Ratios
Leverage ratios	Mortgage debt to property value ratio (loan to value ratio) Debt coverage ratio Default ratio
Operating activity ratios	Total asset turnover ratio Operating expense ratio
Profitability ratios	Profit margin Return to equity on total investment Return on equity

From Jaffe and Sirmans (2001). *Fundamentals of Real Estate Investments*, 3E. © 1995 Delmar Learning, a part of Cengage Learning, Inc. Reproduced by permission. www.cengage.com/permissions.

countries. Certain REITs may develop their own quantitative Preliminary Analysis measures to reflect particular requirements, such as the percentage of income sourced from corporate tenants for use by a REIT that has a Stock Selection criterion to invest in real estate principally leased to corporate tenants.

As simple measures, rules of thumb suffer from significant limitations that should be borne in mind but are often given insufficient weight. Given the simplicity, imprecision and potential for error in such measures, there is considerable uncertainty about the quality of the decision made thereupon and the use of multiple measures is strongly recommended.

Ratio analysis

Those measures adopted in ratio analysis are adapted from financial statement analysis for use in real estate investment and provide a measure of the financial feasibility of the investment through the relationship between various parts of the cash flow statement.

There are, essentially, three groups of ratios for consideration comprising leverage, operating activity and profitability ratios as summarised in Table 3.2. Again, as simple measures, ratio analysis suffers from significant limitations that should be borne in mind but are often given insufficient weight. Reflecting the simplicity, imprecision and potential for error in such measures, the resulting ratios may be distorted by many factors such that it is often difficult to generalise whether a particular ratio is 'good' or 'bad'. Similarly, potential real estate investments may include a mixture of apparently 'good' and 'bad' ratios such that it is often difficult to determine whether or not an investment is financially feasible based on ratio analysis alone. Accordingly, the use of multiple measures is strongly recommended.

Appraisal techniques

Such measures are adapted from conventional appraisal techniques for quick and simple application to available data and may include some of the measures considered above. While investment appraisal techniques and comparative sales appraisal techniques may be commonly used around the world, in the US cost based appraisal techniques may also be considered.

The application of investment or income appraisal techniques parallels the Gross Income Multiplier, Net Income Multiplier and overall capitalisation rate referred to above and so suffer from the same limitations. Comparative sales appraisal techniques compare the subject property to other sales using a broad unit measure, such as sale price per square metre net lettable area. This provides the investor with information about the relative value of the property as a whole or particular attributes of the property in the particular market in which it is located, but suffers the limitations of an inadequate data set if there are insufficient comparable sales and with the relevance of the data diminishing with the passage of time.

Cost based appraisal techniques focus on an estimate of the value of the site and the depreciated cost of the improvements thereon based on the concept of replacement cost, being premised on the assumption that a relationship exists between cost minus depreciation and value which may or may not be the case. Cost based appraisal techniques inherently suffer from many further limitations, including the difficulties in measuring cost and depreciation, which also limit their usefulness for Quantitative Preliminary Analysis.

Reflecting the limitations in the use of each of the above appraisal techniques for Quantitative Preliminary Analysis, the use of multiple measures is strongly recommended.

Limitations of Quantitative Preliminary Analysis

The principal limitation of Quantitative Preliminary Analysis is the reliance upon simplistic, single period, deterministic approaches. The variables adopted for such approaches are often information constrained, rather than detailed and comprehensive, involving some form of averaging or some form of assumed stabilised year. Accordingly, extensive application of implicit adjustment rather than explicit adjustment is required with the risk of error compounded if the data being adjusted is sourced from assumption and assertion rather than fact, historic experience or comparable evidence.

The reliance on single period approaches excludes adjustment for time related variables or future information, not least the time value of money. Accordingly, the potential impact of future rental increases, capital expenditure, periodic maintenance costs, vacancies, incentives, losses from defaulting tenants and so forth are not reflected in Quantitative Preliminary

Analysis unless quantified in some way in the single year income or value data adopted. Such quantification is challenging to undertake, further limiting the usefulness of individual measures and reinforcing the importance of the consideration of multiple measures.

3.3.3 *Preliminary Analysis*

Qualitative Preliminary Analysis may draw on past experience grounded in prior knowledge and may be supplemented by a simple tick/cross table to develop a *'feel'* for the alternative properties. Quantitative Preliminary Analysis comprises simplistic, single period analyses that may be based on heuristics or rules of thumb, ratio analysis and the application of appraisal techniques. The simplicity of such measures and their reliance on current information without regard to future information limits their usefulness and reliability with the consideration of several measures strongly recommended.

Application of Qualitative and Quantitative Preliminary Analysis may indicate a preferable alternative potential property acquisition and provide some information on aspects of the property that may positively or negatively affect the pricing of the property, through being a source of growth or risk potential greater than that which the market may have priced into the property. Effectively, Preliminary Analysis is part of the process of impounding information into pricing in search of a mis-priced asset that has the potential to deliver abnormal returns.

It does not, however, provide information on the risk-return profile of the potential acquisition nor on the extent of possible mis-pricing which may contribute to such abnormal returns. Accordingly, while Preliminary Analysis may provide information as to a preference ranking for alternative investments, it does not provide information on whether the prospective returns from such an investment render it acceptable.

3.4 Structuring

Having completed the Preliminary Negotiation Step, the Capital Transactions Team now embark on intermediate negotiations with the vendors in an endeavour to agree the basis upon which the commercial transaction may be structured to suit both the vendor and the purchaser. This Step overlaps, to a degree, with the documentation undertaken in the Transaction Closure Step of the Executing Stage and with the Settlement Step of the Watching Stage.

Simultaneously, the Fund Management Team embarks on the Structuring of the funding transaction to determine the optimal basis upon which the

REIT may pay for the acquisition of the property at the Settlement Step of the Watching Stage.

Real estate transactions involving large investment properties are complex and lengthy. While the principles of each transaction may be common, the differences between transactions may be considerable resulting in time consuming negotiation and extensive, bespoke documentation for each transaction. As negotiations progress, the terms of the transaction and the position of the parties may change significantly requiring the REIT management team, as purchaser, to continually keep in mind the Goals that the transaction is intended to fulfil. If, at any point in the negotiations, the transaction appears no longer likely to fulfil the Goals intended, then it may be appropriate to consider ceasing negotiation and focusing on an alternative opportunity.

3.4.1 Structuring the commercial transaction

As will be considered in the Watching Stage, Settlement is the Step in which investor capital is exchanged for legal title to the investment property and the rights and responsibilities associated therewith. Accordingly, Structuring the commercial transaction forms the first part of identifying on what basis and how much investor capital will be exchanged for legal title and for exactly which associated rights and responsibilities at Settlement.

Investor capital
Depending on the relative bargaining positions of the respective parties, the basis for the transfer of investor capital may be in full at Settlement on a nominated date or staged as a series of payments over a defined period starting on the date of Settlement. For example, payment in full may be made at Settlement which is to be, say, 90 days after exchange of contracts, or payment of 20% of the agreed purchase price may be made at Settlement which is to be, say, 90 days after exchange of contracts with the balance paid in four equal instalments at periods of, say, 90 days thereafter. Such periods could equally be 30, 60 or 180 days or the staged payments in two or three tranches, depending on the strength of the bargaining position of each party.

The structure of the basis for the transfer of investor capital may have a significant effect on the returns from the investment over the payment period, depending on how the transfer of rights and responsibilities is negotiated. For example, if the purchaser negotiates to receive all income from Settlement but to transfer capital by staged payments, the income return from the property will be significantly enhanced for the duration of the staged payments.

Further, the documentation may be negotiated to be unconditional with neither the vendor nor the purchaser required to fulfil any conditions prior to Settlement. Alternatively, either or both of the parties may be required to fulfil one or more conditions prior to Settlement. Such conditions may include regulatory matters such as the obtaining of formal government approvals or certificates, risk management matters such as the execution of leases by major tenants, commercial matters such as the completion of capital expenditure by the vendor or other matters.

The impact of such conditions may include the shifting of risk and/or return between the parties. For example, a condition requiring the execution of a lease by a major tenant shifts an element of tenant risk from the purchaser to the vendor. Similarly, completion of capital expenditure by the vendor may shift risk from the purchaser to the vendor in addition to potentially enhancing the capital return to the purchaser through the value of the asset acquired by the purchaser at Settlement when the condition has been fulfilled by the vendor.

Following Preliminary Negotiation, the vendor is likely to have nominated a purchase price with associated sale conditions and some negotiation may have been entered into. The purchaser, through Preliminary Analysis, will have an appreciation of whether or not the nominated purchase price and associated sale conditions are within the bounds of negotiation to achieve potential acceptability. However, at this Step, it is too early to determine the price that the purchaser will offer the vendor as this is dependent on the outcome of the commercial Structuring of rights and responsibilities, funding Structuring and outcome of the Advanced Financial Analysis Step.

Rights and responsibilities

Structuring the rights and responsibilities to pass at Settlement is fundamental to the pricing process to determine how much the purchaser should pay for the potential real estate investment. Starting from the premise that the purchaser will have the right to receive all revenue and have the responsibility to pay all expenses from Settlement, the respective revenue and expenses need to be identified and agreed between the parties. This is usually achieved by the exchange of a tenancy schedule, copies of lease documents, historic accounting records for expenditure, copies of relevant invoices and so forth.

Specific Structuring will be required where there are unusual revenue streams, such as rent paid annually in advance, or unusual expense streams, such as capital works underway or new tenants not paying rental during an incentive period. Agreeing what will be borne by the vendor and purchaser, respectively, will determine the cash flow from the property for consideration in the Advanced Financial Analysis Step.

Central to the management of risk in the acquisition of a real estate investment is the Structuring of guarantees, warranties and indemnities. Guarantees comprise pledges or agreements to be responsible for an obligation, while warranties are statements of responsibility and indemnities provide protection from loss whereby a party is no worse off if the indemnified matter occurs than if it had not occurred.

Some guarantees, warranties and indemnities will be sought by the parties for manageable risks, such as the vendor indemnifying the purchaser for events prior to purchase or the purchaser warranting to the vendor to observe the terms and conditions of the existing leases. In such cases, the parties may be prepared to give the guarantees, warranties and indemnities and put in place appropriate risk management operational processes to support these.

However, some guarantees, warranties and indemnities may be sought by the parties to manage unquantifiable risk, such as the vendor indemnifying the purchaser for leases not disclosed in the sale contract or the purchaser warranting to use its best endeavours to collect rental debts on behalf of the vendor. During the Structuring Step, the requirement of both parties for guarantees, warranties and indemnities will become apparent and form a key input into the pricing process for the purchaser.

In some cases, there may be matters which are non-negotiable. For example, the governing documents for some REITs preclude or limit the extent to which guarantees, warranties and indemnities may be given or only permit capital expenditure for certain purposes. Accordingly, the transaction will need to be structured to accommodate non-negotiable matters if the transaction is to proceed. This may be addressed through negotiation between the parties, such as by replacing open indemnities with obligations to pay specific dollar amounts if a specified event occurs or by the vendor undertaking capital expenditure which the purchaser is precluded from undertaking and reflection in the agreed sale price.

Preliminary Negotiation provided a broad outline of the possible transaction for analysis. Intermediate negotiations during the Structuring Step then identify and agree a wide range of issues that directly impact upon which rights and responsibilities will be exchanged with legal title at Settlement in return for what form and basis of payment of investor capital. Details of the commercial Structuring of the transaction are essential to undertake the Advanced Financial Analysis Step necessary to understand the risk-return profile of the potential investment and to determine the extent, if any, of potential mis-pricing.

3.4.2 *Structuring the funding transaction*

Simultaneous with the Capital Transactions Team negotiating the basis upon which the commercial transaction may be structured to suit both the vendor and the purchaser, the Fund Management Team embark on the Structuring of the funding transaction to determine the optimal basis upon which the REIT may pay for the property at the Settlement Step of the Watching Stage.

Issues associated with funding a major real estate transaction are both extensive and complex, being briefly considered in summary form only here. Readers are referred to Hawawini and Viallet (2002) for a more detailed consideration of issues concerning debt/equity mix generally and to Rowland (1997) for a more detailed consideration of the forms and sources of debt for real estate investment.

The initial step in Structuring the funding transaction comprises determining who will be the purchasing entity for the proposed real estate acquisition. While this may often be the principal entity comprising the REIT, certain properties may suit acquisition in a separate trust or company entity to accommodate local taxation or regulatory requirements. For example, if local trust law permits a REIT to hold real estate but not to conduct a business from such real estate, it may be preferable to acquire the title to a trading property such as a hotel in the principal entity comprising the REIT but to acquire the business in a separate company entity.

Briefly, Structuring the funding transaction requires consideration of a variety of issues including the level of debt and equity to be used in the transaction and the form and source of the debt to be used.

Debt and equity mix
Determination of the optimal debt and equity mix is a complex area covered extensively in corporate finance texts, with only a cursory overview provided here. At each extreme, the potential real estate acquisition may be funded entirely from equity or entirely from debt with any combination in between possible.

For example, the purchaser may determine to allocate equity to 70% of the proposed investment and raise the balance 30% as debt. Clearly, the level and cost of debt will determine the amount of interest payable and the level of post-debt cash flow available to the REIT.

Many considerations may impact the debt and equity mix, including the cost and availability of both debt and equity and the level of gearing that results for the REIT. If current market conditions are unsupportive of an equity raising, then the REIT may have to consider higher levels of debt. Conversely, if debt availability is limited and the REIT has cash reserves, it may consider using higher equity levels.

The level of REIT gearing is a measure commonly followed closely by REIT analysts with that level acceptable to the market varying over time. Accordingly, REIT gearing requires management relative not only to that of other REITs but also to the expectations of REIT analysts concerning prudent debt levels at differing stages in market cycles.

Working together with the Chief Financial Officer, the Fund Management Team may be expected to consider a wide range of debt-equity combinations and model each, undertaking both sensitivity and scenario analyses for changes in interest rates and other variables, prior to determining the optimal mix.

Form and source of debt

As with the debt and equity mix, determination of the optimal form and source of debt is a complex area covered extensively in corporate finance texts, with only a cursory overview provided here.

Forms of debt available to REITs are continually evolving and becoming ever more sophisticated. Conventional forms of debt may include:

- some form of **loan** – including unsecured or secured by a mortgage over one or more properties or a charge over the assets of the REIT;
- some form of **note or bond** – including fixed term or perpetual, potentially converting into equity;
- some form of **security** – including mortgage backed securities where the debt instrument is tradeable; and
- some form of **hybrid** combination of one or more of the above,

which may be either pre-arranged or existing in anticipation of a transaction or negotiated as the transaction arises.

Like forms of debt, sources of debt available to REITs are continually evolving and becoming ever more sophisticated. While the international banking sector provides a significant proportion of REIT debt, global debt capital markets are now providing a growing proportion as transaction sizes increase.

With the growing sophistication of both forms and sources of debt, the requirements for debt management and, in particular, interest rate management for fixed and floating rate exposures and exchange rate management for foreign currency denominated debt, are increasing exponentially. It is now common for larger REITs with international real estate portfolios to include treasury and foreign exchange executives within the CFO's team to both originate and then manage debt and currency transactions.

In summary, details of how the funding for the transaction will be structured, including the optimal debt-equity mix and form and source of debt funding, are essential to undertake the Portfolio Impact Assessment Step to determine the extent, if any, of the impact of the proposed acquisition on the REIT portfolio.

3.4.3 Documenting the proposed transaction

Having completed the Preliminary Negotiation Step, the commercial structure and funding structure of the proposed transaction are agreed during the intermediate, iterative negotiations of the Structuring Step. The proposed transaction is shaped to form an in-principle transaction which may then be subject to Advanced Financial Analysis to determine the existence and extent of mis-pricing, followed by an assessment of the potential impact of the transaction on the portfolio.

Though further negotiation may be required following completion of the Advanced Financial Analysis Step, it is likely that the parties will seek to document the transaction as agreed in principle in the Structuring Step. Some form of in-principle documentation, such as heads of terms or short form agreement of intent, may be drafted to record the terms and conditions so far agreed between the parties.

Such in-principle documentation will be an essential part of the purchaser's application for Governing Entity approval for both the commercial transaction and the funding transaction and may be required by the vendor to provide sufficient comfort to remove the property from the market and suspend negotiations with other potential purchasers. The extent and detail of such in-principle documentation will be influenced, in part, by the standing of the respective parties and their respective trust worthiness and credit worthiness.

Following completion of the negotiation and subsequent in-principle documentation of the proposed transaction by the Capital Transactions and Fund Management Teams, the Portfolio Management Team then have a clear summary of the proposed transaction with which to undertake the next step of the Dealing Stage, the Advanced Financial Analysis Step.

3.5 Advanced Financial Analysis

The Advanced Financial Analysis Step seeks to determine if the proposed transaction is mis-priced and so offers the opportunity for the REIT to earn abnormal returns. In essence, the two principal methods of determining if the proposed transaction is mis-priced are to compare the worth of the proposed real estate investment to the purchaser with the acquisition price and/or to compare the expected return from the proposed real estate investment with that required by the purchaser.

To establish whether or not an asset is mis-priced requires a theoretical basis for pricing and a practical tool with which to undertake pricing, with the two principal methods incorporating a range of theoretical and practical issues that are considered further in this Step.

To determine the worth of the proposed real estate investment to the purchaser requires not only an understanding of the concept of worth and how that differs from price and value, but also an understanding of the practical issues associated with pricing models which may also provide an estimate of expected return. Similarly, to compare the expected return from the proposed real estate investment with that required by the purchaser requires an understanding of the theoretical and practical issues associated with the purchaser's determination of a required, or target, rate of return. Finally, in order to ensure a rational and consistent basis, some form of decision rule is required to provide the basis for decision making.

For simplicity, these issues will be approached through a consideration of the theoretical and practical issues associated with target rates of return, the theoretical basis of mis-pricing (being consideration of concepts of worth, price and value), the theory and practice of pricing models with a particular focus on risk and the principles of decision rules.

Underlying the concept of mis-pricing is the notion that market inefficiencies may exist that result in mis-pricing, as considered in Chapter 2. Fundamental to notions of market efficiency is the role of information and the way in which information is processed and impounded into prices, particularly forecast information which is not known with certainty. Continuing on from the Asset Identification Step of the Planning Stage, the role of information processing and impounding information into prices is central to the Advanced Financial Analysis Step. In the Asset Identification Step of the Planning Stage, it was principally current available information that was processed and impounded into pricing, whereas in the Advanced Financial Analysis Step it is also forecast information that is processed and impounded into pricing.

The Advanced Financial Analysis Step is effectively the capital budgeting process considered in corporate finance text books. With real estate investment being slow, difficult and incurring high transaction costs followed by a long holding period with high management responsibilities, it may be paralleled with a company making a capital budgeting decision to allocate capital to a long life project such as a new manufacturing plant. Accordingly, readers may find the discussion of capital budgeting in such corporate finance texts as Hawawini and Viallet (2002) to be informative.

Further, a wide range of research has been undertaken into the evolution of the extent to which REITs and other real estate investment groups use quantitative approaches of the type considered below (see, for example: Page, 1983; Wiley, 1976; Kim and Farragher, 1981; Webb, 1984; Webb and McIntosh, 1986; Louargand, 1992; Brzeski et al., 1993; Farragher and Kleiman, 1996; De Wit, 1996; Farragher and Savage, 2008). While there are differences in the findings, it may be generalised that, as time has passed, the use of quantitative approaches has increased though each of the quantitative approaches considered below may not yet be commonly used by REITs while the use of non-quantitative or heuristic measures continues.

For the REIT management team, determining the basis upon which the proposed acquisition would be commercially structured in the previous Step provides the final pieces of current information necessary to undertake the

Advanced Financial Analysis Step to determine the extent, if any, of potential mis-pricing. Completion of the Advanced Financial Analysis Step is followed by the Portfolio Impact Assessment Step which comprises an assessment of the potential impact of the proposed commercial and funding transactions on the existing risk-return profile of the REIT.

3.5.1 Target rate of return

With one of the principal methods of determining if the proposed transaction is mis-priced being to compare the expected return from the proposed real estate investment with that required by the purchaser, an understanding is necessary of the theoretical and practical issues associated with the purchaser's determination of a required, or target, rate of return.

Theoretical issues
The rate of return that a REIT earns from each property acquired will contribute to the rate of return generated by the REIT as a whole. Accordingly, the REIT is not only concerned about the rate of return from the individual real estate asset to be acquired but also the impact that the acquisition, with its attached funding structure, will have on the REIT's overall return performance.

   The Advanced Financial Analysis Step is primarily concerned with the rate of return from the individual real estate asset to be acquired, without the benefit of any return enhancement contributed by the attached funding structure which is the focus of the following Portfolio Impact Assessment Step.

   Accordingly, the target rate of return is the REIT's required rate of return for a specific individual real estate asset to reflect, among other things, the unsystematic and idiosyncratic risk of that asset, effectively being the risk adjusted return expectation of the REIT for that real estate asset. As such, the target rate of return may vary for each potential acquisition under consideration though a REIT may have generic target rates of return for certain unsystematic risk groupings such as different real estate sectors (being office, retail, industrial and so forth) and geographies.

   As considered in Chapter 2, a REIT could adopt the Capital Asset Pricing Model as an approach to pricing a potential property for acquisition. This focuses attention on the quantification of the appropriate beta for the potential property for acquisition as the main input into the required return. While defining and then measuring the expected return on the market portfolio would be challenging, given the current status and availability of relevant real estate market data, the quantification of beta would be even more challenging given its role as an holistic expression of risk. Accordingly, it is proposed to focus on the derivation of target return through approaches other than the Capital Asset Pricing Model, though it is acknowledged that the role of the Capital Asset Pricing Model in pricing a potential real estate acquisition may be expected to increase over the next few years.

The target rate of return should be distinguished from the REIT's weighted average cost of capital (WACC) which is, effectively, the opportunity cost of capital to the REIT. It is important to note, therefore, that the rate at which a REIT is able to borrow funds is not the opportunity cost of capital for a REIT. As an entity listed on a stock exchange, the WACC for a REIT may be derived by the formula:

$$WACC = w_d r_d (1-t) + w_e r_e$$
[Equation 3.1]

where:

WACC	is the weighted average cost of capital	
w_d	is the market value weight of debt	
r_d	is the cost of debt	
w_e	is the market value weight of equity	
r_e	is the geared or levered cost of equity	
t	is the corporate tax rate	(Brown and Matysiak, 2000)

The WACC for a REIT provides a minimum hurdle rate of return for any potential real estate acquisition, with acquisitions showing an expected rate of return above WACC being accretive to shareholder value and those showing an expected rate of return below WACC being dilutive to shareholder value, only being considered for special reasons such as the prospect of significantly increasing short to medium term returns or greatly diversifying risk.

With the determination of the cost of equity being based on the Capital Asset Pricing Model, WACC only compensates investors for systematic risk. Accordingly, compensation for unsystematic and idiosyncratic risk is required through alternative sources such as the cash flow for the property or the target rate of return.

Through the required or target rate of return, a REIT is seeking compensation for loss of liquidity (through a risk free rate), compensation for risk (through a risk premium) and compensation for expected inflation (Baum and Crosby, 1988; Hoesli and MacGregor, 2000). Accordingly, the formula for the required nominal rate of return may be stated as:

$$R_N = RF_R + RP + i_e$$
[Equation 3.2]

where:

R_N is the required nominal rate of return
RF_R is the real risk free rate of return

RP is the risk premium
i_e is the compensation for expected inflation

This focuses attention on three elements, being the real risk free rate, the risk premium and compensation for expected inflation. However, in practice, the formula is generally simplified through the use of a nominal risk free rate, so combining the contributions of the real risk free rate and the compensation for expected inflation, as follows:

$$R_N = RF + RP$$
[Equation 3.3]

where:
R_N is the required nominal rate of return
RF is the nominal risk free rate of return
RP is the risk premium

Accordingly, this focuses attention on the selection of the nominal risk free rate of return and the risk premium.

Nominal risk free rate
Generally, the central government long term bond rate is adopted as a proxy for the nominal risk free rate. While an apparently simple proposition, this raises issues about which central government bond rate to use and the relevant term of the bond rate to be adopted. In the event of offshore investment, a REIT may choose to use the long term bond rate of the country in which the potential acquisition is situated as that rate will form the basis of pricing in that country. Alternatively, a REIT may choose to use the long term bond rate of its country of listing and reflect the risks associated with offshore investment in the selection of the risk premium.

The relevant term of the bond rate to be adopted is generally agreed to be long, but how long is open to debate. A REIT may choose to match the term of the bond rate with the term of the pricing model, using a ten year bond rate for construction of the target rate for use with a ten year forecast cash flow model. Alternatively, a REIT may consider real estate investment to be a long term proposition and so adopt a bond rate of between 20-50 years as appropriate.

To be theoretically robust, the term structure of interest rates should be taken into account in selecting the nominal risk free rate, being the extent to which interest rates vary by term to maturity as illustrated by the yield curve. If the yield curve is not flat, the use of a constant nominal risk free rate in a pricing model could lead to error and readers are referred to Brown and Matysiak (2000) for a fuller consideration of this issue.

Risk premium

Historically, as noted by Dubben and Sayce (1991), the market applied a 2% risk premium for real estate investment to take into account all of the risks involved in real estate when compared to the central government bond rate, with a greater focus on security of income rather than relative sector volatility.

However, over the last 20 years, the sophistication of both theory and practice in the derivation of the risk premium has developed exponentially. Theoretically, the risk premium should reflect the unsystematic and idiosyncratic risks of the potential real estate investment, which may be generally grouped as sectoral/geographic risks and property specific risks, respectively.

Following the work of Baum (2009), reflection of unsystematic risks such as sectoral and geographic risks in the risk premium may be determined through quantitative and qualitative measures. Working from a risk premium that reflects the real estate market as a whole, the sector premium for commercial, retail, industrial and so forth will be based on the relative position of that sector having regard to the sensitivity of the sector to economic shocks, with particular reference to rental growth and depreciation, the illiquidity of the sector and other relevant factors.

Geographic risks may reflect the state, city or economic basis through an assessment of the riskiness of the economic structure of the state or city and its catchment area, together with a consideration of competing locations. The risk premium range may expand from a minimum premium for diversified states or cities with healthy industries, having a low sensitivity to economic shocks and where real estate market liquidity is high, to a maximum premium for states or cities whose economies are concentrated in weak sectors having a heightened sensitivity to economic shocks and where real estate market liquidity is low.

Further, following the work of Baum (2009), reflection of idiosyncratic risk may be considered through four components being tenant risk, building risk, location risk and other identifiable risk. The relative weighting of each may be assessed by multiple regression analysis, using a large sample of individual property investments to determine the relative importance of each variable at a point in time to explain risk premia and then to hypothesise their respective future importance.

Theoretically, it is important to distinguish between those aspects of unsystematic and idiosyncratic risk that are to be reflected in the cash flow and those that are to be reflected in the risk premium, in order to avoid double counting. For example, if a tenant occupying a large area within a potential acquisition property is found to be of limited credit worthiness this could be reflected in either the risk premium or the cash flow. The risk premium may be increased to reflect additional tenant risk or the cash flow may be adjusted by assumptions such as decreased rental income in anticipation of support being required or a vacancy period is anticipation of tenant collapse and vacation. Adoption of allowances in both the risk premium and the cash flow may over compensate for tenant risk, leading to an underassessment of worth, whereas insufficient allowance may lead to an over assessment of worth such that a careful balance is required.

Practically, having derived a risk premium on the above basis, a REIT may then seek to rationalise the choice through comparison to both historic data and market forecasts. Historic risk premium data provides an objective measure of actual market performance for a given period, though consideration should be given to the extent to which such data may include an expectation premium. Market forecasts of risk premium data may be obtained from the REIT's own original research or from surveys of investors undertaken on a regular basis by fee for service research organisations, though consideration should be given to the subjective nature of such forward looking data and the tendency of respondents to be influenced by their past estimates and by potential optimism bias.

Target rate of return
Consistent with Equation 3.3, the nominal risk free rate and the risk premium will sum to provide a REIT's target rate of return for a given potential real estate acquisition. Significantly, while the Preliminary Analysis Step in the Dealing Stage may determine that a potential real estate acquisition is preferable, it is the target or required rate of return that will determine if it is likely to be acceptable.

Practically, as with the rationalisation of the choice of risk premium, a REIT may seek to reconcile the derived target rate of return through comparison to both historic data and market forecasts for discount rates. With due allowance for potentially differing bases of analysis and the limitations of market surveys, such data should only be considered at a high level to ascertain if the target rate of return is within the realm of current transactions or inexplicably higher or lower requiring further consideration.

Reference may be made to the derivation of prevailing market discount rates from the analysis of capitalisation rates arising from recent transactions or from market forecasts, which may be more readily available, together with an allowance for rental growth. However, the myriad of assumptions underlying such an approach render it highly unsafe.

Having derived a property specific target rate of return, a REIT may then combine this with a pricing model to determine the worth of a potential real estate acquisition for comparison to the acquisition price in order to determine the extent, if any, of mis-pricing leading to the potential for the REIT to earn abnormal returns.

3.5.2 *Theoretical basis of mis-pricing*

To establish whether or not an asset is mis-priced requires a theoretical basis for pricing and a practical tool with which to undertake pricing. With one of the principal methods of determining whether a proposed transaction is mis-priced being to compare the worth of the proposed real estate investment to the purchaser with the acquisition price, an understanding is required of the concept of worth and how that differs from price and value, which together form the theoretical basis of mis-pricing.

Price, value and worth

The terms price, value and worth are often used loosely in differing contexts leading to confusion. Accordingly, the globally accepted and carefully worded definitions of the International Valuations Standards Committee (IVSC) are adopted for the purposes of application.

The International Valuation Standards (IVSC, 2007) consider price to be a term used for the amount asked, offered or paid for a good or service. Because of the financial capabilities, motivations, or special interests of a given buyer and/or seller, the price paid for a good or service may or may not have any relation to the value that might be ascribed to the good or service by others. Price is, however, generally an indication of a relative value placed upon a good or service by the particular buyer and/or seller under particular circumstances.

Further, the International Valuation Standards (IVSC 2007) consider value to be an economic concept referring to the price most likely to be concluded by the buyers and sellers of a good or service that is available for purchase. Value is not a fact, but an estimate of the likely price to be paid for a good or service at a given time in accordance with a particular definition of value. The economic concept of value reflects a market's view of the benefits that accrue to one who owns the good or receives the service as of the effective date of valuation. The IVSC define market value to be:

> *The estimated amount for which a property should exchange on the date of valuation between a willing buyer and a willing seller in an arm's-length transaction after proper marketing wherein the parties had each acted knowledgeably, prudently, and without compulsion.* (IVSC, 2007)

Worth is considered by the International Valuation Standards (IVSC, 2007) to be the value of a property to a particular investor, or a class of investors, for identified investment objectives. This subjective concept relates a specific property to a specific investor, group or groups of investors, or entity with identifiable investment objectives and/or criteria. The worth of a property asset may be higher or lower than the value of a property asset.

For the purposes of determining mis-pricing, it is the relativity of worth to price that is of particular relevance. If, through the application of the target rate of return in a pricing model, a REIT determines that the worth of a potential property acquisition is greater than the price of the property, mis-pricing may be identified and the potential to earn abnormal returns may arise.

Context and relativity

From the viewpoint of the REIT management team, price, value and worth may comprise a scenario for a potential property acquisition as follows:

- **price** – being the amount asked by the vendor of the potential property acquisition;
- **value** – being the estimate of the likely price to be paid for the potential property acquisition by an independent appraiser in accordance with the above definition of market value; and
- **worth** – being the amount that the REIT may be willing to pay for the potential property acquisition to achieve a previously nominated target rate of return.

The key concern for the REIT management team is the relativity of worth to price and value. If the real estate market were efficient, price, value and worth would be equal, but this is unlikely to be the case, as considered above. For a property to be mis-priced for a REIT, worth should be greater than price or value indicating that the REIT may earn abnormal returns if able to acquire the asset at price or value.

Of secondary concern to the REIT management team, in its role as a fiduciary, is that price should not exceed value as acquisition of the asset at price will most likely require the support of an Independent Appraisal of value. Related to the concepts of price and value are the aspects of valuation variation or margin of error (being the range of acceptable valuations for a given property at a given point in time) and valuation accuracy (being the systematic difference between valuation and selling price), which are considered in detail in Chapter 5 concerning the Independent Appraisal Step of the Executing Stage (Hoesli and MacGregor, 2000).

In rising or falling markets the rate of change of price, value and worth may be rapid and the relativity between each may also vary rapidly. Further, in markets where one purchaser group has a systemic advantage over another purchaser group, price, value and worth may be particularly challenging concepts to distinguish in practice. For example, if REITs, as listed real estate funds, have the ability to raise capital more easily than unlisted real estate funds for an extended period of time, a clientele effect may manifest where listed real estate funds pay an apparent premium for assets during a specific time period. The question then arises as to when such listed real estate funds become the market, such that the concept of worth to such listed real estate funds, as manifest in price when they each compete to buy an asset, then becomes value.

Having determined a target rate of return for a potential real estate acquisition, the REIT management team now needs to determine the worth of a potential real estate acquisition for comparison to the acquisition price in order to determine if mis-pricing and the opportunity for the REIT to earn abnormal returns may exist. This may be achieved through the combination of the target rate of return and a pricing model.

3.5.3 Pricing models

To establish whether or not an asset is mis-priced and the extent to which it is mis-priced requires a theoretical basis for pricing and a practical tool with which to undertake pricing, being a pricing model. To determine not only the worth of the proposed real estate investment to the purchaser but also an estimate of the expected return, each being methods of determining mis-pricing, requires an understanding of the theory and practice of pricing models with a particular focus on risk.

To be economically valid, a pricing model should comprise:

* all **cash flows**;
* being discounted at, in this case, the REIT's **target rate of return**;
* with the pricing model aiming to **maximise shareholder wealth**;
* providing a choice between **mutually exclusive projects** on the basis of maximising shareholder wealth; and
* allowing projects to be **capable of analysis separately** (Brown and Matysiak, 2000).

Pricing models serve to formalise the process by which worth is assessed for comparison to price, identifying the critical factors and drawing on the information collated and the economic relationships defined between critical variables. Therefore, the quality of the assessment of worth through a pricing model depends on the quality of the information available and the information processing undertaken.

This is particularly important for forecast information which plays a significant role in pricing models. The preparation and application of forecasts is a key role for the Research Team and presents probably their greatest opportunity to contribute to outperformance by a REIT. Professionally prepared forecasts provide a REIT with a robust, rational, explicit outlook against which to judge reality as it unfolds. Clearly, forecasts may only be prepared with the information available at the time of preparation to which, therefore, differing levels of uncertainty attach. Accordingly, the explicit recognition and treatment of risk is an essential feature within pricing models.

The most commonly used pricing model to determine worth is a discounted cash flow model using the investor's target rate of return as the discount rate, being a multi-period, dollar weighted average total return expectation.

Cash flow
The cash flow combines current information which is principally factual and forecast information which is principally judgmental, being assumption based. Such information will include current and forecast revenues and expenses over the cash flow period with an estimate of the terminal value of the property at the end of the cash flow period, discounted back at the target rate of return to provide a present value estimate which represents the worth of the potential property to that investor based on the scenario adopted.

The mathematics of discounted cash flow are extensively addressed in other texts and readers are referred to Hoesli and MacGregor (2000) and Baum and Crosby (2007) for a detailed explanation. A discounted cash flow facility is generally included within the portfolio management software programmes, such as DYNA™, Circle™, Argus™ and Cougar™ referred to in Chapter 2, which has the benefit of standardising the mathematics and allowing the user to focus more closely on the input data.

Suitability of discounted cash flow
As a pricing model to determine the worth of a potential real estate investment, discounted cash flow offers the ability to:

- reflect the size and timing of each **individual cash flow** into the future;
- measure all cash flows throughout the life of the investment plus the impact of the **sale of the property**;
- measure different **sizes and types** of cash flow, including after debt and after tax cash flow;
- reflect an **equity reversion** taking into account selling expenses, if any, and repayment of outstanding debt principal, if any;
- permit all variables to **change over time** at individual rates, reflecting rent reviews, vacancies, bad debts, borrowing rates, tax rates and so forth;
- incorporate the **time value of money** for future cash flows; and
- **incorporate risk** generally and changing levels of risk over time in particular into the cash flow.

Accordingly, discounted cash flow has become the standard tool in real estate investment analysis. Compared to traditional single period analytical tools, discounted cash flow has the benefits of including more explicit input variables and being less restrictive in their measurement which provides significantly greater transparency and flexibility.

Discounted cash flow guidance

Having now been in use by the real estate investment industry for around 25 years, discounted cash flow has evolved significantly and many of the originally contentious aspects have been resolved.

The *Project Appraisal Using Discounted Cash Flow – International Good Practice Guide*, issued by the International Federation of Accountants (International Federation of Accountants, 2008), provides generic guidance on best practice in discounted cash flow, including both principles and application, to which the reader is referred.

Guidance Note 9 on discounted cash flow, issued by the International Valuation Standards Committee (IVSC, 2007), is real estate specific and provides an excellent balance between prescription of minimum requirements and flexibility for application as the basis of good practice, to which the reader is referred.

Reflecting the widespread adoption of software packages such as DYNA™, Circle™, Argus™ and Cougar™ which provide a template layout for the cash flow and include pre-programmed mathematics, such formalised guidance now emphasises the importance of good quality information for use in information processing and the validation of key data for input into the cash flow. Aspects of information quality including accuracy, relevance, reliability, consistency, completeness, timeliness and supportability by market sources and reasoned judgment are emphasised, being fundamental to effective information processing and the validity of input data.

Cash flow structure

The structure of the cash flow essentially comprises decisions concerning period, revenue, expenses and capital, subject to the fundamental requirement not to double count aspects of the potential real estate acquisition in both the cash flow and the risk premium within the target rate of return.

The period to be used for the cash flow requires consideration of duration, start point and end point. While a period of ten years has evolved as the convention for the duration of a cash flow, periods such as five years, 15 years and 20 years are not uncommon. Care is, however, required with the selection of the start point and end point of the cash flow, particularly for properties with unusual characteristics. For example, a single tenant property with 12 years unexpired lease term may be challenging to adequately consider in a ten year cash flow where all issues associated with the imminent lease expiry would have to be addressed in the assessment of terminal value. Use of a 20 year cash flow would facilitate greater transparency and the opportunity to investigate alternative scenarios, such as lease renewal at varying rental levels, differing periods of vacancy before reletting and so forth.

In considering revenue and expenses, attention should be given to the range of revenue and expense sources, the current quantum of each and the forecast growth rates for each in the cash flow. Passing rentals under existing leases should be reflected in the cash flow, together with increases reflecting the prescribed rent review pattern up to lease expiry, when renewal assumptions and revenue forecasts are required. Care is required to ensure consistency of approach between revenue and expenses with certain expenses, such as rates and taxes, often continuing regardless of the level of occupation. Similarly, as leases expire, assumptions are required in the cash flow for the prospects of reletting and the likely period of vacancy during which, consistently, there will be neither rental revenue nor recovery of expenses.

Capital for consideration may include assumptions for both ongoing capital expenditure and the terminal value of the property at the end of the cash flow period. Care is required to ensure consistency between ongoing capital expenditure assumptions and revenue and expense forecasts. For example, if no ongoing capital expenditure is assumed over the cash flow period, consistent revenue assumptions should include lower levels of growth as the building becomes less attractive and expenses assumptions should include higher levels of growth as the cost of repairs and maintenance increases. Conversely, if ongoing capital expenditure is assumed, the benefits of same in increased revenue growth and decreased expense growth should be reflected in the cash flow.

Assessment of the terminal value of the property at the end of the cash flow period requires particular attention. Regard should be given to forecasts for capitalisation and discount rate trends over the cash flow period together with the relativity to those at acquisition. The profile of the property at the end of the cash flow period, in terms of the lease expiry profile, tenant quality profile and building quality profile, consistent with the level of ongoing capital expenditure, should be carefully considered in determining the terminal value for use in the cash flow. For cash flows of a short duration, the terminal value may have a significant impact on present value but this will diminish as the duration of the cash flow increases.

Role of judgment
Cash flows, in common with other forms of computer generated forecasts, suffer from limitations necessitating the application of common sense as a reality check. Jaffe and Sirmans (2001) validly note that, *'Computers are for calculating: investors are for thinking and analysing.'* (Jaffe and Sirmans,

2001) voicing a common concern that the use of software packages fosters an unjustified level of confidence in the validity of the outputs which are then used to make, rather than support, the decision.

Further, awareness is required of the risk of bias affecting information flows, particularly optimism bias. For example, over exuberance in estimates of current market rental levels may be exacerbated by aggressive forecast rental growth rates contributing to a very optimistic assessment of terminal value and resulting in a significantly increased present value. The compounding effect of optimism bias through the various elements of the cash flow requires careful attention, as does the effect of compounding pessimism.

Accordingly, judgment is required in both the assessment of the reasonableness of the assumptions underlying the input data for the cash flow and the rationality of the present value output. The use of software packages should not preclude or supersede the application of insight and intuition, nor the use of simple rules of thumb to provide a reality check on the output.

Original research by Farragher and Kleiman (1996) found that only 46% of rent forecasts in cash flows were appropriate though 62% of operating cost forecasts were appropriate.

Interestingly, 45% of rent forecasts in cash flows were overstated and 34% of operating cost forecasts were understated.

46% of respondents thought this was because analysts were too involved with the project to objectively evaluate its potential, 34% thought analysts lacked the necessary experience and 20% thought it was because analysts felt they needed to support management's pet projects.

Impounding risk
Risk is implicit within the use of a pricing model that includes forecasts of the future made at a given point in time and which may or may not eventuate. The inability to make perfect forecasts requires the explicit consideration of risk in the use of a pricing model. Risk may be considered within the pricing model either through the risk premium in the target rate of return or through the cash flow.

Consideration of risk in the pricing model should involve an explicit discussion of the uncertainty surrounding the various forecasts within the pricing model and may be conducted on a qualitative or quantitative basis with the objective of gaining an appreciation of the relative level of uncertainty inherent in the pricing model.

A qualitative approach to the assessment of risk within a pricing model may involve verbal scenario analysis through hypothesising a series of '*what if*' scenarios followed by consideration of the possible outcomes. The principal quantitative approaches comprise the use of risk adjusted discount rates and certainty equivalent cash flows, with a range of supporting risk analysis techniques also being available for use.

The use of risk adjusted discount rates involves the re-running of the discounted cash flow using alternative target rates of return, reflecting upward or downward adjustments to the risk premium. Such adjustment of the risk premium may be made subjectively (for example, –50 basis points, –25 basis points, +25 basis points, +50 basis points) based on a qualitative assessment of the perceived optimism or pessimism of the forecasts or may be made objectively through the variation of the unsystematic or idiosyncratic risk premia. While such adjustment may be arbitrary, implicit and lack transparency, the resulting range of present values permits consideration of the magnitude of the impact of changes in the discount rate.

Certainty equivalent cash flows seek to assess risk through the cash flows in the pricing model rather than within the discount rate, by the application of a certainty equivalent coefficient to each cash inflow or outflow. Such coefficients may range from 0.00 to 1.00 depending on the degree of certainty associated with the cash flow, immediate future cash flows being more certain than distant future cash flows (Baum and Crosby, 1988; Jaffe and Sirmans, 2001). With the choice of coefficient being subjective, this is again arbitrary, implicit and lacks transparency, but the resulting present values permit consideration of risk from another viewpoint.

In addition to the use of risk adjusted discount rates and certainty equivalent cash flows, risk may also be considered in a pricing model through the use of traditional risk analysis techniques including:

- **probability analysis** – involving the use of subjectively determined probability distributions attached to various forecast inputs based on perceived levels of confidence;
- **scenario analysis** – through the consideration of a range of different scenarios such as optimistic, base case and pessimistic within which each of the forecast inputs are adjusted consistently and probabilities then ascribed to the respective outcomes;
- **sensitivity analysis** – being the systematic alteration of forecast inputs to observe the impact on present value and so isolate the forecast inputs that have the greatest impact on present value;
- **simulation analysis** – being a computer driven approach in which simulated present values are generated by randomly selecting from a range of possible outcomes, such as through Monte Carlo simulation; and
- **decision tree analysis** – being an estimate of the likelihood of each given outcome at every expected decision point in the future with all events, options and outcomes specified and subjective probabilities assigned to each outcome.

The various types of risk analysis techniques available each serve to assist in determining what might be the impact on present value if one or more of the input variables in the pricing model differs from that forecast. The results provide the user with a level of confidence in the robustness of the pricing model and a clearer understanding of the sources of risk within the assessment of present value. This may lead to a view that confidence in the forecast inputs and the assessment of present value is high and the Advanced Financial Analysis Step may then proceed to the application of a decision rule. Conversely, it may lead to a lower level of confidence in the integrity of the assessment of present value and so require additional research and analysis prior to proceeding further.

3.5.4 Decision rule

In order to ensure a rational and consistent basis of decision making, some form of decision rule is required to provide the basis for decision making on the outcome of the pricing model. Accordingly, it is necessary to have an understanding of the principles of decision rules.

The Advanced Financial Analysis Step seeks to determine if the proposed transaction is mis-priced and so offers the opportunity for the REIT to earn abnormal returns. In essence, the two principal methods of determining if the proposed transaction is mis-priced are to compare the worth of the proposed real estate investment to the purchaser with the acquisition price and/or to compare the expected return from the proposed real estate investment with that required by the purchaser.

In comparing the worth of the proposed real estate investment to the purchaser with the acquisition price, the focus is on the determination of worth relative to the acquisition price and the applicable rule to determine if the potential acquisition is mis-priced is the Net Present Value (NPV) decision rule.

Alternatively, in comparing the expected return from the proposed investment with that required by the purchaser, the focus is on the expected return from the proposed real estate investment relative to the purchasers target rate of return and the applicable rule to determine if the acquisition is mis-priced is the Internal Rate of Return (IRR) decision rule.

NPV decision rule
Operation of the pricing model using the acquisition cost with current and forecast cash flows discounted at the target rate of return will determine the NPV of the proposed real estate investment.

If the NPV is positive, the pricing model indicates that a return greater than the target rate of return may be achieved if the property is acquired at the acquisition price and the current and forecast future cash flows are realised. Accordingly, based on the criteria adopted by the REIT, the potential real estate acquisition is mis-priced and may be acceptable as the forecast return exceeds the target rate of return. Similarly, if the net present value is zero, the potential real estate acquisition is not mis-priced but may be acceptable as the forecast return is equal to the target rate of return.

However, if the net present value is negative, the pricing model indicates that a return less than the target rate of return may be achieved if the property is acquired at the acquisition price and the current and forecast future cash flows are realised. Accordingly, the potential real estate acquisition is mis-priced but is unacceptable as the forecast return does not achieve the target rate of return. In such a circumstance, the potential real estate acquisition may be rejected or the basis of acquisition modified, through further negotiation, in an endeavour to achieve a zero or positive net present value.

Accordingly, the NPV decision rule may be summarised as follows:

NPV > 0   property is mis-priced and acceptable for acquisition
NPV = 0   property is not mis-priced but is acceptable for acquisition
NPV < 0   property is mis-priced but unacceptable for acquisition

The NPV decision rule is consistent with the wealth maximisation motive, with a positive NPV demonstrating contribution to unitholder value as risk adjusted and time adjusted expected cash inflows outweigh expected cash outflows. Further, the NPV decision rule is generally considered to be superior to the IRR decision rule as it can accommodate potential investment alternatives of differing sizes and/or duration, provides an absolute measure of profitability for an individual acquisition and is additive, such that a portfolio of acquisitions with positive NPVs will represent an increase in the value of the REIT in absolute terms.

IRR decision rule
Operation of the pricing model using the acquisition cost with current and forecast cash flows discounted at iterations of the discount rate until a net present value of zero results will determine the IRR of the proposed real estate investment.

If the IRR exceeds the target rate of return, the pricing model indicates that a return greater than the target rate of return may be achieved if the property is acquired at the acquisition price and the current and forecast future cash flows are realised. Accordingly, based on the criteria adopted by the REIT, the potential real estate acquisition is mis-priced and may be acceptable as the forecast return exceeds the target rate of return. Similarly, if the IRR equals the target rate of return, the potential real estate acquisition is not mis-priced but may be acceptable as the forecast return is equal to the target rate of return.

However, if the IRR is below the target rate of return, the pricing model indicates that a return less than the target rate of return may be achieved if the property is acquired at the acquisition price and the current and forecast future cash flows are realised. Accordingly, the potential real estate acquisition is mis-priced but is unacceptable as the forecast return does not achieve the target rate of return. In such a circumstance, the potential real estate acquisition may be rejected or the basis of acquisition modified, through further negotiation, in an endeavour to achieve or exceed the target rate of return.

Accordingly, the IRR decision rule may be summarised as follows:

IRR > Target   property is mis-priced and acceptable for acquisition
IRR = Target   property is not mis-priced but is acceptable for acquisition
IRR < Target   property is mis-priced but unacceptable for acquisition

The IRR decision rule is often preferred for use in practice as it is simple to understand, straight forward to compute, the solution appears to be unique and unambiguous and the resulting rate is in a convenient form for comparison with alternative investment opportunities. However, the IRR decision rule is constrained by the problem of multiple IRRs and the ongoing debate over the reinvestment rate issue. Multiple IRRs may arise when a negative cash flow occurs in a future period with a positive cash flow either side. While such IRRs may be mathematically correct, they are of little, if any, use for decision making resulting in reliance on the NPV decision rule in such circumstances.

Debate over the reinvestment rate has continued unresolved for many years, including debate over whether the reinvestment rate assumption even exists. Proponents of the debate contend that the NPV and IRR approaches each make different assumptions concerning the reinvestment rate, with the NPV approach assuming investors can reinvest at their opportunity cost of capital which is contended to be a correct assumption concerning the reinvestment rate. Conversely, the IRR approach assumes investors can reinvest at the IRR, which may differ between alternative properties under consideration and may be higher than the opportunity cost of capital. To address the alleged reinvestment rate issue within the IRR approach, a range of variants of the IRR, such as the Modified Internal Rate of Return (MIRR) and the Financial Management Rate of Return (FMRR), have been proposed but have generally not been widely adopted in practice.

Accordingly, therefore, in order to ensure a rational and consistent basis of decision making from the outcomes of the pricing model, a decision rule should be adopted with the choice usually being between the NPV decision rule and the IRR decision rule.

3.5.5 Advanced Financial Analysis

The Advanced Financial Analysis Step seeks to determine if a proposed transaction is mis-priced and the extent to which it is mis-priced, so offering the opportunity for the REIT to earn abnormal returns. In essence, the two principal methods of determining if the proposed transaction is mis-priced are to compare the worth of the proposed real estate investment to the purchaser with the acquisition price and/or to compare the expected return from the proposed real estate investment with that required by the purchaser.

The theoretical basis of mis-pricing may be proposed to be the determination of worth to the REIT with the practical basis of determining worth being through the use of a target rate of return in a discounted cash flow pricing model with net present value as the preferred decision rule.

Having determined that a proposed transaction is mis-priced at the individual asset level, it is now necessary to consider the impact of the addition of the asset on the risk-return profile of the portfolio in order to determine its acceptability.

3.6 Portfolio Impact Assessment

By this point of the REIT real estate investment decision making process, it is highly unlikely that analysis of a proposed real estate acquisition in the Portfolio Impact Assessment Step would yield any significant adverse findings. The proposed real estate acquisition has been carefully chosen following a rigorous, quantitatively based process and the impact on the portfolio given initial consideration in the debt and equity mix of the Structuring Step.

Accordingly, the Portfolio Impact Assessment Step seeks to confirm expectations concerning the impact of the proposed acquisition on the existing REIT portfolio and update relevant portfolio metrics. As will be considered further in the Performance Monitoring Step of the Watching Stage, the existing REIT portfolio is carefully modelled on an ongoing basis, making separate iterations to reflect the addition of a proposed real estate acquisition to the portfolio straightforward.

3.6.1 Risk-return balance

Through modelling, the impact of the proposed acquisition and its funding structure on the forecast risk-return of the REIT portfolio will be analysed. Having identified an asset to be mis-priced as structured at the target rate of return, it is likely that its addition to the REIT portfolio will contribute an increase in forecast portfolio returns assuming a prudent funding structure has been negotiated.

However, the quantification of the exact change in forecast portfolio risk-return provides the Portfolio Management Team with the opportunity to consider whether the risk-return balance is worthwhile. For example, Portfolio Impact Assessment modelling may indicate that the forecast portfolio return for each of the next two financial years will increase by only a few basis points while the forecast portfolio risk is effectively unchanged. For the Portfolio Management Team, the question then becomes whether or not an investment of the proposed magnitude is worth the effort for the benefit to be gained? Effectively, this is a question to which the answer may only be subjectively or qualitatively determined.

Having got this far through the REIT real estate investment decision making process and committed considerable internal time resources to the proposed acquisition, it is challenging for the Portfolio Management Team to withdraw at this point though fiduciary responsibility would require them to do so if they considered the risk-return balance not worthwhile. This serves to reinforce the importance of carefully considering the risk premium when setting the target rate of return required by the REIT for the proposed acquisition in the Advanced Financial Analysis Step. If the risk premium and target rate of return are too high, acquisition opportunities may be limited but if they are too low, Portfolio Impact Assessment may serve to question the basis for so many properties being found to be apparently mis-priced.

3.6.2 Portfolio metrics

Relevant portfolio metrics may also be updated for the impact of the proposed acquisition on the portfolio, including:

- portfolio percentage **sectoral** weightings;
- portfolio percentage **geographic** weightings;
- portfolio percentage **building** weightings;
- portfolio percentage **tenant** weightings, including credit worthiness, business sector and so forth;
- portfolio weighted **average lease expiry**;
- portfolio **rent review profile**; and
- portfolio **gearing** or leverage,

each of which should improve marginally as a result of the proposed acquisition. Though unlikely, in the event that a metric marginally deteriorates as a result of the proposed acquisition, the Investor Interface

Team may be forearmed with an appropriate explanation for REIT investors and analysts.

3.6.3 *Short form documentation*

Having completed the Portfolio Impact Assessment Step, the REIT management team now have a commercial and funding transaction that is acceptable and ready for the Governance Decision Step.

Prior to the Governance Decision Step, the Portfolio Management Team and the Fund Management Team will seek to update the in-principle documentation agreed between vendor and purchaser on completion of the Structuring Step to reflect any subsequent negotiations during the Advanced Financial Analysis and Portfolio Impact Assessment Steps and which will then form the basis of the report to be submitted for the Governance Decision.

3.6.4 *Portfolio Impact Assessment Step*

Having confirmed that expectations concerning the impact of the proposed acquisition on the existing REIT portfolio are positive and updated relevant portfolio metrics in the Portfolio Impact Assessment Step, followed by updating the short form commercial and funding documentation, if required, a REIT may now conclude that the proposed acquisition is acceptable and prepare to proceed to the Executing Stage of the Transacting Phase.

3.7 Super REIT

Having completed the Envisioning Stage, Super REIT has developed a Vision to be the premier diversified REIT on the stock exchange, interdependent with its adopted generic and specific investment management Style which is active, top down, growth and value added, respectively. To attain this Vision, Super REIT has identified four Goals including to be within the top quartile return performance with lowest quartile tracking error of the stock exchange REIT index every year. Consistently, Super REITs Strategic Plan focuses on return optimisation at the REIT, portfolio and property level together with effective risk management, supported by a large number of specified Objectives encompassing all REIT management executives in the respective Teams and so aligning the motivations and actions of all REIT management executives with the attainment of Super REIT's Vision.

On completion of the Planning Stage, Super REIT has developed a Property Portfolio Strategy with a Strategic Asset Allocation comprising a sectoral allocation (50% retail, 40% office, 10% industrial) and geographic allocation

Table 3.3   Target list: stock selection criteria.

	Stock Selection Criteria	Lex Plaza	Superman Tower
Asking price	$375 million	$370 million	$385 million
Tenure	Freehold	Freehold	Freehold with easements
Location	Prime, Downtown Precinct	Main Street, Downtown	Side Street, Downtown
Grade	A	A–	A+
Size	High rise	37 500 m² 22 levels	35 000 m² 20 levels
Building quality	Modern	Modern	Green
Age	<10 years	12 years	7 years
Tenant profile	Principally corporate	International accounting and legal firms	50% government 50% listed corporate

(60% northern, 40% southern states), enhanced by a Tactical Asset Allocation of 2.5% to the office sector in the northern city of Metropolis for a period of two years reflecting a forecast undersupply of office accommodation. Within the allocation to the office sector, Super REIT has developed Stock Selection criteria specifying lots of around $375 million each, being freehold title in prime office locations within the downtown precincts of specified cities and A grade, high rise, modern office towers that are less than ten years old, being principally leased to corporate tenants.

On completing the Planning Stage, Super REIT has identified three potential properties for acquisition in Metropolis and a further property has been externally introduced to the Capital Transactions Team through their extensive network of real estate market contacts. Accordingly, on entering the Dealing Stage, Super REIT's management team now embark on the Steps of Preliminary Negotiation, Preliminary Analysis, Structuring, Advanced Financial Analysis and Portfolio Impact Assessment to determine if one or more of the four identified assets may be appropriate and acceptable for acquisition.

3.7.1 Preliminary Negotiation

Given that three of the four potential acquisition properties on the target list were internally identified, it is possible that the owners are not willing to consider sale at the given time. Following discussions, the Capital Transactions Team may ascertain that two such owners are unwilling to consider sale at the given time, resulting in Preliminary Negotiation reducing the target list of potential properties for acquisition to two properties, Lex Plaza and Superman Tower.

As the summary in Table 3.3 indicates, neither of the two properties on the target list of potential properties for acquisition exactly matches the Stock Selection criteria. As may often be the case, both are close to the

Table 3.4 Qualitative Preliminary Analysis: Lex Plaza and Superman Tower.

	Stock Selection Criteria	Lex Plaza	Qual. Prelim. Analysis	Superman Tower	Qual. Prelim. Analysis
Asking price	$375 million	$370 million	√	$385 million	√
Tenure	Freehold	Freehold	√	Freehold with easements	X
Location	Prime, Downtown Precinct	Main Street, Downtown	√	Side Street, Downtown	X
Grade	A	A–	X	A+	√√
Size	High Rise	37 500 m² 22 levels	√	35 000 m² 20 levels	√
Building quality	Modern	Modern	√	Green	√√
Age	<10 years	12 years	X	7 years	√
Tenant profile	Principally corporate	International accounting and legal firms	X	50% gov't 50% listed corporate	√

Stock Selection criteria but each display some positive and some negative characteristics (or growth characteristics and risk characteristics) relative to the Stock Selection criteria.

Accordingly, Preliminary Analysis is required to seek to determine which of the potential acquisition properties may be preferable though, it should be noted, being preferable as an investment is different to being acceptable as an investment.

3.7.2 Preliminary Analysis

Preliminary Analysis offers a quick snapshot of the transaction under consideration, usually through some form of single period analysis using either quantitative or qualitative analysis techniques.

Qualitative Preliminary Analysis
While prior knowledge of each property may assist in developing a *'feel'* for the alternative investments, in the absence of such prior knowledge a simple table of ticks and crosses may assist in Qualitative Preliminary Analysis. In such a table, ticks may reflect positive perceptions and crosses may reflect negative perceptions of the potential acquisition property, with the strength of the perception expressed by the number of ticks or crosses, as shown in Table 3.4.

Very simplistically, Qualitative Preliminary Analysis may attribute a single tick or cross where the potential acquisition property broadly

Table 3.5 Quantitative Preliminary Analysis: Lex Plaza and Superman Tower.

	Lex Plaza	Superman Tower
Gross income	$21.00 million pa	$21.00 million pa
Operating costs	$2.50 million pa	$2.10 million pa
Net income	$18.50 million pa	$18.90 million pa
Asking price	$370.00 million	$385.00 million

accords with the Stock Selection criteria and multiple ticks or crosses where the property exceeds or falls short of the criteria. In Table 3.4, Lex Plaza broadly accords with five criteria, but the building grade, age and tenant profile fall short. Superman Tower broadly accords with four criteria, while the building grade and quality exceed the criteria though the tenure and location fall short. Overall, Lex Plaza is attributed five ticks and three crosses while Superman Tower is attributed eight ticks and two crosses, with qualitative Preliminary Analysis suggesting that Superman Tower may be preferable to Lex Plaza.

This is, however, a very simplistic analysis and makes no allowance for the risk-return relativity of each of the criteria. For example, is the effect of easements on the freehold title for Superman Tower equal in risk-return impact to Lex Plaza being two years older than the Stock Selection criteria building age? Or, is the green building quality of Superman Tower double the risk-return impact of the modern building quality of Lex Plaza?

The answer to both questions is almost certainly 'no'. While the positive and negative features of each will have a risk-return impact, it is not possible at this stage to quantify what that impact might be and hence the extent to which Superman Tower may be preferable to Lex Plaza.

Quantitative Preliminary Analysis
Concerning Quantitative Preliminary Analysis, such analysis may be based on a limited amount of publically available information concerning the income streams of potential acquisition properties, as may be summarised in Table 3.5.

While a range of measures could be considered, as detailed above, it is proposed to focus on the Gross Income Multiplier, Net Income Multiplier and Initial Yield as summarised in Table 3.6. Using Lex Plaza as an example, common quantitative financial analysis measures in the US may include the Gross Income Multiplier (GIM) of 17.62, being an expression of $21.00 million pa relative to the asking price of $370 million, or the Net Income Multiplier (NIM) of 20.00, being an expression of $18.50 million pa relative to the asking price of $370 million. In the UK and other Commonwealth countries, the common quantitative financial analysis measure may be the

Table 3.6 Quantitative Preliminary Analysis: Lex Plaza and Superman Tower.

	Lex Plaza	Superman Tower
Gross income multiplier	17.62×	18.33×
Net income multiplier	20.00×	20.37×
Initial yield	5.00%	4.91%

reciprocal of the NIM, being the Initial Yield of 5.00%, an expression of $18.50 million pa relative to the asking price of $370 million.

While Superman Tower may have been an intuitively preferable building based on qualitative Preliminary Analysis, Table 3.6 indicates that it is also a very marginally more *'expensive'* building with an Initial Yield of 4.91% or Net Income Multiplier of 20.37× compared to Lex Plaza at 5.00% or 20.00x, respectively. Though Superman Tower may also have a higher Gross Income Multiplier (18.33× compared to 17.62× for Lex Plaza), it is a more financially efficient property with a smaller proportion of operating expenses lost, as shown in the relativity of Gross Income Multiplier to Net Income Multiplier.

Accordingly, on the criterion of maximising Initial Yield, Lex Plaza may appear marginally preferable to Superman Tower for potential acquisition. However, this also illustrates the limitations of simplistic, single period measures as the resulting Initial Yield or Net Income Multiplier is very close to identical, given the nature of the base data, with no account being taken of potential future cash flows. It may be that the green building quality of Superman Tower will significantly benefit future cash flows relative to the modern building quality of Lex Plaza, resulting in the future year yields of Superman Tower exceeding those of Lex Plaza. As with Qualitative Preliminary Analysis, there is no allowance for risk-return relativity, with no indication whether the extent of potential future higher returns from Superman Tower may be appropriate for the risk assumed in such an investment.

Accordingly, having regard to the target list of potential real estate acquisitions, Qualitative Preliminary Analysis suggests that Superman Tower may be preferable with Quantitative Preliminary Analysis indicating that, while each are very similar in terms of initial return, Superman Tower is very marginally more *'expensive'* but more financially efficient and may offer the advantage of superior longer term returns.

Following Preliminary Analysis, Superman Tower may be preferred for further negotiation to verify existing information, collate further information and establish how the acquisition transaction might be structured. However, Lex Plaza does not appear sufficiently inferior at this stage to reject completely, such that further negotiation on Lex Plaza as a fall back potential real estate acquisition may be prudent.

Prior to undertaking the Advanced Financial Analysis necessary to understand the risk-return profile of the potential investment and determine the extent of any potential mis-pricing, a clear understanding of the proposed basis upon which the transaction will be structured is essential.

3.7.3 Structuring

The Capital Transactions Team now embark on intermediate negotiations with the vendors of Superman Tower and Lex Plaza in an endeavour to agree the basis upon which the commercial transaction for each may be Structured to suit both vendors and Super REIT as purchaser.

Both commercial transactions may be structured, for convenience, on the basis of 100% of the purchase price being payable at Settlement, subject to adjustments for rent and service contracts paid in advance, with Settlement 90 days after exchange of contracts.

Simultaneously, the Fund Management Team embarks on the Structuring of the funding transaction to determine the optimal basis upon which Super REIT may pay for the acquisition of each property at the Settlement Step of the Watching Stage.

For convenience, it may be assumed that the structure of the funding transaction is common for both Superman Tower and Lex Plaza. The funding transaction may be structured to match the REIT debt-equity profile, with 40% of the acquisition cost funded by debt and 60% by equity. The form of debt may comprise a general loan facility, secured over a pool of REIT real estate assets, sourced from an existing syndicate of bank lenders at a floating rate of 75 basis points over the Bank Bill Swap Bid Rate (BBSY) subject to five-yearly renewal. Equity may be raised from existing cash reserves, avoiding the need for an equity raising from REIT unitholders.

Having now determined the commercial and funding structures for each potential property acquisition and that both are appropriate as real estate investments for Super REIT, the Portfolio Management Team at Super REIT now embark on the Advanced Financial Analysis Step to determine if either or both is mis-priced and so potentially acceptable for acquisition.

3.7.4 Advanced Financial Analysis

Combining Tables 3.4, 3.5 and 3.6 into Table 3.7 provides a summary of Lex Plaza and Superman Tower as a starting point for consideration of the Advanced Financial Analysis Step. To determine if either property is mis-priced requires Super REIT to assess the worth of each property using a cash flow pricing model, adopting Super REIT's target rate of return as the discount

Table 3.7   Qualitative and Quantitative Preliminary Analysis: Lex Plaza and Superman Tower.

	Stock Selection Criteria	Lex Plaza	Superman Tower
Asking price	$375 million	$370 million	$385 million
Tenure	Freehold	Freehold	Freehold with easements
Location	Prime, Downtown Precinct	Main Street, Downtown	Side Street, Downtown
Grade	A	A–	A+
Size	High Rise	37 500 m²	35 000 m²
		22 levels	20 levels
Building quality	Modern	Modern	Green
Age	< 10 years	12 years	7 years
Tenant profile	Principally corporate	International accounting and legal firms	50% government 50% listed corporate
Gross income		$21.00 million pa	$21.00 million pa
Operating expenses		$2.50 million pa	$2.10 million pa
Net income		$18.50 million pa	$18.90 million pa
Gross income multiplier		17.62 ×	18.33 ×
Net income multiplier		20.00 ×	20.37 ×
Initial yield		5.00%	4.91%

rate and applying a decision rule. Effectively, this comprises information processing by impounding forecast information into pricing to determine if, at the asking prices of $370.00 million and $385.00 million respectively, Lex Plaza and Superman Tower are mis-priced on Super REIT's criteria.

Accordingly, Super REIT needs to determine its target rate of return and the forecast cash flows that may be derived from each property. Each of the characteristics that differ for the respective properties from the Stock Selection criteria, such as location, building quality and so forth as described in Table 3.7, require reflection as a source of either growth or risk in either the target rate of return or the cash flow but with care required to ensure that no double counting arises by inclusion in both.

Having considered the various characteristics and the current information available, Super REIT decides to reflect the differences in location, building grade and tenant profile through the risk premium in the target rate of return. Reflecting their potential impact on cash flow and inter-related nature, Super REIT decides to reflect building quality and building age through the cash flow while acknowledging that these could alternatively be reflected in the risk premium. While both properties have the same title or tenure, being freehold, the impact of easements on Superman Tower requires recognition and Super REIT decides that this should be reflected through the risk premium as it represents an identifiable risk aspect of the property that is unlikely to have a cash flow impact.

While the acquisition of an office property in Metropolis comprises a Tactical Asset Allocation decision with a two year time frame, Super REIT needs to be cognisant of the potential returns from the property if it cannot be sold after two years and has to be retained in the portfolio. Accordingly, Super REIT decides to complete a three year cash flow to reflect the Tactical Asset Allocation period and a conventional ten year cash flow in order to consider each scenario.

Target rate of return

Super REITs weighted average cost of capital (WACC) forms the minimum hurdle rate of return for any potential real estate acquisition. Given Super REITs capital structure comprising approximately 60% equity capital and 40% debt capital with no tax applicable for Super REIT, following Equation 3.1 the WACC may be approximated as follows:

Cost of equity	11.50%
Cost of debt	6.50%
WACC	9.50% being $(0.4 \times 6.50\%) + (0.6 \times 11.50\%)$

Therefore, any potential real estate acquisition should have a total return of or in excess of 9.50% in order to be accretive to the returns of Super REIT.

To determine the target rate of return for each property, Super REIT needs to determine the nominal risk free rate, the unsystematic risk premium for the office sector and geographic location of Metropolis, which is common to both properties, as well as the idiosyncratic risk premium which will differ for each of Lex Plaza and Superman Tower.

As a proxy for a nominal risk free rate, Super REIT decides to adopt the central government nominal bond rate for periods to reflect the cash flows, being three years and ten years. Presently, the central government nominal bond rate is 5.75% for three years and 6.00% for ten years reflecting the current shape of the yield curve, being common to both of Lex Plaza and Superman Tower.

Super REIT's previous research has determined that an appropriate risk premium to reflect the unsystematic risk of the office sector is 2.00% and of Metropolis is 1.00%, reflecting the low liquidity of the Metropolis office market and the relative weakness of the local Metropolis economy which gives a heightened sensitivity to economic shocks. This sums to a risk premium to reflect unsystematic risk of 3.00% which is common to both of Lex Plaza and Superman Tower and is assumed, for simplicity, to be common to both a three year and ten year holding period though, theoretically, the unsystematic risk premium for the respective time periods may differ.

Table 3.8 Target rate of return: Lex Plaza and Superman Tower.

Risk type		3 year Lex Plaza	3 year Superman Tower	10 year Lex Plaza	10 year Superman Tower
Risk free		5.75%	5.75%	6.00%	6.00%
Unsystematic risk	Office sector	2.00%	2.00%	2.00%	2.00%
	Geog. sector	1.00%	1.00%	1.00%	1.00%
Idiosyncratic risk	Location	0.00%	0.50%	0.00%	0.50%
	Building grade	0.25%	0.00%	0.25%	0.00%
	Tenant profile	0.75%	0.25%	0.75%	0.25%
	Tenure	0.00%	0.50%	0.00%	0.50%
Risk premium		4.00%	4.25%	4.00%	4.25%
Target rate of return		9.75%	10.00%	10.00%	10.25%

The idiosyncratic risk premium for each potential acquisition is summarised in Table 3.8 and considered further, below. The idiosyncratic risk premium differs for each of Lex Plaza and Superman Tower but it is assumed, for simplicity, to be common to both a three year and ten year holding period though, theoretically, the idiosyncratic risk premium for the respective time periods may differ.

Super REIT determines the respective idiosyncratic risk premiums based on analysis of past transactions and internal research and analysis. Having regard to location, Superman Plaza is considered to exhibit greater risk as it is located in Side Street, rather than Main Street, resulting in a premium of 50 basis points being attributed. With building quality and building age being reflected through the cash flow, Super REIT attributes a risk premium of 25 basis points for building grade for Lex Plaza which is considered to exhibit greater risk as it is an A– grade building. It should be noted that no adjustment was made for Superman Plaza which is an A+ grade building, allowing reflection in the cash flow through the inter linked effects of building quality and building age.

Concerning tenant profile, Super REIT's Stock Selection criteria identified a corporate tenant profile as being of greater credit worthiness than professional services firms and willing to pay higher rents than government. Accordingly, Lex Plaza with a tenant profile comprising international accounting and legal firms is considered to exhibit considerably greater credit risk and so is attributed a premium of 75 basis points. While the 50% corporate tenant profile of Superman Tower accords with the Stock Selection criteria, the 50% government tenant profile, while not impacting credit risk, may result in diminished rental growth leading to the attribution of a premium of 25 basis points.

Reflecting the impact of the easements on title upon the risk inherent within Superman Tower is somewhat challenging. Depending on the nature of the easement, there may be a greater or lesser effect on an investment property. It is assumed, for simplicity, that the easements are easements for access allowing neighbours to pass and re-pass over the property and which are currently accommodated through the design of the building which provides for pedestrian walkways at ground level. Accordingly, there is little, if any, impact on the current property but there may be constraints to redevelopment in the future which creates a risk within the title to Superman Tower that is absent from the unencumbered title of Lex Plaza. To reflect this risk, which is currently relatively minor but may impact the future marketability of the property, Super REIT attributes a 50 basis points premium.

Therefore, the total idiosyncratic risk premium for Lex Plaza is 1.00% and for Superman Tower is 1.25% which provides an assessment of relativity between the idiosyncratic characteristics for the respective properties. Added to the risk free rate and the unsystematic risk premium produces a target rate of return for Lex Plaza of 9.75% over three years and 10.00% over ten years and for Superman Tower of 10.00% and 10.25%, respectively. The target rates of return may be rationalised through comparison to historic data and market forecasts from investor surveys, potentially requiring reconsideration if anomalies become apparent.

With the target rate of return for each potential real estate acquisition being greater than Super REITs WACC of 9.50%, both could be accretive acquisitions if found to be mis-priced.

Cash flow
For the purposes of this example, a very simplified cash flow pricing model is considered with only one gross income, operating expense and capital expenditure line. In reality, the lease structure of a property would result in many individual cash flows for gross income with a range of service providers potentially resulting in numerous individual operating expense cash flows and with the prospect of further individual cash flows for recurrent capital expenditure.

Similarly, for simplicity, it is assumed that rentals are received annually in advance, may be reviewed annually by a fixed percentage reflecting market movement, that 100% occupancy is maintained throughout the cash flow period and that transaction costs are ignored. Further, for the purposes of illustrating various principles in the example, large round numbers are adopted for forecast rental growth leading to large differences in NPV between the respective properties whereas, in reality, the forecasts and the NPVs may be expected to be very considerably closer.

As previously noted, being a Tactical Asset Allocation decision, disposal after three years is considered together with a conventional ten year holding period to allow explicit consideration of a scenario where the property

Table 3.9 Cash flow forecast: key variables.

	Lex Plaza	Superman Tower
Forecast rental growth rate – yrs 1–3	10.00% pa	12.50% pa
Forecast rental growth rate – yrs 4–8	3.00% pa	5.00% pa
Forecast rental growth rate – yrs 9–10	5.00% pa	6.25% pa
Forecast operating expense growth rate	5.00% pa	4.00% pa
Forecast capital expenditure	$25 million	$15 million
	Yr 8	Yr 3
Forecast terminal capitalisation rate – 3 yrs	5.75%	5.66%
Forecast terminal capitalisation rate – 10 yrs	5.50%	5.25%

cannot be sold and has to be retained in the portfolio. For the purposes of a very simplified cash flow, the key inputs are the acquisition price, gross income and operating expenses, as detailed in Table 3.7, together with the forecast rental and operating expense growth rates, capital expenditure allowance and terminal capitalisation rate, which are summarised in Table 3.9.

The inter linked effects of differing building quality and building age, together with the A+ grade of Superman Tower may be reflected in the cash flow through the forecasts for rental and operating expense growth and for capital expenditure. As a green building and newer building, Superman Tower is forecast to generate higher levels of annual rental growth and lower levels of annual operating expense growth. A foyer refurbishment in Year 3, when Superman Tower is ten years old, at a cost of $15 million will cushion the impact of the declining local office market as greater levels of supply become available, allowing Superman Tower to achieve higher levels of rental growth after Year 3 than Lex Plaza. Similarly, an allowance for $25 million capital expenditure on foyer and services in Year 8, when Lex Plaza is 20 years old, will allow greater rental growth in Years 9 and 10 and support the terminal value on sale. For both properties, the impact of oversupply of new office accommodation is forecast to last for five years and result in significant dampening of forecast rental growth rates. For simplicity, the operating expense growth rate is assumed to be constant over the cash flow forecast period.

It should be noted that the terminal capitalisation rates differ for the three year period and the ten year period. For the three year period, the terminal capitalisation rate should reflect a scenario wherein the period of under supply of office accommodation in Metropolis is close to conclusion and a period of over supply is imminent. Accordingly, Super REIT adopts a 75 basis points weakening in the capitalisation rates for each property compared to the initial yield at acquisition.

However, after ten years, the market is assumed to have normalised and the terminal capitalisation rate should reflect the characteristics of the respective properties. Lex Plaza will be a recently upgraded, 22-year-old

Table 3.10   Three year cash flow: Lex Plaza.

Year	0	1	2	3	4
Growth pa – gross income		10.00%	10.00%	10.00%	3.00%
Growth pa – operating expenses		5.00%	5.00%	5.00%	5.00%
Cash flow					
Gross income		$21.00	$23.10	$25.41	$27.95
Operating expenses		–$2.50	–$2.63	–$2.76	–$2.89
Net income		$18.50	$20.48	$22.65	$25.06
Capital expenditure					
Terminal capital value				$435.77	5.75%
Cash flow		$18.50	$20.48	$458.43	
Target rate of return	9.75%				
Present value	$380.64				
Acquisition price	–$370.00				
Net present value	$10.64				

building whereas Superman Tower will be a 17-year-old building facing upgrading in around three years time but still a green building. Accordingly, Super REIT adopts a 50 basis points weakening in the capitalisation rate for Lex Plaza to 5.50% compared to the initial yield at acquisition and a 34 basis points weakening to 5.25% for Superman Tower, principally recognising the impact of Superman Tower being a green building.

The three and ten year cash flows for Lex Plaza are set out in Tables 3.10 and 3.11, respectively, with those for Superman Tower set out in Tables 3.12 and 3.13, respectively. It should be noted that these are very simplified cash flows and that, in reality, such cash flows would be considerably longer and more detailed.

Assessment of worth

The application of the target rate of return to the cash flows in the pricing model results in a determination of present value or worth, as summarised in Table 3.14. The present value represents the worth of the proposed property investment to Super REIT based on Super REIT's forecasts in order to achieve Super REIT's target rate of return. It should be noted that Lex Plaza has an apparently greater worth to Super REIT for a three year holding period than for a ten year holding period, whereas Superman Tower has an apparently greater worth for a ten year holding period. This should immediately focus attention on the significance of the three year holding period for Lex Plaza and prompt further risk analysis.

For the determination of mis-pricing through the use of the NPV decision rule, it is the net present values of the potential property acquisitions that are of relevance, being the present value less the acquisition price, as shown in Table 3.15. It should be noted that the NPV decision rule is preferable to

Table 3.11 Ten year cash flow: Lex Plaza.

Year	0	1	2	3	4	5	6	7	8	9	10	11
Growth pa – gross inc.		10.00%	10.00%	10.00%	3.00%	3.00%	3.00%	3.00%	3.00%	5.00%	5.00%	
Growth pa – op. exp.		5.00%	5.00%	5.00%	5.00%	5.00%	5.00%	5.00%	5.00%	5.00%	5.00%	
Cash flow												
Gross income		$21.00	$23.10	$25.41	$27.95	$28.79	$29.65	$30.54	$31.46	$32.40	$34.02	$35.72
Operating expenses		–$2.50	–$2.63	–$2.76	–$2.89	–$3.04	–$3.19	–$3.35	–$3.52	–$3.69	–$3.88	–$4.07
Net income		$18.50	$20.48	$22.65	$25.06	$25.75	$26.46	$27.19	$27.94	$28.71	$30.14	$31.65
Capital expenditure									–$25.00			
Terminal capital value											$575.49	
Cash flow		$18.50	$20.48	$22.65	$25.06	$25.75	$26.46	$27.19	$2.94	$28.71	$605.63	
Target rate of return	10.00%											
Present value	$359.80											
Acquisition price	–$370.00											
Net present value	–$10.20											

Table 3.12   Three year cash flow: Superman Tower.

Year	0	1	2	3	4
Growth pa – gross income		12.50%	12.50%	12.50%	5.00%
Growth pa – operating expenses		4.00%	4.00%	4.00%	4.00%
Cash flow					
Gross income		$21.00	$23.63	$26.58	$29.90
Operating expenses		–$2.10	–$2.18	–$2.27	–$2.36
Net income		$18.90	$21.44	$24.31	$27.54
Capital expenditure				–$15.00	
Terminal capital value				$486.54	5.66%
Cash flow		$18.90	$21.44	$495.85	
Target rate of return	10.00%				
Present value	$407.44				
Acquisition price	–$385.00				
Net present value	$22.44				

the IRR decision rule where the cash flows include a negative cash flow in a future period, with a positive cash flow either side, which may cause the problem of multiple IRRs referred to previously.

Application of the NPV decision rule:

$NPV > 0$ property is mis-priced and acceptable for acquisition
$NPV = 0$ property is not mis-priced but is acceptable for acquisition
$NPV < 0$ property is mis-priced but unacceptable for acquisition

indicates that both Lex Plaza and Superman Tower are mis-priced on a three year holding period and may be acceptable for acquisition but that, on a ten year holding period, only Superman Tower is mis-priced and may be acceptable for acquisition with Lex Plaza being mis-priced but unacceptable for acquisition.

However, on a three year holding period, with a narrow NPV of $10.64 million and $22.44 million or only 2.88% and 5.83% of acquisition price, respectively, small changes in the variables within the pricing model could potentially result in either property indicating a negative NPV and so being mis-priced but unacceptable for acquisition. This supports concerns about the significance of the three year holding period for Lex Plaza and so should prompt further risk analysis.

Risk analysis
The inability to make perfect forecasts within a pricing model requires the explicit consideration of risk within a cash flow. For the purposes of this example, a small selection of the techniques for impounding risk,

Table 3.13 Ten year cash flow: Superman Tower.

Year	0	1	2	3	4	5	6	7	8	9	10	11
Growth pa - gross inc.		12.50%	12.50%	12.50%	5.00%	5.00%	5.00%	5.00%	5.00%	6.25%	6.25%	
Growth pa - op. exp.		4.00%	4.00%	4.00%	4.00%	4.00%	4.00%	4.00%	4.00%	4.00%	4.00%	
Cash flow												
Gross income		$21.00	$23.63	$26.58	$29.90	$31.40	$32.97	$34.61	$36.34	$38.16	$40.55	$43.08
Operating expenses		-$2.10	-$2.18	-$2.27	-$2.36	-$2.46	-$2.55	-$2.66	-$2.76	-$2.87	-$2.99	-$3.11
Net income		$18.90	$21.44	$24.31	$27.54	$28.94	$30.41	$31.96	$33.58	$35.29	$37.56	$39.97
Capital expenditure				-$15.00								
Terminal capital value											$761.37	5.25%
Cash flow		$18.90	$21.44	$9.31	$27.54	$28.94	$30.41	$31.96	$33.58	$35.29	$798.93	
Target rate of return	10.25%											
Present value	$442.36											
Acquisition price	-$385.00											
Net present value	$57.36											

Table 3.14   Summary of present values.

	Lex Plaza	Superman Tower
3 year present value	$380.64 million	$407.44 million
10 year present value	$359.80 million	$442.36 million
Acquisition price	$370.00 million	$385.00 million

Table 3.15   Summary of net present values.

	Lex Plaza	Superman Tower
3 year present value	$10.64 million	$22.44 million
10 year present value	–$10.20 million	$57.36 million
Acquisition price	$370.00 million	$385.00 million

considered previously, will be applied to the analysis of Lex Plaza and Superman Tower. In reality, a wider range of techniques would be applied and the results analysed in much greater detail.

Reflecting the narrow NPV found for each property over a three year holding period, a sensitivity analysis may be undertaken to determine the potential impact of changes in the terminal capitalisation rate and forecast rental growth rate individually, together with a scenario analysis to determine the potential impact of both.

The sensitivity analysis in Table 3.16 clearly shows that the NPV for Lex Plaza is much more sensitive to changes in the forecast rental growth rate than to changes in the forecast terminal capitalisation rate. Significantly, the pessimistic sensitivity for each forecast variable and the pessimistic scenario for both forecast variables results in a negative NPV indicating that the property is mis-priced but unacceptable for acquisition. Accordingly, a 250 basis points weakening in the forecast rental growth rate or 25 basis points in the forecast terminal capitalisation rate would render the potential property investment unacceptable, leading the Portfolio Management Team to further consider the potential for over statement in their forecasts.

Similarly, the sensitivity analysis in Table 3.17 shows that the NPV for Superman Tower is much more sensitive to changes in the forecast rental growth rate than to changes in the forecast terminal capitalisation rate. Significantly, the pessimistic sensitivity for forecast rental growth and the pessimistic scenario for both forecast variables result in a negative NPV indicating that the property is mis-priced but unacceptable for acquisition. Accordingly, a 250 basis points weakening in the forecast rental growth rate would render the potential property investment unacceptable, leading the Portfolio Management Team to further consider the potential for over statement in their forecasts.

Table 3.16   Sensitivity analysis and scenario analysis: Lex Plaza.

Three year holding period		NPV optimistic	NPV base case	NPV pessimistic
Sensitivity: forecast rental growth	+/– 250 basis points	$37.60 million	$10.64 million	–$15.17 million
Sensitivity: terminal capitalisation rate	+/– 25 basis points	$25.62 million	$10.64 million	–$3.10 million
Scenario: forecast rental growth and terminal capitalisation rate	Both +/– 250 basis points +/– 25 basis points	$53.75 million	$10.64 million	–$27.88 million

Table 3.17   Sensitivity analysis and scenario analysis: Superman Tower.

Three year holding period		NPV optimistic	NPV base case	NPV pessimistic
Sensitivity: forecast rental growth	+ / – 250 basis points	$50.82 million	$22.44 million	–$4.75 million
Sensitivity: terminal capitalisation rate	+ / – 25 basis points	$39.33 million	$22.44 million	$6.98 million
Scenario: forecast rental growth and terminal capitalisation rate	Both + / – 250 basis points + / – 25 basis points	$68.96 million	$22.44 million	–$19.12 million

Subsequently, having reconsidered their forecasts based on a clearer understanding of risk in the cash flow, the Portfolio Management Team have a high level of confidence in their forecasts and form the view that, on balance, they are both robust and reasonable but that there is a greater risk of over statement than understatement. Accordingly, they attach a 60% probability of occurrence to the base case with a 15% probability of occurrence to the optimistic case and a 25% probability of occurrence to the pessimistic case. Such probabilities may be applied to the NPVs derived from scenario analysis as follows:

Lex Plaza
   ($53.75 million × 15%) + ($10.64 million × 60%) + (–$27.88 million × 25%)
   = $8.06 million + $6.38 million – $6.97 million
   = $7.47 million probability weighted NPV
   = 2.02% acquisition price

Superman Tower
   ($68.96 million × 15%) + ($22.44 million × 60%) + (–$19.12 million × 25%)
   = $10.34 million + $13.46 million – $4.78 million
   = $19.02 million probability weighted NPV
   = 4.94% acquisition price

The probability weighted NPVs indicate that Superman Tower offers a superior positive NPV margin to Lex Plaza, relative to acquisition price, indicating that Superman Tower may be both acceptable and preferable.

If the same risk analysis is undertaken using a ten year holding period, the following probability weighted NPVs may be derived:

Lex Plaza
($86.92 million × 15%) + (−$10.20 million × 60%) + (−$86.28 million × 25%)
= $13.04 million − $6.12 million − $21.57 million
= −$14.65 million probability weighted NPV
= −3.96% acquisition price

Superman Tower
($174.58 million × 15%) + ($57.36 million × 60%) + (−$34.37 million × 25%)
= $26.18 million + $34.42 million − $8.59 million
= $52.01 million probability weighted NPV
= 13.5% acquisition price

Accordingly, for a three year holding period, Lex Plaza is mis-priced and may be acceptable for acquisition, but only narrowly so, while for a ten year holding period is mis-priced but unacceptable for acquisition. However, for both a three year and ten year holding period, Superman Tower is mis-priced and acceptable for acquisition and so preferable.

Acceptable property for acquisition
Super REIT, therefore, decides to proceed further with the acquisition of Superman Tower and to suspend negotiations on Lex Plaza for the time being. However, prior to moving into the Executing Stage of the Transacting Phase, Super REIT needs to confirm the potential impact of the proposed acquisition on its existing portfolio and its risk-return forecasts.

3.7.5 Portfolio Impact Assessment

Having identified Superman Tower to be mis-priced as structured at the target rate of return, it is likely that its addition to the REIT portfolio will contribute an increase in forecast portfolio returns assuming a prudent funding structure has been negotiated. Similarly, as the identification of a Tactical Asset Allocation to the office sector in Metropolis was based on capital market theory, it is likely that Superman Tower will contribute a decrease in forecast portfolio risk.

The addition of Superman Tower to the portfolio model for Super REIT is found to show a forecast increase in portfolio return of around 6.6 basis points in Year 1, reflecting the strong rental growth forecasts for Metropolis. It should be noted that the forecast increase in portfolio return is both modest and incremental, reflecting the limited impact of adding further individual properties to an already substantial $15 billion REIT. Similarly, the enhanced diversification resulting from the addition of an office property in a northern state shows a decrease in forecast portfolio risk with a reduction of around 5 basis points in Year 1 (reflecting Super REIT's 40% weighting to the office sector and 60% weighting to northern states). While Superman Tower will require an investment of $385 million, given that the total open market value of assets in Super REIT is currently $15 billion, Super REIT determines the risk-return balance to be worthwhile.

Updating portfolio metrics allows Super REIT to determine the exact level of improvements in sectoral, geographic, building and other weightings for use by the Investor Interface Team in marketing the proposed property acquisition to Super REIT's existing major investors and analysts. While the principal rationale for the acquisition, to be marketed to investors and analysts, will be the Tactical Asset Allocation for short term enhanced returns, positive changes in portfolio metrics for sectoral, geographic and building weightings may be useful in shifting the focus of attention from the minor deterioration of the portfolio metric for tenant profile resulting from the addition of a property with 50% government tenants.

Accordingly, the potential acquisition of Superman Tower is found to be not only appropriate but also acceptable, being consistent with the Goals and Vision of Super REIT and so should be well received by investors and analysts and so be positive for Super REIT's unit price on the stock exchange.

3.7.6 Outcomes of implementing the Dealing Stage

In the context of Super REIT, the Planning Stage determined the Strategic Asset Allocation to be enhanced by a Tactical Asset Allocation of 2.5% to the office sector in the city of Metropolis for a period of two years. Within the allocation to the office sector, Super REIT developed Stock Selection criteria specifying lots of around $375 million each, being freehold title in prime office locations within the downtown precincts of specified cities and A grade, high rise, modern office towers that are less than ten years old and being principally leased to corporate tenants. Having completed the Asset Identification Step, Super REIT had developed a target list of assets for potential acquisition that were consistent with the Stock Selection criteria and may be mis-priced.

In order to identify a specific asset for acquisition that is considered mis-priced:

- Super REIT used its extensive network of market contacts to identify properties that may be available and that were consistent with the Stock Selection criteria, with four possible properties for acquisition identified. Through the **Preliminary Negotiation** Step, the respective vendor's willingness to sell and the nature of terms upon which a transaction may take place were established, reducing the target list to two potential properties for acquisition, being Lex Plaza and Superman Tower;
- neither Lex Plaza nor Superman Tower exactly matched the Stock Selection criteria, with Qualitative **Preliminary Analysis** suggesting Superman Tower may be preferable to Lex Plaza. Application of Quantitative Preliminary Analysis indicated that Superman Tower was preferable but that Lex Plaza was not sufficiently inferior to be discarded for potential acquisition based on simplistic, single period measures;
- commercial transaction **Structuring** resulted in agreement to pay 100% of the purchase price at Settlement, 90 days after exchange of contracts for both Superman Tower and Lex Plaza, with funding for both to be structured on the basis of 40% debt and 60% equity contribution by Super REIT and both the commercial and funding structures documented in a heads of terms agreement;
- **Advanced Financial Analysis** determined that Superman Plaza was acceptably mis-priced by a significant extent over both a three and ten year holding period, while Lex Plaza was only acceptably mis-priced to a limited extent over a three year period, with risk analysis identifying the vulnerability of both to changes in forecast rental growth. Following sensitivity and scenario analysis, Superman Tower was found to be preferable for acquisition; and
- Superman Tower was confirmed to be acceptable for acquisition through **Portfolio Impact Assessment** which found its addition to the portfolio to be positive for both forecast return and risk and for the majority of portfolio metrics.

Completion of the Dealing Stage results in Super REIT having identified a specific asset for acquisition, Superman Tower, that is considered mis-priced by a significant extent over both a three and ten year holding period and so capable of generating abnormal returns. Following Portfolio Impact Assessment, Superman Tower was confirmed to be acceptable for acquisition at $385 million on the basis of the commercial and funding structures proposed. Accordingly, Super REIT now needs to seek the necessary internal approvals to comply with governance requirements, close the transaction, document the transaction and undertake due diligence including independent appraisal which, together, comprise the Executing Stage that will then conclude the Transacting Phase.

3.8 Summary

The first Phase of the REIT real estate investment decision making process, the Preparing Phase, comprised the Envisioning Stage (considered in Chapter 1) and the Planning Stage (considered in Chapter 2). On completion of the Preparing Phase, the REIT has articulated where it is going and how it is going to get there, providing unitholders with a clear understanding of the risk-return profile to expect from the managers investment of their funds.

The second phase of the REIT real estate investment decision making process, the Transacting Phase, comprises the Dealing Stage (considered in this chapter) and the Executing Stage (considered in Chapter 4). The Dealing Stage comprises the Steps of Preliminary Negotiation, Preliminary Analysis, Structuring, Advanced Financial Analysis and Portfolio Impact Assessment.

The emphasis of the Dealing Stage is firmly on identifying a mis-priced asset that is capable of generating abnormal returns. The Dealing Stage starts with a target list of assets for potential acquisition and comprises a lengthy, repetitive process of Preliminary Negotiation and Preliminary Analysis in order to identify a preferred potential property for acquisition that appears likely to be mis-priced.

Following Structuring and through Advanced Financial Analysis, the existence and extent of such mis-pricing may be identified through the use of a pricing model, such as a discounted cash flow model, to determine the worth of a potential property acquisition using the REIT's target rate of return as the discount rate. Application of the NPV decision rule will identify a mis-priced asset and may indicate that the preferred potential property acquisition is acceptable. Portfolio Impact Assessment will serve as the final determinant of acceptability, through quantification of the extent of increase in return and decrease in risk at the portfolio level arising from the incorporation of the potential property acquisition and funding structure into the REIT portfolio.

Such an approach, while rigorous and transparent, is lengthy and complex. Great care is required in the treatment of risk in Advanced Financial Analysis as risk may be reflected in the pricing model through the cash flow and the discount rate risk premium, which should not be double counted, or through explicit risk management techniques. Too great an allowance for risk may result in few, if any, properties appearing acceptable while insufficient allowance may lead to the basis for so many properties being found to be apparently mis-priced being questioned in the Portfolio Impact Assessment Step.

The Dealing Stage brings into sharp focus the imperfect nature of the real estate market and the tension between theoretical ideals and practical outcomes in REIT portfolio management. While such features as weak form market efficiency create the opportunity for the REIT to earn abnormal returns in the real estate market and the adoption of modern portfolio theory, capital market theory and the Capital Asset Pricing Model identify the ideal profile of assets for acquisition, other real estate market features such as limited supply of properties and high time and monetary costs of transacting make the realisation of such opportunities challenging. A balance is, therefore, required to maintain and protect the integrity of the theoretical basis of real estate portfolio management while also developing a Property Portfolio Strategy capable of implementation in practice.

Completion of the Dealing Stage may result in the REIT having converted a target list of specific property assets for potential acquisition into an in-principle transaction for the acquisition of a nominated asset, leading into the Executing Stage which is considered in the next chapter.

Completion of the Dealing Stage and the Executing Stage mark the completion of the second of the three Phases, the Transacting Phase, wherein the REIT manager seeks to implement the outcomes of the Preparing Phase through the creation of a tangible real estate portfolio. This then leads to the third and final Phase of the REIT real estate investment decision making process, the Observing Phase.

3.9 Key points

- The Dealing Stage is the first Stage of the **Transacting Phase**, with the Executing Stage being the second Stage, following successful completion of the Preparing Phase (comprising the Envisioning and Planning Stages) and preceding the Observing Phase (comprising the Watching and Optimising Stages).
- The **Dealing Stage** comprises the Preliminary Negotiation, Preliminary Analysis, Structuring, Advanced Financial Analysis and Portfolio Impact Assessment Steps.
- To be undertaken effectively, the Dealing Stage requires the Portfolio Management Team, Strategy Team, Research Team and Capital Transactions Team to work as an **interactive group**, maintaining very close links to strong real estate market networks.
- The iterative Steps of **Preliminary Negotiation** and Preliminary Analysis seek to reduce the target list of potential properties for acquisition to a short list of preferred properties through a repetitive cycle of search, suggestions and filtering.
- **Preliminary Analysis** comprises simplistic, single period comparative analyses which may be qualitative or quantitative, with an expression of the relativity of income to capital, such as a form of the capitalisation rate, being the most commonly used.

- The **Structuring Step** seeks to shape the commercial terms of the proposed transaction, comprising identification of those rights and responsibilities to be transferred in exchange for investor capital, together with the basis upon which the transaction is to be funded, to form an in-principle transaction for Advanced Financial Analysis.
- The **Advanced Financial Analysis** Step seeks to determine, through the use of a pricing model, the existence and extent of mis-pricing of the potential real estate acquisition and the opportunity for the REIT to earn abnormal returns.
- Discounted cash flow has become the standard **pricing model** in real estate investment analysis, being included in pre-programmed form within various portfolio management software packages.
- The two principal methods of determining if the proposed transaction is **mis-priced** are to compare the worth of the proposed real estate investment to the purchaser with the acquisition price and/or to compare the expected return from the proposed real estate investment with the purchasers target or required rate of return.
- The terms **price, value and worth** may be used loosely in differing contexts but have specific definitions and roles for the purposes of real estate investment analysis.
- The **unsystematic and idiosyncratic risk** within a potential real estate acquisition may be reflected in the pricing model through the cash flow or the risk premium within the target rate of return, but care is required to avoid double counting through reflection in both.
- Reflecting the role of forecasts or future information within a pricing model, which are inherently uncertain, an appreciation of the level of uncertainty should be sought through an **explicit consideration of risk**.
- The **NPV decision rule** is generally considered superior to the IRR decision rule for real estate investment analysis.
- The final Step of the Dealing Stage, the **Portfolio Impact Assessment** Step, determines the impact of the potential real estate acquisition and funding structure on the REIT portfolio as a whole, being the final determinant of acceptability of the proposed investment.
- Completion of the Dealing Stage may result in the REIT having converted a target list of specific real estate assets for potential acquisition into an **in-principle transaction** for the acquisition of a nominated asset.
- The Dealing Stage is followed by the **Executing Stage**, where the REIT verifies all information relied upon and assumptions made in the pricing process and reflects this in the documentation necessary to protect the interests of unitholders at Settlement, with completion of the Dealing Stage and the Executing Stage completing the second Phase, the Transacting Phase, so positioning the REIT to then enter the third and final Phase, the Observing Phase.

References

Further information concerning issues considered in this chapter may be found in the following texts:

Baum, A.E. (2009) *Commercial Real Estate Investment*, Second Edition (First Edition 2002), Estates Gazette, London.

Baum, A. and Crosby, N. (2007) *Property Investment Appraisal*, Third Edition (Second Edition 1995, First Edition 1988), Routledge, London.

Brown, G.R. and Matysiak G.A. (2000) *Real Estate Investment: A Capital Market Approach*, Financial Times, Prentice Hall, Harlow.

Brzeski, W.J., Jaffe, A.J. and Lundtrom, S. (1993) Institutional Real Estate Investment Practices: Swedish and United States Experiences, *Journal of Real Estate Research*, **8**(3), p.293.

De Wit, D.P.M. (1996) Real Estate Portfolio Management Practices of Pension Funds and Insurance Companies in the Netherlands: A Survey, *Journal of Real Estate Research*, **11**(2), p.131.

Dubben, N. and Sayce, S. (1991) *Property Portfolio Management: An Introduction*, Routledge, London.

Farragher, E.J. and Kleiman, R.T. (1996) A Re-Examination of Real Estate Investment Decisionmaking Practices, *Journal of Real Estate Portfolio Management*, **2**(1), p.31

Farragher, E.J. and Savage, A. (2008) An Investigation of Real Estate Investment Decision-Making Practices, *Journal of Real Estate Practice and Education*, **11**(1), p.29.

Gallimore, P., Gray, A. and Hansz, J.A. (2000) *Sentiment in Property Investment Decisions: A Behavioural Perspective*, Pacific Rim Real Estate Society Conference, Sydney.

Hawawini, G. and Viallet, C. (2002) *Finance for Executives: Managing for Value Creation*, South-Western Thomson Learning, Cincinnati.

Hoesli, M. and MacGregor, B. (2000) *Property Investment – Principles and Practice of Portfolio Management*, Longman, Harlow.

International Federation of Accountants (2008) *International Good Practice Guidance – Project Appraisal Using Discounted Cash Flow*, International Federation of Accountants, New York.

International Valuation Standards Committee (2007) *International Valuation Standards*, Eighth Edition, International Valuation Standards Committee, London.

Jaffe, A. and Sirmans, C.F. (2001) *Fundamentals of Real Estate Investment*, South-Western Thomson Learning, Mason.

Kim S.H. and Farragher E.J. (1981) Current Capital Budgeting Practice, *Management Accounting*, **62**(12), p.26.

Louargand, M.A. (1992) A Survey of Pension Fund Real Estate Portfolio Risk Management Practices, *Journal of Real Estate Research*, **7**(4), p.361.

Page, D.E. (1983) Criteria for Investment Decision Making: An Empirical Study, *Appraisal Journal*, October–December, **52**(4), p.498.

Rowland, P. (1997) *Property Investments and Their Financing*, Thomson Lawbook Co, North Ryde.

Roulac, S. (2001) *Stephen Roulac on Place and Property*, Property Press, California.

Webb, J. (1984) Real Estate Investment Acquisition Rules for Life Insurance Companies and Pension Funds: A Survey, *AREUEA Journal*, **12**(4), p.495.

Webb, J. and McIntosh, W. (1986) Real Estate Acquisition Rules for REITs: A Survey, *Journal of Real Estate Research*, **1**(1), p.67.

Wiley, R.J. (1976) Real Estate Investment Analysis: An Empirical Study, *Appraisal Journal*, October, **44**(4), p.586.

4

Executing

Chapter 1 outlined the Envisioning Stage of the REIT real estate investment decision making process comprising the Steps of development of a Vision, Goals, Style, Strategic Plan and Objectives for the REIT. On completion of this Stage, the REIT should have a clearly articulated destination together with a high order route map by which to get to the destination and some measurable outcomes to determine whether or not the REIT has arrived at the destination.

Having completed the Envisioning Stage, Super REIT has developed a Vision to be the premier diversified REIT on the stock exchange, interdependent with its adopted generic and specific investment management Style which is active, top down, growth and value added, respectively. To attain this Vision, Super REIT has identified four Goals including to be within the top quartile return performance with lowest quartile tracking error of the stock exchange REIT index every year. Consistently, Super REIT's Strategic Plan focuses on return optimisation at the REIT, portfolio and property level together with effective risk management, supported by a large number of specified Objectives encompassing all REIT management executives in the respective Teams and so aligning the motivations and actions of all REIT management executives with the attainment of Super REIT's Vision.

Chapter 2 then outlined the Planning Stage of the REIT real estate investment decision making process comprising the Steps of development of the Property Portfolio Strategy, Strategic Asset Allocation, Tactical Asset Allocation, Stock Selection and Asset Identification. On completion of this Stage, the REIT should have converted its Vision into an identified target list of specific property assets for potential acquisition that meet the Stock Selection criteria and may be mis-priced.

Global Real Estate Investment Trusts: People, Process and Management,
First Edition. David Parker.
© 2011 David Parker. Published 2011 by Blackwell Publishing Ltd.

On completion of the Planning Stage, Super REIT has developed a Property Portfolio Strategy with a Strategic Asset Allocation comprising a sectoral allocation (50% retail, 40% office, 10% industrial) and geographic allocation (60% northern, 40% southern states), enhanced by a Tactical Asset Allocation of 2.5% to the office sector in the northern city of Metropolis for a period of two years reflecting a forecast undersupply of office accommodation. Within the allocation to the office sector, Super REIT has developed Stock Selection criteria specifying lots of around $37.5 million each, being freehold title in prime office locations within the downtown precincts of specified cities and A grade, high rise, modern office towers that are less than ten years old, being principally leased to corporate tenants.

Completion of the Envisioning Stage and the Planning Stage mark the completion of the first of the three Phases, the Preparing Phase, wherein the REIT articulates where it is going and how it is going to get there, providing unitholders with a clear understanding of the risk-return profile to expect from the managers investment of their funds. Having completed the Preparing Phase the REIT then moves into the second of the three phases, the Transacting Phase, comprising the Dealing Stage and the Executing Stage.

Chapter 3 then outlined the Dealing Stage of the REIT real estate investment decision making process comprising the Steps of Preliminary Negotiation, Preliminary Analysis, Structuring, Advanced Financial Analysis and Portfolio Impact Assessment. On completion of this Stage, the REIT should have converted a target list of specific assets for potential acquisition into an in-principle transaction for the acquisition of a nominated asset.

Having completed the Dealing Stage, Super REIT has identified a specific asset for acquisition, Superman Tower, that is considered mis-priced by a significant extent over both a three and ten year holding period and so capable of generating abnormal returns. At a portfolio level, Superman Tower was confirmed to be acceptable for acquisition at $385 million on the basis of the commercial and funding structure proposed.

The REIT now enters the Executing Stage of the REIT real estate investment decision making process which is the subject of this chapter. The Executing Stage comprises the Steps of the Governance Decision, Transaction Closure, Documentation, Due Diligence and Independent Appraisal (valuation).

Completion of the Executing Stage may result in the REIT having verified all information relied upon and assumptions made in the pricing process and having reflected this in the Documentation necessary to protect the interests of unitholders at Settlement, leading into the Watching Stage of the REIT real estate investment decision making process which is considered in the next chapter.

Completion of the Dealing Stage and the Executing Stage mark completion of the second of the three Phases, the Transacting Phase, wherein the

REIT manager seeks to implement the outcomes of the Preparing Phase through the creation of a tangible property portfolio. This then leads to the third and final Phase of the REIT real estate investment decision making process, the Observing Phase.

It should be noted that the Dealing and Executing Stages may be commonly applied to real estate acquisitions, real estate disposals and other real estate transactions. For the sake of simplicity, this and the previous chapter consider the Dealing and Executing Stages in the context of a real estate acquisition. Arguably, given not only the financial costs of real estate disposal but also the loss of sunk costs of considerable intellectual capital from past management of the real estate asset, real estate disposal requires as much if not more careful analysis and consideration than real estate acquisition.

Accordingly, by the end of this chapter, the reader should understand:

- the **nature of the relationship** between the REIT Governing Entity and the REIT management team to effectively facilitate the management of risk in a transaction;
- the **continual balance** required between risk mitigation and commercial practicality in each Step of the Executing Stage, together with the importance of a REIT managers fiduciary duty to unitholders;
- the role and importance of the Due Diligence and Independent Appraisal Steps in **verifying information** and **supporting assumptions** relied upon in the Dealing Stage;
- the significance of rapidly rising or falling real estate markets in the reconciliation of **assessments of value and worth**, together with an awareness of the potential impact of the powers of an appraisal client upon an appraiser; and
- the **iterative processes** underlying both of the Transaction Closure and Documentation Steps and of the Due Diligence and Independent Appraisal Steps, each of which may necessitate the repeat of all or part of the Dealing Stage.

4.1 People

While the Portfolio Management Team, Strategy Team and Research Team were actively involved in the Planning Stage with the Capital Transactions Team participating in the Dealing Stage, the Executing Stage principally involves the Portfolio Management Team and Capital Transactions Team working together in the Governance Decision, Transaction Closure and Documentation Steps with the Portfolio Management Team then undertaking the Due Diligence and Independent Appraisal Steps.

Effectively, the Portfolio Management Team takes responsibility for the carriage of the Executing Stage by undertaking a project management role with co-ordination of the Governance Decision, Transaction Closure, Documentation, Due Diligence and Independent Appraisal Steps being common to both the acquisition of and disposal of real estate, to major capital expenditure projects and to other major transactions.

However, following the Governance Decision Step where the REIT makes a decision to proceed with the proposed transaction, the requirements for transparency and continuous disclosure for listed entities may be likely to make it necessary for some form of statement to be provided to the stock exchange, regulators, investors and other relevant stakeholders which is likely to be developed by the Investor Interface Team.

4.1.1 Investor Interface Team

The role of the Investor Interface Team is to co-ordinate the provision of information to the market and to stakeholders, with the principal purpose of the role being to provide the interface between the REIT and investors, analysts and the media and the scope of the role including all portfolios and funds within the REIT.

The Investor Interface Team usually reports to the CEO, without any direct reports but usually responsible for managing a wide range of external service providers including graphic designers, annual report editors, printers, share registry, hotels and conference centres and so forth.

The principal contribution of the Investor Interface Team is to facilitate the positive presentation of the REIT to external parties, with the functions of the role including:

- **sales** – comprising promotional initiatives, often in association with the stock exchange, investor advisory groups or special interest groups, whereby the opportunity to invest in the REIT is presented, usually through some form of information exchange or briefing;
- **marketing** – comprising management of the REIT's brand, sponsorship opportunities, social and sporting event participation and other activities designed to facilitate the positive presentation of the REIT to external parties; and
- **investor relations** – comprising a wide range of activities from provision of call centre facilities for retail unitholders to targeted briefings for institutional unitholders, from production of the annual report for all unitholders to targeted presentations for specific unitholder or stakeholder groups, liaison with and management of external stakeholders such as analysts and media and the development and maintenance of crisis management procedures.

Reflecting the national and international spread of existing and potential REIT stakeholders, the activities of the Investor Interface Team are often repetitive for consistent reinforcement, expensive to execute (given the extent and frequency of travel), require senior management participation for authentic communication and may have a lengthy lead time before manifestation in increased investment in the REIT, uplift in the REIT unit price and so forth.

Depending on the size of the REIT, the Investor Interface Team may be arranged as generalists by portfolio or fund or as specialists by function for the REIT itself. Readers are referred to Garrigan and Parsons (1997) for a detailed consideration of the activities of the Investor Interface Team.

4.2 Governance Decision

The first Step of the Executing Stage comprises the Governance Decision, where the REIT will summarise the findings of the pricing process to secure the requisite internal and external approvals for the acquisition to proceed. This will be followed by the Transaction Closure, Documentation, Due Diligence and Independent Appraisal Steps to verify the information relied upon and to support the assumptions made in the Dealing Stage. Completion of the Executing Stage will result in the protection of the interests of unitholders in the exchange of their capital at Settlement in return for legal title to the investment property and the rights and responsibilities associated therewith.

The Governance Decision may include both internal approvals by the relevant decision maker within the REIT itself and external approvals by relevant bodies, such as regulatory body approvals, foreign investment approvals, stock exchange approvals and so forth. The principal components of the Governance Decision Step comprise the determination of who will make the decision and the information that the decision maker requires in order to make a decision. From the viewpoint of internal approvals, the determination of who will make the decision will be based on the delegation of authority policy adopted by the Governing Entity which may, in turn, influence the extent of information required by the decision maker.

4.2.1 Delegation of authority

As a publicly listed enterprise, a REIT Governing Entity may be likely to approve a range of policies to facilitate effective risk management for adherence by the CEO and the various REIT management teams, being monitored by the Compliance and Risk Management Team.

Reflecting the commercial reality of directing a large organisation, the Governing Entity may be likely to reserve major decisions for itself and delegate the balance to the CEO and various officers, with such arrangements usually specified in the delegation of authority policy approved by the Governing Entity. Delegations of authority are usually based on a combination of financial and risk limits which vary depending on the nature of the matter. For example, a Governing Entity may delegate authority for approval of leases of less than 25% of a property or for a term of five years or less to the CEO for approval and reserve the right to approve leases for the majority of space in a building or for a lengthy term, as such leasing transactions may be expected to have a more significant impact on the risk profile of the REIT.

Similarly, with acquisitions, disposals, major capital expenditure, redevelopment or refurbishment and other large transactions, the Governing Entity may delegate authority for approval to the CEO where the transaction is less than a specified amount or a threshold level. A balance is, of course, required between retention of prudent risk control by the Governing Entity and impediment of effective business operations – if the delegations are too low, a large volume of matters may come to the Governing Entity for decision which would slow the operation of the business and divert the attention of the Governing Entity whereas, if the delegations are too high, the Governing Entity may lose control of risk management in the business.

4.2.2 Information required by decision maker

The determination of who will make the decision based on the delegation of authority policy adopted by the Governing Entity may, in turn, influence the extent of information required by the decision maker. For example, if the decision is delegated to the CEO, who has been closely involved in negotiation of the matter subject to decision, less information may need to be provided to the CEO as decision maker.

Usually, where the delegation of authority policy requires reference to the Governing Entity as decision maker, the CEO will be the nominal presenter of the proposal to the Governing Entity with the proposal having been canvassed generally with the Governing Entity in prior meetings to gauge potential support, areas of concern and issues that may require specific attention in the proposal.

While the CEO may be the nominal presenter of the proposal, preparation of the proposal is likely to have been co-ordinated by the Portfolio Management Team with the assistance of the Strategy, Research and Asset Management Teams and subject to input by the Fund Management Team.

Different Governing Entities will have different requirements for the structure and content of Governing Entity proposals, being a balance between receiving enough information with which to make a balanced, prudent and rational decision but without so much information that the key risk management issues become challenging to identify. Similarly, with the legal obligations that fall upon a Governing Entity in decision making, the REIT management team will wish to ensure that all relevant issues that may influence the decision are included within the proposal and given appropriate attention. Some Governing Entities may issue templates for Governing Entity proposals with suggested headings and indications of appropriate length, others may prefer to receive proposals of whatever length is required to address the matter for decision while some may require the proposal to be limited to a single A4 sheet.

On the assumption that matters reserved by the Governing Entity for decision have a level of complexity, a common structure for a Governing Entity proposal may be:

- **recommendation** for approval;
- **report** supporting the proposal; and
- **appendices** supporting the report.

While the recommendation for approval should be clearly and unambiguously stated in a form capable of approval, a balance is again required given the practicalities of real estate investment management. While an ideal form of recommendation might be: '*That the Governing Entity approves the acquisition of (property name) for (amount).*' the practicalities of real estate investment management may result in a recommendation such as: '*That the Governing Entity approves the acquisition of (property name) for (amount) subject to satisfactory due diligence and supporting independent appraisal.*' illustrating the balance required in Governing Entity decision making. To undertake Due Diligence and obtain an Independent Appraisal before submission to the Governing Entity for approval would allow the Governing Entity to approve the acquisition unconditionally but may result in the REIT incurring very significant costs. Conversely, a conditional approval based on *satisfactory* Due Diligence and *supporting* Independent Appraisal avoids incurring such costs prior to Governing Entity approval but provides sources of potential risk to the Governing Entity due to the scope for interpretation of such terms.

While *supporting* could be restated as 'not less than the purchase price', this may result in other un-supporting aspects or warning bells in the Independent Appraisal report not being referred back to the Governing Entity for consideration. Similarly, *satisfactory* Due Diligence could be replaced by specified limits for financial risks but this would not adequately safeguard against non-financial risks. As both the Governing Entity and the REIT management team need to know how far matters may go before being referred back to the Governing Entity for further consideration, a level of trust needs to be established between the REIT Governing Entity and management team to facilitate a workable balance between the retention of prudent risk control by the Governing Entity while not impeding the effective operation of the business by the REIT management team.

Report and appendices supporting the proposal

Having succinctly stated the recommendation for approval, the report to the Governing Entity should provide a clear and logical flow of ideas leading to a conclusion in support of the recommendation with relevant, ancillary material contained in appendices. Effectively, as the Governing Entity would have been closely involved with the Envisioning Stage and aware from previous Governing Entity reports of the Planning Stage, the report and appendices are a summary of the analysis undertaken in the Asset Identification Step and then in the Dealing Stage of the real estate investment decision making process.

While the Governing Entity report effectively includes all of the risk-return issues considered by the Portfolio Management Team in the Advanced Financial Analysis and Portfolio Impact Assessment Steps of the Dealing Stage, these may not necessarily be presented as such but incorporated within other descriptive categories more familiar to the Governing Entity. The content of the Governing Entity report and appendices may vary by real estate type, with a report for the acquisition of a retail property likely to include demographic, spending and related analyses while a report for the acquisition of an industrial property may include analysis of road and rail infrastructure. The following aspects may be included within either the report or the appendices:

Factual information

Address	Street name and number, suburb.
Legal Title	Freehold – real property description, registered owner, easements.
	Leasehold – epitome of head lease.
	Subject to leases – may be summarised in a tenancy schedule in an appendix.
Site	Description of site including area and regularity of shape.
Services	Mains water, power, telephone.
Planning	Zoning, Development Approval, special Development Approval conditions and compliance, constraints, heritage, contamination.
Location	Geographic – road frontages, surrounding development.

Sector specific information:
○ Office – train stations, buses, car parks;
○ Retail – demographics, competing centres;
○ Industrial – road systems, airports, ports.

Building	Description of construction and building materials. Building Approval – special conditions, compliance. Deleterious materials. Sector specific information: ○ Office – lifts, common areas; ○ Retail – mall widths, escalators, travelators; ○ Industrial – clear span, eaves height.
Tenancy Profile	Description of tenancy mix, lease terms, rentals passing. Sector specific information: ○ Office – assignment constraints, liability for make good; ○ Retail – majors and specialty stores; ○ Industrial – liability for environmental issues.

Economic and real estate market commentary

- Systematic risks-general economic overview:
  - ○ Office – employment economic data;
  - ○ Retail – consumer spending, consumer sentiment economic data;
  - ○ Industrial – manufacturing, inventory data.
- Unsystematic risks-real estate market overview:
  - ○ Office – vacancy rate and trend, current and forecast construction levels, current face and effective rental levels and trend, current capitalisation and discount rates and trend;
  - ○ Retail – moving annual turnover relative to market levels, competing centres, potential competing developments, occupancy cost/affordability, mix relative to other properties;
  - ○ Industrial – vacancy rate, supply of land, level of building approvals, level of construction underway.

SWOT analysis
Being a useful way to capture various growth and risk influences on the property:

- Strengths – should be reflected in growth assumptions in the cash flow forecasts;
- Opportunities – should be considered further in a separate section such as the asset management plan;
- Weaknesses – should be reflected in growth assumptions in the cash flow forecasts or in the risk analysis;
- Threats – should be reflected in the risk analysis and have a separate section on mitigation.

Asset management plan
Being developed out of the opportunities from the SWOT analysis, including future plans for the property asset, such as lease renewals, rental increases or refurbishment, which should link with cash flow forecasts.

Commercial transaction
Being a summary of the commercial structure of the transaction, any conditions such as Due Diligence and Independent Appraisal and details of warranties, indemnities and guarantees both given and received.

Financial analysis
Being the relevant summary property level cash flow with the basis of each of the forecasts for rental income, operating expense, capital expenditure and terminal capitalisation rate explained. This should tie in with the strengths, opportunities and weaknesses from the SWOT analysis and the proposals contained within the asset management plan.

The target rate of return, discount rate, IRR and NPV should be detailed together with sensitivity and scenario analyses focusing on the weaknesses and threats from the SWOT analysis but with care to avoid double counting.

Funding transaction
Being a summary of the property level funding structure of the transaction, with details of the source and cost of funds and any related taxation issues arising such as stamp duty liability. If debt funding is to be used, details of lenders, terms and covenants should be included. If an equity raising is required, this may be a condition of approval and the subject of a separate Governing Entity report.

Portfolio impact
Being a summary of the Portfolio Impact Assessment of the transaction in portfolio risk-return and portfolio metrics terms. A clear loop should be evident whereby undertaking the proposed transaction contributes to achieving the Goals and so attaining the REIT's Vision.

Risk management
Being an analysis of the weaknesses, threats and risks identified and the basis upon which each risk will be managed and mitigated.

Given the enormous diversity of property types and matters that may be subject to reports for Governing Entity approval, the above is not intended to be comprehensive. In preparing a Governing Entity report, the REIT management team will consider the matter from the viewpoint of the Governing Entity and seek to include such information as the Governing Entity may be likely to require and which may vary considerably depending on the nature of the property and matter requiring Governing Entity approval.

4.2.3 Governance Decision

The proposal may be likely to be included with the Governing Entity papers and circulated to members ahead of the Governing Entity meeting to allow time for reading, review and questions of the REIT management team.

At the Governing Entity meeting, the CEO may talk to the proposal or the Fund Management Team may make a presentation. Following discussion, the Governing Entity may decide to approve or reject the proposal on the basis submitted or on a modified basis or may defer a decision pending the provision of further information.

The Governance Decision comprised the first Step of the Executing Stage, where the REIT summarised the findings of the pricing process to secure the requisite internal and external approvals for the acquisition to proceed. This Step is now followed by the Transaction Closure, Documentation, Due Diligence and Independent Appraisal Steps.

4.3 Transaction Closure

Having completed the Governance Decision Step, the next Step of the Executing Stage comprises Transaction Closure, where the REIT completes final negotiations with the vendor in order to close the transaction. This will be followed by the Documentation, Due Diligence and Independent Appraisal Steps to verify the information relied upon and to support the assumptions made in the Dealing Stage. Completion of the Executing Stage will result in the protection of the interests of unitholders in the exchange of their capital at settlement in return for legal title to the investment property and the rights and responsibilities associated therewith.

4.3.1 Commercial Transaction Closure

Negotiation of the commercial terms of a real estate transaction is an ongoing iterative process starting in the Preliminary Negotiation Step and then continuing during the Structuring, Advanced Financial Analysis and Portfolio Impact Assessment Steps of the Dealing Stage. The Capital Transactions Team established the broad parameters of the transaction during the Preliminary Negotiation Step, but these were then negotiated and renegotiated as the Portfolio Management Team undertook the Structuring, Advanced Financial Analysis and Portfolio Impact Assessment Steps and identified issues requiring attention.

Ideally, all matters requiring negotiation with the vendor would have been resolved prior to seeking the Governance Decision in order to permit clarity and certainty in the decision making process. In the event that the Governance Decision is conditional or other matters arise, the Capital Transactions Team may negotiate relevant issues as required during the Transaction Closure Step.

Documentation

As the iterative process of negotiating and renegotiating during the Structuring, Advanced Financial Analysis and Portfolio Impact Assessment Steps unfolded, the transaction took shape and was summarised within in-principle documentation which then formed the basis of the report submitted for the Governance Decision.

In the event that further negotiation during Transaction Closure varies such in-principle documentation, this may require redrafting with care needed to ensure that such redrafting does not materially alter that which was approved during the Governance Decision Step.

4.3.2 Funding Transaction Closure

In the Structuring Step of the Dealing Stage, the Fund Management Team determined and then negotiated the structure of the funding transaction to provide the optimal basis upon which the REIT may pay for the property to be acquired.

During the Transaction Closure Step, the Fund Management Team will seek to confirm that funding on the basis proposed still remains available. For the equity contribution, the Fund Management Team will liaise with the CFO and treasury function to confirm availability of funds at the proposed date of settlement. For the debt contribution, the Fund Management Team will seek to confirm with the debt providers that the proposed facility is still available at the quoted rate and on the quoted basis.

Documentation

Similar to the commercial transaction closure, the structure of the funding transaction agreed with the debt providers was summarised within in-principle documentation which then formed the basis of the report submitted for the Governance Decision.

In the event that further negotiation during Transaction Closure varies such in-principle documentation, this may require redrafting with care needed to ensure that such redrafting does not materially alter that which was approved during the Governance Decision Step.

4.3.3 Transaction Closure

The Transaction Closure Step comprised the final negotiation of commercial terms and funding terms for the transaction, with renegotiation of the transaction where necessary, prior to documenting the transaction in a commonly agreed form. Having completed the Transaction Closure Step, the next Steps comprise Documentation, Due Diligence and Independent Appraisal to verify the information relied upon and to support the assumptions made in the Dealing Stage.

4.4 Documentation

Having completed the Governance Decision and Transaction Closure Steps, the next Step of the Executing Stage comprises preparation of transaction Documentation – in the case of an acquisition, this may comprise a contract of sale and purchase. This will be followed by the Due Diligence and Independent Appraisal Steps with completion of the Executing Stage resulting in the protection of the interests of unitholders in the exchange of their capital at Settlement in return for legal title to the property and the rights and responsibilities associated therewith.

4.4.1 Negotiation of Documentation

Having completed the Transaction Closure Step, the REIT management team should have updated two documents, variously referred to as the in-principle agreements, heads of terms, terms sheets or short form agreements, which summarise the proposed commercial and funding transaction respectively and which formed the basis of the report submitted for the Governance Decision.

The next Step for the Portfolio Management Team and the Fund Management Team is to convert the updated short form documentation of the commercial transaction and the funding transaction, respectively, into a full set of documents for each, in a commonly agreed form using a risk management approach, which, when executed, will then bind the parties to the transaction.

Documentation of commercial transaction

Negotiation of Documentation forces the parties to a transaction to refocus on risk management, as the document requires the parties to agree, amongst other things, what will happen in a wide range of 'what if' scenarios. This often serves to create an inherent tension both within each party and between each party where the desire to complete the transaction needs to be tempered by prudent risk management.

It is usually expeditious to agree as soon as possible which party will prepare the Documentation as it may be expected that, whichever party does so, the other party will require amendments. Amendments to Documentation may be required for the entire range of risk management issues including logistics, financial issues, non-financial issues, guarantees, warranties, indemnities and so forth. As matters are identified, the Portfolio Management and Capital Transactions Teams will be required to negotiate an agreement, usually through a process of prioritisation by risk impact and progressive trade-offs. Given the proximity of completion and the weariness of the parties by time this Step arrives, considerable fortitude, patience and calm is usually required to agree Documentation.

By way of example, a typical sale and purchase contract may be expected to incorporate a wide range of clauses including the following:

Parties	nominate vendor and purchaser
Property	identify the property being bought and sold
Obligation	vendor to sell and purchaser to buy
Sale price	nominate the sale price
Deposit	nominate the amount of the deposit and timing of payment
Settlement	nominate the date and place of Settlement
Inclusions	nominate that which is included in the sale and anything that may be excluded
Tenancies	detail all existing tenancies, licenses and so forth and the basis upon which rent reviews, lease renewals, requests for assignment, letting of vacant accommodation and other tenancy matters will be managed between exchange of contracts and Settlement
Management	nominate the approach to be adopted to management of the property, collection of rent, payment of operating expenses, repairs and maintenance and so forth between exchange of contracts and Settlement
Actions	specify any particular actions to be taken by either party, such as completion of building works by the vendor, between exchange of contracts and Settlement
Events	outline a process to be adopted, such as discussion in good faith, if an unexpected event arises between exchange of contracts and Settlement
Risk	detail all warranties, indemnities, guarantees and other undertakings together with the point at which the purchaser is at risk
Conditions	nominate any matters upon which the contract is conditional
Default	nominate the approach to be adopted in the event of default by the vendor or purchaser under the contract
Notices	specify the process by which one party is deemed to have given notice to the other concerning matters under the contract

in addition to many other detailed clauses addressing relevant legal issues specific to the jurisdiction within which the transaction takes place. The above list is not intended to be exhaustive and individual transactions may require further, specific clauses to address risk management issues arising in the transaction.

Satisfactory Due Diligence and supporting Independent Appraisal
In the event that the Governing Entity gave conditional approval for the transaction, such as subject to '*satisfactory Due Diligence*' and '*supporting independent appraisal*', these conditions will require reflection in the Documentation. While the Governing Entity may have relied on such subjective descriptions as *satisfactory* and *supporting* in addition to trust

when giving a decision to the CEO and the Fund and Portfolio Management Teams to proceed with the transaction, this effectively transfers the obligation for crafting objective descriptions in Documentation to the Portfolio Management Team.

The Portfolio Management Team should adopt a risk management approach to both issues, comprising analysis of the range of possible risks arising and development of a risk management strategy to deal with each which may or may not include the drafting of contract clauses.

For example, in terms of *satisfactory* Due Diligence, the Portfolio Management Team may have a clearly defined purpose and objectives wherein issues for investigation may be identified based on likely risks. As the role of Due Diligence is to verify information relied upon in the pricing process during the Dealing Stage, matters arising during the Due Diligence Step may be more likely to be matters of fact rather than matters of opinion, though a question of degree may arise. These may include financial risks, such as incorrect details of leases to tenants, or non-financial risks, such as the property not being built in accordance with the approved building application. Financial risks may be addressed within the contract by either a specified monetary amount, a formula to calculate such an amount, an indemnity for losses arising and so forth. Non-financial risks may be addressed within the contract by a warranty or guarantee, depending on the nature of the risk.

Each identified Due Diligence risk may be matched with a mitigating contract clause for effective risk management. A general clause that the vendor provides information in the contract to the *'best of its knowledge'* provides a risk management base line, which may be supplemented by a warranty that the vendor has provided full disclosure of all matters with which a prudent purchaser may be concerned.

The risk management approach used for *supporting* Independent Appraisal by the Portfolio Management Team may address both the assumptions adopted by the independent appraiser and the assessment of value resulting. The assessment of value may be absolute, for example if the REITs governing documents do not allow acquisition at more than Independent Appraisal, or it may be relative, such as with reference to the NPV determined by the Portfolio Management Team in the Advanced Financial Analysis Step. Through the Independent Appraisal, the Portfolio Management Team seek to support the assumptions made in the Dealing Stage and material differences between the assumptions of the independent appraiser and the Portfolio Management Team will requires analysis. If significant, the commercial structure of the transaction may require renegotiation by the Capital Transactions Team.

Reflecting the nature of risk management, it is rare for all parties to a transaction to achieve a perfect outcome, with the final text of the

Documentation representing a compromise based on risk prioritisation. The outcome of the Documentation Step is an agreed commercial transaction document that is then ready for execution by the parties.

Documentation of funding transaction

Having completed the Transaction Closure Step, the REIT management team should have updated the in-principle document summarising the proposed funding transaction and which formed the basis of the report submitted for the Governance Decision.

The Fund Management Team now need to convert the in-principle document into a full set of lending and security documents, using a risk management approach, in a form agreed with the debt providers and which, when executed, will then bind the parties to the transaction.

If the debt is sourced from an existing syndicate of bank lenders, further loan documentation may not be required other than that to add additional properties to the pool of security assets if necessary.

In other circumstances, loan documentation may need to be negotiated and drafted with a risk management approach adopted in common with that adopted for documentation of the commercial transaction. Similarly, if the basis of the funding transaction differs from that proposed with an impact on the risk-return profile of the transaction, renegotiation may be required and reference back to the Governing Entity if the resulting changes are considered significant.

4.4.2 Sign-offs

Prior to formal execution of the commercial and funding transaction Documentation, REIT risk management policies usually seek to ensure that those upon whom reliance has been placed provide some form of sign-off that appropriate care and attention has been given, that services have been provided in a professional manner and that the advice or services may be relied upon.

For example, the legal advisors to the REIT as a purchaser or vendor may provide sign-off that due care and attention has been provided in a professional manner and that the legal documents prepared reflect the instructions of their client and are enforceable at law. Similar sign-offs may be provided by other consultants who have provided services upon which reliance has been placed.

Depending on the governance structure of the REIT, risk management policies may also require members of the REIT management team to provide sign-offs that the commercial and funding details of the transaction accord with those approved by the Governing Entity in the Governance Decision Step.

4.4.3 Execution and exchange

The delegations of authority, referred to above, usually include delegations for the execution of documents on behalf of the REIT that commit the REIT to some form of obligation.

Given the significant commitment entered into on execution of documents such as a contract to purchase an investment property, such execution will be recorded by the REIT Company Secretary and a copy of the contract held in security pending provision of the original for retention after payment of stamp duty.

Having assembled the accompanying sign-offs, two copies of the document will usually then be submitted to the REIT's signatory for execution under delegated authority. Following execution of both copies by the other party, the parties will exchange documents and retain one copy each. Such sequential execution may be done by the parties together in one room, if the transaction is of a notable magnitude, or separately through their legal advisors if the transaction is more in the nature of business as usual.

Prior to document execution, the Investor Interface Team would have prepared statements for release to the stock exchange, unitholders and the media and obtained approval for same from the Governing Entity, CEO and relevant members of the REIT management team in accordance with the REIT's policy on public statements. On execution and exchange of documents, such statements would be released to the relevant parties and the Investor Interface Team may be expected to follow up media outlets to provide further information, arrange CEO interviews and so forth as part of REIT marketing.

4.4.4 Documentation

Following a lengthy and often frustrating period of repetitive negotiation and analysis, completion and exchange of Documentation usually marks a significant achievement for the Capital Transactions Team and the Portfolio Management Team. While conditions may remain to be fulfilled prior to Settlement, the transaction is now substantially complete and the REIT may start to consider issues associated with the probable incorporation of the property within the REIT's portfolio.

Having completed the Governance Decision, Transaction Closure and Documentation Steps, the REIT is now ready to undertake the Due Diligence and Independent Appraisal Steps of the Executing Stage of the real estate investment decision making process.

4.5 Due Diligence

Having completed the Governance Decision, Transaction Closure and Documentation Steps, the next Step of the Executing Stage comprises Due Diligence, where the REIT seeks to verify information relied upon in the Dealing Stage. This will be followed by the final Independent Appraisal Step which seeks to support the assumptions made in the Dealing Stage.

The Due Diligence Step may be considered to be a balance between process and outcomes, being a conscious decision by the REIT management team regarding the level of resources to be invested relative to the nature of the risks to be investigated. The costs of Due Diligence should be balanced against the long term savings of poor performance with aspirational goals balanced against practical resource, information and time constraints. While Due Diligence does not provide an insurance policy, it should be comprehensive in coverage though succinct in ultimate communication (Roulac in Pagliari, 1995).

Effective completion of the Due Diligence Step should increase the prospect that investment performance will align with expectations, offering the prospect of superior performance generally and mitigating the exposure to substantial loss specifically (Roulac in Pagliari, 1995). As such, the Due Diligence Step offers a method of addressing imperfect knowledge and reducing uncertainty in the transaction (Seabrooke et al., 2004) for, as Roulac (in Pagliari, 1995) observes:

> *Without effective due diligence prior to an acquisition, no amount of strategic insight and/or operational/dispositional brilliance can overcome the debilitating risk associated with a marginal (or worse) property acquisition and the consequences of overlooking a major infirmity in the property, market, manager or investment structure.* (Roulac in Pagliari, 1995)

Through the process of the Due Diligence Step, the REIT management team seeks to verify information relied upon in the Dealing Stage through a structured process of risk management. However, appropriate Due Diligence cannot be prescribed by formula and must be determined based on the investment structure and real estate type (Roulac in Pagliari, 1995).

Within the primary purpose of information verification, the Due Diligence Step may confirm:

- the economic **integrity** of investment;
- the **veracity** of representations;
- the **completeness** of information included; and
- the **general compliance** with prudent investment standards,

with the objectives of:

- **assessment** of regulatory compliance;
- **performance** of appropriate financial and other analyses;
- **detection** of sources of potential problems; and
- **gaining insights** crucial to managing the property (Roulac in Pagliari, 1995).

4.5.1 Fiduciary duty

Given the fiduciary relationship between the REIT management team and unitholders, there is an expectation that the REIT management team will act consistently with the prudent man standard by employing appropriate Due Diligence prior to transferring capital for the acquisition of a property at Settlement. The critical issue then becomes how the REIT management team chooses to operationalise its fiduciary duty through the process and practice of the Due Diligence Step, which is considered further below (Roulac in Pagliari, 1995).

This is part of the balance between process and outcomes whereby the REIT manager chooses between undertaking the minimum processes to 'tick the boxes' and optimal processes to confirm requisite tasks have been performed, pertinent issues identified, critical information disclosed, designated standards confirmed and legal and regulatory compliance achieved:

> *'Effective implementation of the due diligence priority is the explicit substance of prudent investing in the fiduciary context…'* (Roulac in Pagliari, 1995)

4.5.2 Operationalising Due Diligence

With no prescriptive formula and the appropriate process and practice of the Due Diligence Step differing between situations and changing over time, fiduciary duty suggests that the guiding principle should be seeking to replicate that process which a prudent person would employ prior to a major financial commitment (Roulac in Pagliari, 1995).

The Due Diligence process may be operationalised by either high order or specific groupings of issues or themes (Roulac in Pagliari, 1995) or by the specialism of professional advisors engaged to undertake Due Diligence activities on behalf of the REIT (Baum, 2002).

High order groupings of issues or themes as a guide to the process of Due Diligence may include:

- **economic factors** – including demand, market conditions, taxation, inflation;
- **market factors** – including new building, sale prices, rental levels;

- **investment factors** – including vendor reputation, market knowledge, market confidence;
- **property characteristics** – including tenant quality, building condition, location;
- **financial factors** – including lease terms, projected future income, sensitivity analysis; and
- **legal and documentation factors** – including environmental reports, construction documents and title report (Roulac in Pagliari, 1995).

Alternatively, specific groupings of issues or themes as a guide to the process of Due Diligence may include:

- **property definition and description** – including provision of an understanding of the property interests being acquired;
- **site analysis** – including analysis of all aspects of the land;
- **design and functionality** – including the built envelope on the land;
- **assessment of physical** components and their condition – including the structure, services and finishes comprising the built envelope;
- **property use and activity** – including impact on future performance and associated risks;
- **building services and amenities** – including air conditioning, lifts and other services, garbage collection and telecommunications;
- **access and transportation services** – including walkways, roadways and public transport;
- **neighbourhood analysis** – including surrounding uses that impact on the subject property;
- **market size** – including absolute size and shape of relevant market;
- **demand source** – including alternative sources of occupier demand and space use objectives;
- **competitive market supply analysis** – including macro analysis of market conditions and micro analysis of demand and pricing conditions;
- **financing and ownership** – including consideration of relevant lenders and documentation;
- **financial structure** – including the relationships between the financial participants in the project;
- **tenants** – including capacity to pay rental and prospects for expansion;
- **lease arrangements** – including those lease features that define current income, prospective value and risk;
- **property operations** – including historic performance and prospective future performance;
- **management** – including asset, property and facilities management;
- **financial performance** – including analysis of historical operating and financial statements for the property;

- **health, safety and environmental quality** – including assessment of the site and physical components and condition;
- **legal issues** – including compliance with relevant legislation, current and pending litigation and contingent liabilities; and
- **risk assessment** – including identification and assessment of risks associated with each of the above (Roulac in Pagliari, 1995).

The Due Diligence process may be operationalised by the specialism of professional advisors engaged to undertake Due Diligence activities on behalf of the REIT (Baum, 2002), with the REIT manager then focusing on such questions as:

- who is to be **involved**?
- what are their **qualifications**?
- what are the specifications for their **roles and responsibilities**?
- which **issues** are being addressed?
- what **types** of investigation will be pursued?
- what **depth** of investigation is needed?
- what **documentation** is desired?
- what form of **final work product** is desired? and,
- are any **recommendations** required? (Roulac in Pagliari, 1995)

Following risk analysis, Due Diligence tasks may then be divided between professional advisers on the basis of their skill sets, including:

- **legal advisors** – including title, leases;
- **accountants** – including tenant creditworthiness, review of financial modelling;
- **planners** – including development approval compliance, zonings, heritage issues;
- **environmentalists** – including land contamination, flora and fauna protection;
- **building surveyor** – including building approval compliance, building condition, identification of deleterious materials (such as asbestos);
- **structural engineer** – including structural stability, building integrity;
- **mechanical and electrical engineer** – including lifts, escalators, air conditioning;
- **hydraulics engineer** – including water supply, waste removal;
- **sector specialists** – such as demographers and trade area spending analysts for retail property; and
- **other specialists** – such as art or sculpture consultants.

Whichever Due Diligence process is operationalised, some form of report or output is required which describes or states the current position and compliance with relevant regulation to facilitate comparison with that information relied upon by the Portfolio Management Team in the Dealing Stage. In the event that differences are identified as a result of Due Diligence, the Advanced Financial Analysis and Portfolio Impact Assessment Steps may need to be revisited to determine the risk-return impact with reference back to the Governing Entity if necessary.

4.5.3 Due Diligence

As a practice and process for information verification, Due Diligence must be carefully designed to suit each individual transaction to a level and in a form appropriate to meet the prudent man standard and fiduciary obligations. In the event that Due Diligence verifies that information adopted, the transaction may proceed with greater confidence in the forecast outcomes. Conversely, in the event that Due Diligence identifies something different to that which was anticipated, fiduciary duty requires the REIT management team to take action appropriate to the nature of that identified.

Having verified the information relied upon in the Dealing Stage, the final Step in the Executing Stage of the real estate investment decision making process is the Independent Appraisal Step. Completion of the Executing Stage will result in the protection of the interests of unitholders in the exchange of their capital at settlement in return for legal title to the investment property and the rights and responsibilities associated therewith, being the first step in the Watching Stage considered in the next chapter.

4.6 Independent Appraisal

Having completed the Governance Decision, Transaction Closure, Documentation and Due Diligence Steps, the final step of the Executing Stage comprises Independent Appraisal (generally referred to as valuation in Commonwealth countries), where the REIT management team seeks to support the assumptions made in the Dealing Stage.

In the event that the assumptions made in the Dealing Stage are found to be unsupported by Independent Appraisal, then renegotiation may be required together with reiteration of the Advanced Financial Analysis and Portfolio Impact Assessment Steps of the Dealing Stage. Depending on the significance of the changes to the transaction then resulting, it may be necessary to complete the Governance Decision Step of the Executing Stage again and amend Documentation accordingly.

Reflecting the globalisation of capital markets and of real estate markets, appraisal standards and guidance are now internationalised through the pronouncements and publications of the International Valuation Standards Committee (IVSC, 2007) and harmonised with International Financial

Reporting Standards (http://www.ifrs.org/Home.htm). Generally, individual countries then have national appraisal standards and guidance which are harmonised with those of the IVSC, such as:

- the RICS *Red Book* in the United Kingdom; (http://www.rics.org/redbook);
- the Appraisal Institute *Standards of Professional Appraisal Practice* in the USA; (http://www.appraisalinstitute.org/ppc/ethics_standards.aspx); and
- *Professional Practice* in Australia and New Zealand (Australian Property Institute, 2006).

The Independent Appraisal Step of the Executing Stage may be considered to be a process comprising determination of the requirement for appraisal, appointment and instruction of the appraiser and receipt and review of the appraisal report. However, over the last 25 years, extensive research has been undertaken into issues associated with appraisal leading to a greater understanding of important issues such as appraisal smoothing, accuracy and variation, margin of error and negligence, point estimates vs. ranges, price, value and worth and issues associated with appraiser behaviour.

4.6.1 Requirement for appraisal

Within the governing documents of some REITs, Independent Appraisal is mandatory whereas for others it is a matter for the Governing Entity. Accordingly, the Portfolio Management Team needs to determine the requirement for an Independent Appraisal, either as a matter of legal or regulatory obligation or as a matter of voluntary good practice.

In the interests of transparency and risk management, it is prudent for a REIT to obtain an Independent Appraisal prior to acquisition, disposal or other major transaction, as well as during the holding period for capital return performance measurement as considered in Chapter 5. An Independent Appraisal provides an external opinion of the value of a property, effectively providing a benchmark which allows the REIT management team to not only determine that it is not paying too much or accepting too little for a property but also to be able to prove this to relevant stakeholders.

However, within this apparently straightforward concept of not paying too much or accepting too little lies a wide range of appraisal issues for consideration.

A survey of 125 large US real estate investors found only 41% of pension funds, insurance companies, private investment companies and REITs used appraisal reports. (Farragher and Kleiman, 1996)

4.6.2 Appraisal issues

Extensive research over the last 25 years has provided significant insights into various aspects of appraisal leading to a greater understanding of issues including price, value and worth, point estimates vs. ranges, appraisal smoothing, accuracy and variation, margin of error and appraiser negligence together with issues associated with appraiser behaviour.

Price, value and worth

Issues associated with the distinction between price, value and worth were considered in Chapter 3 in the context of the theoretical basis of mis-pricing.

In the context of Independent Appraisal, the independent appraiser will generally be instructed to determine value, being the economic concept referring to the price most likely to be concluded by buyers and sellers of a good or service that is available for purchase (IVSC, 2007) and usually based on the IVSC's definition of market value:

The estimated amount for which a property should exchange on the date of valuation between a willing buyer and a willing seller in an arm's-length transaction after proper marketing wherein the parties had each acted knowledgeably, prudently, and without compulsion.

(IVSC, 2007)

The independent appraiser's opinion of value will form a benchmark for comparison by the REIT management team with its assessment of worth, being the amount that the REIT may be willing to pay or accept for a property to achieve its nominated target rate of return.

In this sense, an Independent Appraisal not only provides evidence of what other active market participants might hypothetically pay or accept for a property but also confirmation that such value is greater than the REIT management team's assessment of worth.

Point estimate vs. range

While there has been extensive debate for several decades concerning the wisdom of a single nominated appraised value figure (or point estimate) compared to a range of figures, the REIT industry, in common with the real estate investment industry generally, remains focused on the point estimate.

While a point estimate provides a comparative benchmark for decision making or entry into financial statements, it is relatively uninformative from a risk management viewpoint. Consistent with the definition of market value, a point estimate provides the appraisers assessment of the estimated amount at which there is the greatest probability of the willing buyer and willing seller reaching agreement.

The point estimate, however, provides limited information on a range of aspects including:

- **the magnitude of such probability** – for example, is there a probability of 10% with 45% probability either side? Or a probability of 90% with a 5% probability either side? and,
- **the range of potential estimates of value and potential probabilities on either side** – for example, could the value be up to 20% higher but with a lesser probability or up to 10% lower but with a higher probability?

From the viewpoint of transparency, risk management and informed decision making, it may be contended that it would be both beneficial and informative for the real estate investment industry generally, including the REIT industry, to seek the independent appraisers opinion of not only a point estimate of value but also the range of values within which the point estimate lies and an opinion of the attached probabilities as part of the Independent Appraisal process.

Appraisal smoothing, accuracy, variation and margin of error
The traditional claim that appraisal is an art, not a science, has been subject to extensive research over the last 25 years, particularly concerning the aspects of appraisal smoothing, accuracy and variation with a consequent impact on appraiser negligence. While such research provides a clearer understanding of the impact of each, appraiser behaviour (considered below) and the opinion based nature of an appraisal result in a continued role for judgment in addition to scientific method.

The impact of appraisal smoothing on real estate returns is considered in Chapter 5, together with appraisal accuracy, being the effectiveness of an appraisal as a proxy for likely selling price, which research has found to demonstrate a high level of validity. Assessment of real estate returns may also be affected by appraisal variation, which concerns issues associated with the simultaneous appraisal of the same property by multiple appraisers on a common basis.

Related to appraisal variation, Brown and Matysiak (2000) investigate the distinction between the margin of error between two equally informed appraisers and negligence in appraisal. Reflecting that market imperfections give rise to dispersion in appraisals, the authors argue that the degree of confidence in an appraisal will vary depending on circumstances including the level of uncertainty in each appraisal and the level of commonality of opinion between appraisers on expected outcomes, with each appraisal being a reflection of the quality of available information and expectations formed therefrom. As expectations are uncertain, the appraisal implies both a probability and a range of possible outcomes with the question then being at what point does a large range become negligent?

As a range of values is required to exist for there to be an active market with trading, the authors contend that this implies a margin of difference exists as a normal aspect of the real estate market and which may comprise two components, being:

- **uncertainty** in individual appraisals; and
- the **correlation** between different appraisers assumptions used in their calculations – for example, if information is poor or incomplete, this will impact upon how appraisers consider certain factors influence value.

Such information may be used to quantify the uncertainty surrounding the margin of error with the probability of the difference between two appraisals of the same property lying within the given margin of error then capable of calculation. As such, the authors contend that issues associated with the margin of error should be severed from issues associated with negligence, as it is possible to have a large margin of error without negligence, with negligence then depending on an examination of the assumptions used to estimate value.

Appraiser negligence
Case law on appraiser negligence is a feature of most developed economies around the world with the basis upon which a negligence claim may be grounded varying by individual case and jurisdiction. In Commonwealth jurisdictions, Norris and Joyce (1994), (to which readers are referred for comprehensive coverage of issues associated with appraisers' liability), outline the finer details of each of a range of issues, including relationship of proximity and foreseeability of loss, requiring consideration in grounding a claim for negligence in tort law.

From the viewpoint of real estate investment decision making, issues surrounding the margin of error and negligence are of particular significance in rapidly rising or falling markets, especially when such markets move close to an inflection point, usually coming to the fore after the point of inflection has occurred to the disadvantage of one party to the transaction.

It may, therefore, not be surprising to see divergence emerge between the Portfolio Management Team's assessment of worth and an independent appraiser's assessment of value at such inflection points, which should provide a trigger for careful review and reconsideration of assumptions by the Portfolio Management Team.

Appraiser behaviour

Matters associated with appraiser behaviour in the context of Independent Appraisal and Performance Measurement (which are considered in Chapter 5) raise ethical issues surrounding the influence of an appraiser by the Portfolio Management Team with the principles of openness and transparency, coupled with fiduciary duty, applying to prevent the Portfolio Management Team from influencing an appraiser in the context of either Independent Appraisal and/or Performance Measurement.

In order to avoid undue influence, Portfolio Management Teams should be aware of the four types of power exercisable by appraisal clients over appraisers (Levy and Schuck, 1999), being:

- **expert power** – appraisal clients may have a greater amount of expertise and knowledge about real estate markets in which they invest, with expertise in valuation techniques and methodologies further assisting in identifying inconsistencies and inaccuracies when reviewing draft reports;
- **information power** – appraisers may be dependent on clients for information, with appraisal clients exerting power by providing what they consider relevant information that may change an appraisers opinion;
- **reward and coercive power** – appraisal clients may own large portfolios and so be able to provide an appraiser with a substantial amount of revenue over a number of years. Similarly, the appraiser may be tempted to please the client to ensure future instructions; and
- **procedural power** – such as the appraisal clients control over appraisal instructions, choice of appraiser, length of contract, amount of fee, appraisal regularity and the requirement to submit a draft appraisal report for comment.

Of critical importance from the viewpoint of fiduciary duty, great care is required by the Portfolio Management Team to avoid any form of influence or pressure upon the independent appraiser when REIT management team remuneration is linked to appraisal outcomes (Levy and Schuck, 1999).

4.6.3 Appraiser appointment

Having determined the requirement for an Independent Appraisal, either as a matter of legal or regulatory obligation or as a matter of voluntary good practice, the Portfolio Management Team now needs to appoint an external appraiser.

Such an appraiser should be independent of the REIT and be appropriately academically qualified, appropriately licensed or registered and be a member of the relevant national and/or international professional bodies (Pagliari, 1995).

As part of a REIT's risk management policy, it is usual practice to maintain a panel of suitably qualified appraisers with sectoral and/or geographic expertise, created following an expressions of interest process with selection based on pre-determined criteria. Further, effective risk management usually requires a rotating panel of appraisers with staggered, limited terms of appointment and constraints over the frequency of reappointment.

4.6.4 Appraiser instruction

An external appraiser should be formally appointed in writing by the Governing Entity, through the Portfolio Management Team, to prepare an Independent Appraisal report addressed to and for the Governing Entity.
The written instructions should include:

- the names of the Governing Entity and the appraiser;
- the address of the property;
- the date of instruction and the date of appraisal;
- the purpose of the appraisal and the use to which the report will be put;
- the basis of the appraisal, particularly if other than open market value consistent with the IVSC definition;
- the legal description of the property, including title details and the legal interest to be appraised;
- the nature of the property;
- a requirement that the appraisal be undertaken in accordance with IVSC and local jurisdictional practice standards and guidance notes;
- any additional matters specific to the individual property;
- the basis of and obligation for payment of the appraisers fee;
- details for access to the property and contacts for further information; with
- attached summary of tenancies and status report on relevant tenancy matters;
- attached operating expenditure and capital expenditure budgets for the property; and
- attached other information as may be relevant to the particular property. (Australian Property Institute, 2006)

Given the amount of information required to be provided to the independent appraiser before and during the appraisal process, careful co-ordination is required to avoid inadvertent error. For acquisition, such coordination may be undertaken by the Portfolio Management Team, with the Asset Management Team and the Property and Facilities Management Teams undertaking such coordination for disposal and ongoing performance measurement appraisal.

4.6.5 *Appraisal report*

The appraisal report is an important document in the real estate investment decision making process as it summarises the external appraisers assumptions on a range of issues for comparison to those of the Portfolio Management Team adopted in the Dealing Stage.

These may include assumptions concerning the state of the market, such as:

- **rent** for comparable premises;
- **vacancy rates** and trends in the sub-market;
- **rental rates** and trends in the sub-market;
- **lease terms** and concessions on competing properties;
- **sale prices** of comparable properties;
- **new competitive building** and construction trends;
- **local restrictions** on new building;
- **limitations** of land availability; and
- **corporate expansion** and relocation decisions (Roulac in Pagliari, 1995),

which, if they differ from those adopted by the Portfolio Management Team, will necessitate careful review and reconsideration.

The report will also include the external appraiser's assumptions concerning important financial variables for the subject property, such as:

- current **occupancy** levels;
- tenant **quality**;
- tenants' **improvements** and requirements;
- **market rental** levels;
- projected **future income**, including revenue and expense growth rates;
- **lease terms**;
- **capitalisation rate**;
- required **IRR** and/or discount rate;
- projected **future value**;
- **initial yield**;
- **price per unit area** (per square metre, per square foot, etc.); and
- **sensitivity analysis**.

As with assumptions concerning the state of the market, if assumptions concerning financial variables are found to differ from those adopted by the Portfolio Management Team in the Dealing Stage, then careful review and reconsideration will be required. Having regard to openness and transparency, fiduciary duty and appraisal client power, as referred to above, the Portfolio Management Team should take care to restrict comments on the external appraisers draft report, if provided for comment, to matters of fact only and not comment on matters of appraiser opinion with which they may differ.

Depending on the nature and extent of any differences found, renegotiation may be required together with reiteration of the Advanced Financial Analysis and Portfolio Impact Assessment Steps of the Dealing Stage. Further, depending on the significance of the changes to the transaction then resulting, it may be necessary to complete the Governance Decision Step of the Executing Stage again and amend Documentation accordingly.

4.6.6 Independent Appraisal

Having completed the Governance Decision, Transaction Closure, Documentation and Due Diligence Steps, the final Step of the Executing Stage comprised Independent Appraisal (valuation), where the REIT sought to support the assumptions made in the Dealing Stage.

The Independent Appraisal Step of the Executing Stage may be considered to be a process comprising determination of the requirement for appraisal, appointment and instruction of the appraiser and receipt and review of the appraisal report. Fiduciary duty and prudent risk management require the Portfolio Management Team to implement the process objectively, with careful regard to such issues as appraisal smoothing, accuracy and variation, margin of error and negligence, point estimates vs. ranges, price, value and worth and issues associated with appraiser behaviour.

In the event that the assumptions made in the Dealing Stage are found to be unsupported then, following review and reconsideration, it may be necessary to reiterate the Advanced Financial Analysis and Portfolio Impact Assessment Steps of the Dealing Stage and possibly complete the Governance Decision Step of the Executing Stage again and amend Documentation accordingly.

Completion of the Independent Appraisal Step marks completion of the Executing Stage which results in the protection of the interests of unitholders in the exchange of their capital at Settlement in return for legal title to the property and the rights and responsibilities associated therewith, being the first step in the Watching Stage considered in the next chapter.

4.7 Transacting Phase

Completion of the Dealing Stage and the Executing Stage finalise the Transacting Phase of the REIT real estate investment decision making process, wherein the REIT management team seeks to implement the outcomes of the Preparing Phase through the creation of a tangible property portfolio.

Having completed the Transacting Phase, the REIT now moves into the third and final Phase, the Observing Phase, comprising the Watching Stage and the Optimising Stage, wherein the REIT management team seeks to ensure that the REIT's performance will achieve its Goals and so attain its Vision, thereby completing the cyclical process of REIT real estate investment decision making.

4.8 Super REIT

Having completed the Envisioning Stage, Super REIT has developed a Vision to be the premier diversified REIT on the stock exchange, interdependent with its adopted generic and specific investment management Style which is active, top down, growth and value added, respectively. To attain this Vision, Super REIT has identified four Goals including to be within the top quartile return performance with lowest quartile tracking error of the stock exchange REIT index every year. Consistently, Super REIT's Strategic Plan focuses on return optimisation at the REIT, portfolio and property level together with effective risk management, supported by a large number of specified Objectives encompassing all REIT management executives in the respective Teams and so aligning the motivations and actions of all REIT management executives with the attainment of Super REIT's Vision.

On completion of the Planning Stage, Super REIT has developed a Property Portfolio Strategy with a Strategic Asset Allocation comprising a sectoral allocation (50% retail, 40% office, 10% industrial) and geographic allocation (60% northern, 40% southern states), enhanced by a Tactical Asset Allocation of 2.5% to the office sector in the northern city of Metropolis for a period of two years reflecting a forecast undersupply of office accommodation. Within the allocation to the office sector, Super REIT has developed Stock Selection criteria specifying lots of around $375 million each, being freehold title in prime office locations within the downtown precincts of specified cities and A grade, high rise, modern office towers that are less than ten years old, being principally leased to corporate tenants.

Having completed the Dealing Stage, Super REIT has identified a specific asset for acquisition, Superman Tower, that is considered mis-priced by a significant extent over both a three- and ten-year holding period and so capable of generating abnormal returns. At a portfolio level, Superman Tower was confirmed to be acceptable for acquisition at $385 million on the basis of the commercial and funding structure proposed.

Entering the Executing Stage, Super REIT now needs to obtain approval for the acquisition of Superman Tower from the Governing Entity before embarking on the Steps of Transaction Closure, Documentation, Due Diligence and Independent Appraisal.

4.8.1 Governance Decision

For the purposes of Super REIT, where the Governing Entity policy specifies no individual property investment is to be more than 2.5% of the REIT total portfolio, the delegation of authority policy for acquisitions and disposals may require any proposal over $375 million to be subject to Governing Entity approval. Accordingly, the proposed acquisition of Superman Tower for $385 million requires submission to the Governing Entity for approval under Super REIT's delegations of authority policy.

Super REIT then collates and summarises the findings of the pricing process for Superman Tower in a Governing Entity report with appendices. Having discussed the report with members of the Governing Entity prior to the formal meeting, the REIT management team considered the preliminary feedback received and amended the report where appropriate.

The Portfolio Management Team determines that no external approvals are required and the report is then submitted by the CEO to a formal meeting of the Governing Entity, with a presentation by the Fund Management Team, including the following recommendation: *'That the Governing Entity approve the acquisition of Superman Tower for $385 million subject to satisfactory Due Diligence and supporting Independent Appraisal'*, which is approved by the Governing Entity.

4.8.2 Transaction Closure

Having received Governing Entity approval for the proposed transaction, Super REIT's Portfolio Management Team now move to the Transaction Closure Step. The Capital Transactions Team undertake final negotiations with the vendor for the commercial terms of the transaction and the Fund Management Team undertake final negotiations with the debt provider for the funding terms of the transaction.

Given the experience of the Capital Transactions Team and the Fund Management Team, the negotiation of commercial and funding terms progresses smoothly and without need for reference back to the Governing Entity. Having agreed the terms of the commercial transaction and the funding transaction, the Capital Transactions Team and the Fund Management Team now agree minor amendments to the in-principle documents prepared in the Structuring Step and which will now form the basis for the Documentation Step.

4.8.3 Documentation

Starting from the amended in-principle documents, the Portfolio Management Team and the Fund Management Team focus on the identification and management of risks to Super REIT while drafting and negotiating the contract for sale of Superman Tower with the vendor and the loan documentation with the debt provider.

Reflecting the lease profile of Superman Tower, the absence of vacancy, the lack of ongoing capital works and so forth, drafting and negotiating the contract of sale is relatively straightforward, requiring very limited special clauses or additional guarantees, indemnities and warranties other than such usual indemnities as the vendor indemnifying the purchaser for events prior to purchase and warranties such as the purchaser warranting to observe the terms and conditions of existing leases.

Having assembled the required internal and external sign-offs, the final contract Documentation and funding Documentation are then executed by the CEO under delegated authority from the Governing Entity.

In the case of Super REIT, exchange of contracts for the acquisition of Superman Tower would result in the issue of a statement to the stock exchange, announcement to unitholders and issue of a media release by the Investor Interface Team together with the vendor of Superman Tower removing the property from the market and Super REIT also informing the vendors of Lex Plaza that it does not intend to proceed further.

4.8.4 Due Diligence

In order to protect the interests of unitholders, Super REIT undertakes exhaustive Due Diligence to verify the information relied upon in the Dealing Stage. Based on a risk analysis, the Portfolio Management Team divided the Due Diligence tasks between their retained professional advisers.

Accordingly, the legal adviser's verified title and lease information, the accounting adviser's verified tenant information and financial modelling and so forth, with each professional adviser providing a report of findings to the Portfolio Management Team. Such reports verified the majority of information adopted with only minor issues identified which were not significant to the risk-return profile of Superman Tower and could be addressed by way of vendor undertakings rather than amendment to the contract Documentation.

4.8.5 Independent Appraisal

To support the assumptions made in the Dealing Stage, the Portfolio Management Team commission an Independent Appraisal of Superman Tower from a member of Super REIT's panel of appraisers who was independent of all those parties involved in the transaction.

The Independent Appraisal report identified minor differences in growth rates and allowances from those adopted by the Portfolio Management Team in the Dealing Stage, though these were found to have negligible impact on the risk-return profile of Superman Tower.

4.8.6 Outcomes of implementing the Executing Stage

In the context of Super REIT, the Dealing Stage resulted in the identification of a specific asset for acquisition, Superman Tower, that was considered mis-priced by a significant extent over both a three- and ten-year holding period and so capable of generating abnormal returns. At a portfolio level, Superman Tower was confirmed to be acceptable for acquisition at $385 million on the basis of the commercial and funding structure proposed.

Completion of the Executing Stage results in Super REIT having summarised the findings of the pricing process to secure the requisite internal and external approvals for the acquisition to proceed and negotiated Transaction Closure and Documentation. Super REIT has also undertaken Due Diligence to verify information relied upon in the Dealing Stage and commissioned an Independent Appraisal to support the assumptions made in the Dealing Stage.

Having now completed the Transacting Phase, comprising the Dealing and Executing Stages, Super REIT is ready to move into the third and final Phase, being the Observing Phase, commencing with the transaction proceeding to Settlement, being the first Step in the next Stage, the Watching Stage.

4.9 Summary

The first Phase of the REIT real estate investment decision making process, the Preparing Phase, comprised the Envisioning Stage (considered in Chapter 1) and the Planning Stage (considered in Chapter 2). On completion of the Preparing Phase, the REIT has articulated where it is going and how it is going to get there, providing unitholders with a clear understanding of the risk-return profile to expect from the managers investment of their funds.

The second phase of the REIT real estate investment decision making process, the Transacting Phase, comprises the Dealing Stage (considered in Chapter 3) and the Executing Stage (considered in this chapter).

The Executing Stage comprises the Steps of the Governance Decision, Transaction Closure, Documentation, Due Diligence and Independent Appraisal (valuation).

The focus of the Executing Stage is on summarising the findings of the pricing process to secure the requisite internal and external approvals for the acquisition to proceed and then reflecting these in Documentation, followed by Due Diligence and Independent Appraisal to verify information relied upon and assumptions made in the Dealing Stage. Completion of the Executing Stage will result in the protection of the interests of unitholders in the exchange of their capital at Settlement in return for legal title to the investment property and the rights and responsibilities associated therewith.

In the event that the information relied upon and/or the assumptions made in the Dealing Stage are found to be unsupported in Due Diligence and/or Independent Appraisal, then renegotiation may be required together with reiteration of the Advanced Financial Analysis and Portfolio Impact Assessment Steps of the Dealing Stage. Depending on the significance of the changes to the transaction then resulting, it may be necessary to complete the Governance Decision Step of the Executing Stage again and amend Documentation accordingly.

The Executing Stage comprises an essential and fundamental component of REIT risk management, emphasising the fiduciary role of the REIT management team. Prior to handing over unitholder capital to a vendor, the REIT management team must not only determine that the proposed acquisition is a prudent investment for the REIT but also that there is a supportable basis for all assumptions made and that a rigorous process has been undertaken to validate all information relied upon in the analysis of the proposed investment.

Completion of the Executing Stage may result in the REIT having verified all information relied upon and assumptions made in the pricing process and reflected this in the Documentation necessary to protect the interests of unitholders at settlement, leading into the Watching Stage of the REIT real estate investment decision making process which is considered in the next chapter.

Completion of the Dealing Stage and the Executing Stage mark completion of the second of the three Phases, the Transacting Phase, wherein the REIT manager seeks to implement the outcomes of the Preparing Phase through the creation of a tangible property portfolio. This then leads to the third and final Phase of the REIT real estate investment decision making process, the Observing Phase.

4.10 Key points

- The Executing Stage is the second and final Stage in the **Transacting Phase**, following successful completion of the Preparing Phase (comprising the Envisioning and Planning stages) and preceding the Observing Phase (comprising the Watching and Optimising Stages).
- The **Executing Stage** comprises the Governance Decision, Transaction Closure, Documentation, Due Diligence and Independent Appraisal (valuation) Steps.

- To be undertaken effectively, the Executing Stage requires the Portfolio Management Team and Capital Transactions Team to **work closely** with the CEO and Governance Entity to complete the Governance Decision and Transaction Closure Steps, with the assistance of the Investor Interface Team to complete the Documentation Step and the Portfolio Management Team then project managing completion of the Due Diligence and Independent Appraisal Steps.
- The **Governance Decision** Step represents the formal accept/reject decision by the REIT's Governing Entity, to which a formal report and recommendation is submitted for consideration, together with securing such external approvals as may be required.
- The formal report includes a summary of the findings of the pricing process, comprising a **balance** between sufficient risk disclosure to permit prudent decision making and brevity, with the Governing Entity's approval being absolute or conditional and the latter requiring established trust between the REIT Governing Entity and the REIT management team to be practically effective.
- The **Transaction Closure** and **Documentation** Steps comprise an iterative process of negotiation and Documentation with the other party to the transaction to accommodate any requirements of the REIT's Governing Entity and to balance the risk management requirements of both parties, undertaken simultaneously with the negotiation and Documentation of the requisite funding.
- Following exchange of Documentation, the transaction is **substantially complete** and the REIT may start to consider issues associated with the probable incorporation of the property within the REIT's portfolio.
- The **Due Diligence** Step comprises the verification of all information relied upon by the Portfolio Management Team in the Dealing Stage, being a balance between process and outcomes. As a key aspect of the REIT management team's fiduciary duty, Due Diligence may be operationalised by a thematic or grouping approach or by an approach based on the specialisms of professional advisors engaged.
- The **Independent Appraisal** Step comprises the verification of support for all assumptions relied upon by the Portfolio Management Team in the Dealing Stage, which may be a mandatory requirement of the governance structure of the REIT or voluntary as a matter of good governance practice.
- In the event that the information and assumptions relied upon in the Dealing Stage are found to be unsupported, then **renegotiation** may be required together with **reiteration** of the Advanced Financial Analysis and Portfolio Impact Assessment Steps of the Dealing Stage. Depending on the significance of the changes to the transaction then resulting, it

may be necessary to complete the Governance Decision Step of the Executing Stage again and amend Documentation accordingly.

- Completion of the Executing Stage may result in the REIT having **verified all information relied upon and assumptions made** in the pricing process and reflected this in the Documentation necessary to protect the interests of unitholders at settlement.
- Completion of the Dealing Stage and the Executing Stage mark completion of the second Phase, the Transacting Phase, wherein the REIT management team seek to implement the outcomes of the Preparing Phase through the **creation of a tangible property portfolio**, positioning the REIT to then enter the third and final Phase, the Observing Phase.

References

Further information concerning issues considered in this chapter may be found in the following texts:

Australian Property Institute (2006) *Professional Practice: Client Focus 2, Instructing Valuers*, Australian Property Institute, Deakin.

Baum, A.E. (2002) *Commercial Real Estate Investment*, Estates Gazette, London.

Brown, G.R. and Matysiak G.A. (2000) *Real Estate Investment: A Capital Market Approach*, Financial Times Prentice Hall, Harlow.

Farragher, E.J. and Kleiman, R.T. (1996) A Re-Examination of Real Estate Investment Decisionmaking Practices, *Journal of Real Estate Portfolio Management*, **2**(1), p.31.

Garrigan, R.T. and Parsons, J.F.C. (eds.) (1997) *Real Estate Investment Trusts*, McGraw Hill, New York.

International Valuation Standards Committee (2007) *International Valuation Standards*, 8th Edition, International Valuation Standards Committee, London.

Levy, D. and Schuck, E. (1999) The Influence of Clients on Valuations, *Journal of Property Investment and Finance*, **17**(4), p.380.

Norris, K. and Joyce, L. (1994) *Valuers Liability*, Australian Institute of Valuers and Land Economists, Deakin.

Pagliari, J.L. (ed.) (1995) *The Handbook of Real Estate Portfolio Management*, Irwin, Chicago.

Seabrooke, W., Kent, P. and Hebe, H.H.H. (ed.) (2004) *International Real Estate: An Institutional Approach*, Blackwell Publishing Ltd., Oxford.

5

Watching

Chapter 1 outlined the Envisioning Stage of the REIT real estate investment decision making process comprising the Steps of development of a Vision, Goals, Style, Strategic Plan and Objectives for the REIT. On completion of this Stage, the REIT should have a clearly articulated destination together with a high order route map by which to get to the destination and some measurable outcomes to determine whether or not the REIT has arrived at the destination.

Having completed the Envisioning Stage, Super REIT has developed a Vision to be the premier diversified REIT on the stock exchange, interdependent with its adopted generic and specific investment management Style which is active, top down, growth and value added, respectively. To attain this Vision, Super REIT has identified four Goals including to be within the top quartile return performance with lowest quartile tracking error of the stock exchange REIT index every year. Consistently, Super REIT's Strategic Plan focuses on return optimisation at the REIT, portfolio and property level together with effective risk management, supported by a large number of specified Objectives encompassing all REIT management executives in the respective Teams and so aligning the motivations and actions of all REIT management executives with the attainment of Super REIT's Vision.

Chapter 2 then outlined the Planning Stage of the REIT real estate investment decision making process comprising the Steps of development of the Property Portfolio Strategy, Strategic Asset Allocation, Tactical Asset Allocation, Stock Selection and Asset Identification. On completion of this Stage, the REIT should have converted its Vision into an identified target list of specific property assets for potential acquisition that meet the Stock Selection criteria and may be mis-priced.

Global Real Estate Investment Trusts: People, Process and Management,
First Edition. David Parker.
© 2011 David Parker. Published 2011 by Blackwell Publishing Ltd.

On completion of the Planning Stage, Super REIT has developed a Property Portfolio Strategy with a Strategic Asset Allocation comprising a sectoral allocation (50% retail, 40% office, 10% industrial) and geographic allocation (60% northern, 40% southern states), enhanced by a Tactical Asset Allocation of 2.5% to the office sector in the northern city of Metropolis for a period of two years reflecting a forecast undersupply of office accommodation. Within the allocation to the office sector, Super REIT has developed Stock Selection criteria specifying lots of around $375 million each, being freehold title in prime office locations within the downtown precincts of specified cities and A grade, high rise, modern office towers that are less than ten years old, being principally leased to corporate tenants.

Completion of the Envisioning Stage and the Planning Stage mark completion of the first of the three Phases, the Preparing Phase, wherein the REIT articulates where it is going and how it is going to get there, providing unitholders with a clear understanding of the risk-return profile to expect from the managers investment of their funds.

Having completed the Preparing Phase, the REIT then moves into the second of the three Phases, the Transacting Phase, comprising the Dealing Stage and the Executing Stage. Chapter 3 then outlined the Dealing Stage of the REIT real estate investment decision making process comprising the Steps of Preliminary Negotiation, Preliminary Analysis, Structuring, Advanced Financial Analysis and Portfolio Impact Assessment. On completion of this Stage, the REIT should have converted a target list of specific assets for potential acquisition into an in-principle transaction for the acquisition of a nominated asset.

Having completed the Dealing Stage, Super REIT has identified a specific asset for acquisition, Superman Tower, that is considered mis-priced by a significant extent over both a three- and ten-year holding period and so capable of generating abnormal returns. At a portfolio level, Superman Tower was confirmed to be acceptable for acquisition at $385 million on the basis of the commercial and funding structure proposed.

Chapter 4 then outlined the Executing Stage of the REIT real estate investment decision making process comprising the Steps of the Governance Decision, Transaction Closure, Documentation, Due Diligence and Independent Appraisal. On completion of this Stage, the REIT should have verified all information relied upon and assumptions made in the pricing process and reflected this in the Documentation necessary to protect the interests of unitholders at Settlement.

On completion of the Executing Stage, Super REIT has summarised the findings of the pricing process to secure the requisite internal and external approvals for the acquisition to proceed and negotiated Transaction Closure and Documentation. Super REIT has also undertaken Due Diligence to verify information relied upon in the Dealing Stage and commissioned an Independent Appraisal to support the assumptions made in the Dealing Stage.

Completion of the Dealing Stage and the Executing Stage mark completion of the second of the three Phases, the Transacting Phase, wherein the REIT manager seeks to implement the outcomes of the Preparing Phase through the creation of a tangible property portfolio.

Having completed the Transacting Phase, the REIT then moves into the third and final of the three Phases, the Observing Phase, comprising the Watching Stage (considered in this chapter) and the Optimising Stage (considered in Chapter 6), wherein the REIT ensures that its performance will achieve its Goals and so attain its Vision, thereby completing the cyclical process of REIT real estate investment decision making.

Accordingly, the REIT now enters the Watching Stage of the REIT real estate investment decision making process which is the subject of this chapter. The Watching Stage comprises the Steps of Settlement, Post Audit, Performance Monitoring, Performance Measurement and Portfolio Analysis.

Completion of the Watching Stage may result in the REIT being able to clearly determine whether or not the Goals will be achieved and hence the Vision for the REIT will be attained, leading into the Optimising Stage of the REIT real estate investment decision making process which is considered in the next chapter.

Accordingly, by the end of this chapter, the reader should understand:

- the **rights and responsibilities** that come with property Settlement and the transition from vendor into the REIT management structure;
- the importance of Post Audit in understanding the **validity of assumptions** made and forecasting approaches adopted, together with benefits of feedback to the REIT management team as the basis for continuous improvement to future assumptions and forecasting;
- the relevance of **cyclical Performance Monitoring** to ongoing REIT management, the hierarchy of prospective and retrospective reporting bases and their inter-relationship;
- the **theory and practice** of Performance Measurement, its relationship with the Envisioning Stage and importance for Portfolio Analysis; and
- the principal **approaches to Portfolio Analysis** and the relevant quantitative tools for use.

5.1 People

With the Portfolio Management Team, Strategy Team, Research Team, Capital Transactions Team and Investor Interface Team all having been involved at various points through the Planning, Dealing and Executing Stages, the Watching Stage is principally undertaken by the Portfolio Management

Team with the support of the Compliance and Risk Management Team following completion of the Settlement Step.

5.1.1 Compliance and Risk Management Team

The role of the Compliance and Risk Management Team is to monitor adherence by the REIT management team to Governing Entity risk management policies, with the principal purpose of the role being to identify and report non-adherence or breach and the scope of the role including all portfolios and funds within the REIT.

The Compliance and Risk Management Team usually reports to the CFO, with additional reporting to the internal audit function and Governing Entity Audit Committee for larger REITs, without any direct reports but usually responsible for managing a wide range of external service providers including environmental specialists, occupational health and safety specialists, privacy advisers, lawyers and accountants.

The principal contribution of the Compliance and Risk Management Team is to facilitate the mitigation of risk by the REIT, with the functions of the role being potentially diverse, depending on the nature and extent of Governing Entity risk management policies, including:

- **financial risk mitigation** – comprising roles undertaken by an internal audit function in larger REITs, such as monitoring adherence with invoicing, receipting, purchasing, action within delegated authority, maintenance of adequate records and so forth, together with review of the reports from the Performance Monitoring Step in the Watching Stage;
- **regulatory risk mitigation** – comprising monitoring adherence with the requirements of stock exchange, government body, industry body and other relevant regulatory bodies;
- **environmental risk mitigation** – comprising monitoring adherence with government body and regulatory body environmental requirements, being of increasing importance given the global trend to criminal penalties applying to breach;
- **occupational health and safety risk mitigation** – comprising monitoring adherence with government body and regulatory body occupational health and safety requirements, also being of increasing importance given the global trend to criminal penalties applying to breach; and
- **REIT specific risk mitigation** – comprising those risks that a specific REIT may face such as consumer protection risks, privacy risks, money laundering risks and so forth.

Depending on the size of the REIT, the Compliance and Risk Management Team may be arranged as generalists by portfolio or fund or as specialists by function for the REIT itself. Given the continuously increasing level of issues that governments and Governing Entities are including within the scope of risks to be managed by REITs around the world, the functions of the Compliance and Risk Management Team may be expected to continue to expand in the future.

5.2 Settlement

While this chapter focuses on the application of the REIT real estate investment decision making process to the acquisition of a property, it is acknowledged that the process is equally applicable to the disposal of a property or other major transaction such as a large lease renewal or the letting of a substantial area of vacant accommodation.

The Settlement Step is the point at which investor capital is exchanged for legal title to the property acquired and the rights and responsibilities associated therewith. As such, a range of activities may happen simultaneously in the provision of equity and debt capital and the receipt of legal title, leases and licenses to the property. Accordingly, it is not uncommon for Settlement to involve a large number of people including lawyers for all parties and their representatives, with practice Settlement on the day prior often undertaken for larger transactions to ensure no unforeseen problems occur at the actual Settlement.

The sale contract will usually specify that which is to pass at Settlement. The provision of equity and debt capital usually involves representatives of the acquiring REIT and the debt providers. The debt provider representatives seek to ensure that all lending Documentation has been completed and executed to enable the asset to provide security for the loan and will generally seek to have their interest recorded on the title for the property as a mortgage or charge prior to releasing a cheque for the requisite funds at Settlement.

The REIT, as equity provider, seeks to ensure that all the rights associated with the investment property such as leases, licenses and so forth are transferred to the REIT as purchaser in order to receive rental income and license fees. Simultaneously, through the sale contract, the REIT as equity provider will seek to take no more responsibilities for the property than the vendor requires. Accordingly, the responsibility to honour leases and licenses and to pay rates and taxes might be expected to pass at Settlement, but the REIT management team may seek to exclude the transfer of responsibilities for such issues as the vendor's prior breaches of leases, damage to adjoining properties, disputes with other parties and so forth. As equity provider, the REIT will usually endeavour to ensure that rights have been maximised and responsibilities minimised prior to releasing a cheque for the requisite funds at Settlement.

The cheques tendered at Settlement will sum to an amount after adjustment for quantifiable rights and responsibilities. Such rights as rentals and operating cost recoveries together with such responsibilities as rates, taxes and operating costs will be apportioned between the vendor and the purchaser on the basis of days before and after Settlement and summed to an adjustment payment by one party to the other. As such, the calculation of adjustments brings the transfer of rights and responsibilities at Settlement into sharp focus.

On receipt of a cheque from the debt provider and a cheque from the equity provider, the vendor's representatives will usually hand over the title document for the property with most jurisdictions then having an established process for recording the transfer of title, often with a requirement to pay stamp duty, transfer tax or similar government charge.

Settlement is symbolic as the point at which the REIT's plans and proposals for the property start to become reality and require implementation. It is usually the point at which the REIT's Capital Transactions Team transfers functional responsibility to the Portfolio, Asset, Property and Facilities Management Teams. As with any transfer, there are risks of issues being missed, forgotten or disregarded and the use of a Settlement check list may contribute to mitigating such risks.

5.2.1 Settlement check list

The Settlement check list should include details of who will receive and hold original legal documents, keys, service agreements, manuals, warranties and so forth as well as who will manage any issues arising from Settlement. While the Due Diligence Step will have confirmed all relevant details, such as terms of leases, the Settlement check list may address exactly who is going to hold the physical lease documents. For example, will the original copies of the leases be stored in the Company Secretary's safe as legal documents, in the property manager's file as operational documents or elsewhere?

> *'A misplaced document could cost Macquarie Office Trust more than half a million dollars.'* When a misplaced whole building original lease document could not be located for handover at settlement, the purchaser sought to enforce its right to claim a 9% pa fee for delay in settlement. (Australian Financial Review, 16 July 2009)

Further, there may be a range of issues arising from Settlement requiring attention in the future such as apportionment of turnover rents, refund of deposits from utility authorities and so forth. A Settlement check list may not only record who is responsible for administering such tasks but may serve as a useful reminder to ensure such tasks are not inadvertently forgotten in the future.

Following Settlement, a range of practical activities is undertaken by the REIT management team to assume control of the investment property as part of the portfolio. The Portfolio Management Team will include the property in the Performance Measurement process for the REIT, ensuring periodic appraisals are scheduled and all relevant income and expense data captured. The Property and Facilities Management Teams will usually contact all tenants and licensees and arrange for payment of rent and fees direct to the REIT while also contacting all utilities, service providers, tradesmen and so forth to arrange for invoices to be sent direct to the REIT.

5.2.2 Asset management plan

A significant level of practical activity post Settlement is undertaken by the Asset Management Team. The Governing Entity report included an asset management plan for the property which the Asset Management Team will now start to implement through the Optimising Stage, considered in greater detail in Chapter 6.

Elements of an asset management plan such as negotiating lease renewals with expiring tenants, leasing vacant space or undertaking minor upgrade works may be managed by the Asset Management Team as part of asset management activities on a business as usual basis. However, larger refurbishment or redevelopment projects may require the appointment of a specific project manager to ensure implementation on time and on budget (Farragher and Kleiman, 1995). Where such refurbishment or redevelopment is central to the forecast future performance of the property within the portfolio, a prompt and keen focus on implementation is essential as any delay may adversely affect forecast returns.

Careful attention is, of course, also required where the asset management plan includes works that are greater than business as usual but not so great as to warrant the appointment of a specific project manager, in order to ensure that such works are undertaken in a timely and cost effective manner and not deferred due to a focus on business as usual asset management activities.

5.2.3 Settlement

The Settlement Step provides not only the point at which the rights and responsibilities of property ownership pass from the vendor to the purchaser, but also the point at which management transitions from the vendor and the Capital Transactions Team to the REIT Portfolio, Asset, Property and Facilities Management Teams.

5.3 Post Audit

Having completed and settled a transaction, at some point the REIT should determine if the assumptions made in the pricing process and summarised in the Governing Entity report advocating the transaction actually happened in reality.

The Post Audit Step is a review, expressed in terms of initial assumptions, of a property's operational performance (Farragher and Kleiman, 1995). It comprises the process of comparing and reconciling the assumptions made in the pricing process against the actual observed outcomes in the period following the Settlement Step.

5.3.1 Timing

The nature of the assumptions made in the pricing process will determine the appropriate time frame for the Post Audit Step. If, for example, the transaction was premised on benefiting from short term rental growth, Post Audit after three or six months may be appropriate to determine if such short term rental growth has occurred and to the extent assumed. Conversely, if the transaction was premised on refurbishment and subsequent reletting, Post Audit after 12 months may be appropriate in order for the refurbishment to have been completed and the reletting undertaken.

While adoption of a 12 month Post Audit period is common for REITs, Settlement during a financial year may result in a preliminary Post Audit being undertaken at the end of the financial year. The use of a 12 month Post Audit period is consistent with the Advanced Financial Analysis Step often being based on annual periods, asset management plans focusing on the initial year after acquisition and property and facilities management budgets being for 12 month periods.

Following completion of Post Audit, where the assumptions made in the pricing process are compared against the actual outcomes following Settlement, the property will become subject to the ongoing cycle of annual budgeting and planning and monthly, quarterly, half-yearly and annual reporting and review considered in the Performance Monitoring Step, below.

Post Audit is most effective when it is undertaken on a predetermined basis and so comprises an integral part of a rigorous real estate investment decision making process. It is least effective when carried out on an optional basis or on a crisis basis, as even apparently successful transactions may have shortcomings.

5.3.2 *Basis*

The Post Audit process should be a comparison of like with like. Whatever basis of assumptions was adopted in the pricing process should be the same basis of assumptions adopted for Post Audit. For example, if the Governing Entity report forecast an annual total return for the property with comparison to a forecast of an annual direct property total return benchmark, then the Post Audit should adopt the same metrics. This ensures transparency and rigor in Post Audit, rather than adopting an alternative measure that may make the transaction appear more successful in retrospect.

For completeness, every assumption in the pricing process should be tabulated for comparison against the actual observed outcome, including both financial and non-financial assumptions. Financial assumptions may include all forms of growth assumptions (such as income, expenses, and cost of debt), occupancy assumptions (such as lease renewal, reletting periods, and vacancy periods) and so forth. Non-financial assumptions may include assumptions for the prospect of competing properties entering the market, assumptions concerning the economic outlook and so forth.

In addition to tabulating the assumption and the observed outcome, a column comprising commentary on the difference may be added to increase understanding of where and why the principal differences occurred. Simple analysis will then highlight which differences had the greatest contribution to outperformance or underperformance. Such differences may be a series of small differences that sum to a significant difference or an individual significant difference that solely impacted performance. Whether the result was outperformance or underperformance is of lesser relevance from a risk management viewpoint, where the emphasis is on an understanding of whether that which led to the difference was a one-off event or a systemic feature of the REIT's forecasting and pricing process.

5.3.3 *Learning process*

While understanding the sources and causes of differences between assumptions and observed outcomes is important, it is also important to use the Post Audit Step as a learning process for the Portfolio Management, Strategy and Research Teams. If outperformance or underperformance resulted from a specific call by the Portfolio Management, Strategy or Research Teams, how can the thought processes and approaches adopted in making that call be embedded or eliminated in the real estate investment decision making process for future benefit? If outperformance or underperformance was the result of the overlap between assumptions made by different Teams, how can greater co-ordination and cohesion be developed to optimise or minimise such overlaps?

At the individual REIT management executive level, Post Audit provides an excellent basis for constructive and valuable feedback within the performance plan and Objectives process administered by the HR Team. With the Portfolio Management, Strategy and Research Teams comprising executives for whom making assumptions and forecasts is a key part of their job and upon which major financial decisions will be made, the reliability and accuracy of the assumptions and forecasts made is a central issue in performance feedback. Issues such as consistent over or under estimating of assumptions and forecasts deserve discussion, together with the significantly more risky issue of erratic over or under estimation.

Embedding Post Audit as a learning process for the Portfolio Management, Strategy and Research Teams encourages more realistic and honest preparation of assumptions and forecasts by the Teams through increasing accountability by letting Team members know that they will be held responsible for their decisions (Farragher and Kleiman, 1995). Such responsibility may be reinforced by including a measure of the proximity of assumptions and forecasts to observed outcomes as an Objective to which performance based remuneration is linked.

A study in the US found 66% of REITs undertake Post Audit, indicating that it is an embedded part of the real estate investment decision making process, with 72% of REITs using Post Audit to track individual's abilities to make accurate forecasts and to make good investment decisions in US REITs (Farragher and Kleiman, 1995).

In addition to considering the validity of assumptions and forecasts, the Post Audit Step serves to periodically review the validity of the forecasting approaches adopted. This may, for example, highlight that a different time period for forecasting or the use of a different basis of forecasting may be appropriate to more effectively contribute to the real estate investment decision making process.

The Post Audit Step can, of course, also contribute to risk management by indicating when corrective action may be needed to bring an investment to full potential (Farragher and Kleiman, 1995). Identifying where there is a significant gap between the assumed or forecast state of affairs and the actual state of affairs allows the REIT management team to intervene and take whatever action may be appropriate to remedy the situation.

5.3.4 Post Audit

The Post Audit Step, when rigorously and consistently adopted, can play a vital role in the process of understanding the validity of assumptions made and forecasting approaches adopted and in providing feedback to the Portfolio Management, Strategy and Research Teams as the basis for continuous improvement.

5.4 Performance Monitoring

Following completion of the Settlement Step, the property becomes part of the REIT portfolio and together with other assets in the portfolio is subject to the sequential process of ongoing Performance Monitoring, Performance Measurement and Portfolio Analysis.

The Performance Monitoring Step is a cyclical process of planning, comparative analysis and reporting, considered further respectively below, whereby the Portfolio Management Team seek to determine if the Goals are being achieved such that the Vision may be attained and if the market conditions continue to be as anticipated in the Planning Stage (Pagliari, 1995). Where the Goals include quantitative performance measures, Performance Measurement is required and this is considered further next.

Periodically, the Portfolio Management Team will need to take stock on the fulfilment of the REIT's Goals and the prevailing market conditions through the Portfolio Analysis Step which is considered thereafter and take remedial action if required through the Portfolio Rebalancing Step, which is considered in Chapter 6.

As with all aspects of REIT portfolio management, equal focus on each of the risk and return aspects in the Performance Monitoring and Performance Measurement Steps is essential. Similarly, the aspirations identified in the Envisioning Stage require continual balancing with the realities of prevailing market conditions.

In order to effectively monitor portfolio performance against target outcomes, clear statements of such target outcomes are required. Following completion of the Envisioning Stage, the REIT should have a clearly articulated destination together with a high order route map by which to get to the destination and some measurable outcomes to determine whether or not the REIT has arrived at the destination. Accordingly, such measurable outcomes provide the framework within which the various REIT management teams are working and are readily apparent to each.

5.4.1 Planning

Each year, a property and facilities management, asset management and portfolio management plan may be prepared consistent with the framework of the Strategic Plan and with the identified Goals and through the achievement of which the Vision of the REIT may be attained.

Such plans should, however, be cognisant of the differences in market conditions currently emerging to those that prevailed when the Planning Stage was undertaken. For example if, during the Planning Stage, the resource industry was buoyant and office properties within the portfolio in those cities depending on the resource industry were forecast to show significant rental growth, but now the resource industry has slowed and such cities are experiencing over supply with increasing vacancy and decreasing rental growth, regard to such market conditions would be required.

Accordingly, in preparation of an annual property and facilities management, asset management and portfolio management plan, each team would undertake a prior updating real estate market analysis to determine current conditions and expectations and incorporate the results of same in their respective annual plans (Pagliari, 1995).

Working from the individual property level up to the portfolio level, the Property and Facilities Management Teams would prepare an operational budget for each property for the upcoming year including income and expenditure forecasts with resulting net income contribution to the portfolio. The operational budget would be informed by the annual asset management plan, prepared by the Asset Management Team, which focuses on major rent reviews, lease renewals, letting vacancies, capital expenditure, refurbishment and so forth, providing input for the net income budget and for the portfolio management capital budget for each property.

The operational budgets for each property in the portfolio may then be combined by the Portfolio Management Team together with the capital expenditure budgets into an overall budget for the entire portfolio, to which the Portfolio Management Team may add forecasts of property appraisals, acquisitions, disposals and other transactions or portfolio rebalancing as the basis of an ex ante or forward looking annual portfolio performance plan and budget. Finally, the Fund Management Team may combine the portfolio budgets into fund budgets including capital management and then into a single REIT budget as input into the CFO's REIT budgeting process (Geltner et al., 2007).

Thus, each year, the Property and Facilities Management Teams, Asset Management Team, Portfolio Management Team and Fund Management Team rigorously and consistently update their plans and budgets within the context of prevailing market conditions, forming both the Objectives for individual performance plans and the budget with which the Performance Monitoring Step may then be undertaken.

5.4.2 Comparative analysis

Again, working from the individual property level up to the portfolio level, the operational income and expenditure budget is compared to actual income and expenditure by the Property and Facilities Management Teams on a monthly basis. Following completion of the first month, the Property and Facilities Management Teams will prepare a forecast for the balance of the year which comprises a combination of the actual income and expenditure for the month(s) to date and the budget (updated, if necessary) for the balance of the year.

The same process of comparative analysis and forecasts is also adopted by the Asset Management Team, the Portfolio Management Team and the Fund Management Team. The forecasts are then used by each Team to update forecast returns for the respective properties, the cumulative portfolios and the funds as the year progresses.

From a risk management perspective, while minor differences between budget and actual outcomes for various items of income or expenditure are inevitable, at the total level for the property approximate equivalence is sought as a minimum. In the event of income being significantly below budget or expenditure being significantly above budget, the Property and Facilities Management Teams would take appropriate remedial action. As such remedial action may impact both the performance of the asset and the portfolio, close liaison with the Asset Management and Portfolio Management Teams is required.

While the Asset Management and Portfolio Management Teams would monitor the monthly operational budget and forecast performance, particularly in the context of monthly portfolio income returns, the principal focus of both Teams in Performance Monitoring is quarterly. Each quarter, the Asset Management Team will formally review the asset management plan for each property to determine whether performance is in line with, running ahead of or slipping behind that forecast in the asset management plan.

From a risk management viewpoint, as the asset management plan identifies strategies for REIT portfolio performance sensitive items such as major capital expenditure, large lease renewals and leasing of vacant space, any slippage between actual and plan may have a significant effect on REIT portfolio performance for the year as a whole. If remedial action is necessary, close liaison with the Portfolio Management Team is essential to manage the consequential impact on the portfolio forecasts.

Depending on the appraisal policy, the Portfolio Management Team may arrange appraisals of the capital value of all or a portion of the REIT's portfolio each quarter. Together with the capital expenditure identified through monitoring the asset management plan, this provides the capital return data for use in the Performance Measurement Step and so allows the Portfolio Management Team to monitor the total return of the REIT portfolio on a quarterly basis.

Following this cyclical process repeated consistently every quarter, after four quarters the Property and Facilities Management, Asset Management, Portfolio Management and Fund Management Teams have then monitored the performance of the portfolio for a complete year and then commence the process again for the next year.

5.4.3 Reporting

Consistent with the fiduciary responsibility of the REIT management team, continuous and transparent reporting is essential. Therefore, each level of the REIT management team reports the findings of their comparative analysis to the next level of the REIT management team at each time period. Accordingly, the Property and Facilities Management Team report to the Asset Management Team, the Asset Management Team to the Portfolio Management Team, the Portfolio Management Team to the Fund Management Team and the Fund Management Team to the CEO and Governing Entity on a monthly basis with more substantial reporting on a quarterly, half-yearly and annual basis.

5.4.4 Performance Monitoring

The Performance Monitoring Step is a continuous, dynamic, cyclical process (Pagliari, 1995) comprising both prospective and retrospective activities. Budgets and plans are prepared by the Property and Facilities Management, Asset Management and Portfolio Management Teams at the beginning of the year and then monitored on a monthly, quarterly, half-yearly and annual basis with comparative analysis and the preparation of forecasts, in order to ensure that the REIT performance is on track to achieve the Goals and so attain the REIT's Vision.

5.5 Performance Measurement

Each asset within and the REIT portfolio as a whole are continuously subject to the sequential and cyclical process of the ongoing Performance Monitoring Step (considered above), Performance Measurement Step (considered in this section) and Portfolio Analysis Step (considered below).

The Performance Measurement Step is the process of objectively, accurately and quantitatively measuring the past or delivered income, capital and total returns and risk performance of properties, portfolios, funds and the REIT as a whole for comparison to indices or benchmarks.

At each progressively higher level, an increasing range of issues impact performance that cannot be controlled by the REIT management teams. At the REIT level, while strong individual asset and portfolio performance will be positive for REIT stock performance, the general trend in the equity market is likely to be a key performance variable that is beyond the control of the REIT management teams.

Similarly, the REIT management teams can control the impact on REIT performance of cash holdings, debt, tax, various types of REIT level costs and management fees (Hudson-Wilson and Wurtzebach, 1994) through the development of appropriate policies.

At the sectoral or geographic portfolio level, there is little that the REIT management teams can control, outside of the asset allocation decision, with key performance variables being local economic and real estate market conditions which impact all assets in a sector or geography.

At the individual asset level, the REIT management teams can exercise considerable control over key performance variables such as operating expenses and vacancy levels but cannot control variables such as local market occupier demand or the outcome of the independent appraisal process to determine capital value.

However, the REIT management teams can exercise some control over the relevant time period for Performance Measurement, including not only the start and end dates of the performance period but also through an understanding of events during the period that may influence both absolute and relative performance (Hudson-Wilson and Wurtzebach, 1994). For example, a minor refurbishment project may not positively influence REIT returns measured over a quarter but may have a positive impact when returns are measured over a year. Similarly, a Tactical Asset Allocation decision to take an overweight position to office property in a particular geographic location may not benefit returns within one year but the benefit may be evident over a three year period.

Further, the frequency of formal comparison requires careful consideration (Hudson-Wilson and Wurtzebach, 1994). In addition to one-off events such as refurbishment, ongoing Performance Measurement impacts performance particularly through the REIT's appraisal policy. Managing the timing of appraisals to minimise the lag between completion and reporting and so optimise the pricing effect, through information availability and reliability, has a potentially significant impact on REIT performance.

The inclusion or exclusion of properties from a portfolio for Performance Measurement may also influence returns, particularly for large development projects. The risk-return profile of the portfolio will differ significantly if a large development project is undertaken within the portfolio over a long period of time or if it is separated and only measured on completion. If undertaken within the portfolio, Performance Measurement will first include land costs and then building costs as they are progressively incurred as capital expenditure or negative capital returns with a positive capital return only achieved through independent appraisal on completion leading to an extended, volatile period of returns. Alternatively, if the development is separated and only measured on completion, the REIT performance will show only the positive capital return margin between costs and independent appraisal on completion during one time period of performance measurement, leading to potentially lower return volatility.

In addition to asset, portfolio, fund and REIT performance measurement purposes, the Performance Measurement Step may also be undertaken for a range of other purposes, including financial reporting, regulatory compliance, investor communications, marketing and determination of REIT executive performance linked remuneration (Hudson-Wilson and Wurtzebach, 1994). Importantly, the Performance Measurement Step also contributes significantly to increasing the accountability of the REIT management team to investors for achieving the Goals and thus attaining the Vision to which the REIT's investors subscribed (Brown and Matysiak, 2000).

Further, the Performance Measurement Step makes an important contribution for research purposes into improving the understanding of REITs and of real estate as an asset class (Brown and Matysiak, 2000). As such, the Performance Measurement Step demands rigour and objectivity and must be undertaken at arm's length (Hudson-Wilson and Wurtzebach, 1994). It would, for example, be inappropriate for those REIT executives for whom the majority of remuneration was performance linked to be responsible for undertaking Performance Measurement.

The Performance Measurement Step addresses only past or delivered returns and may be distinguished from the Portfolio Analysis Step (considered below) which is concerned with the present (Baum, 2002). The Performance Measurement Step is concerned with calculating changes, expressed either as absolute numbers or as a relative quantitative measure over a specified time period (Hudson-Wilson and Wurtzebach, 1994). It is not only that a REIT may have delivered absolute performance of x% over a given time period that is important, but also the relativity of such absolute performance to that of the relevant index or benchmark.

Issues associated with performance relative to an index or benchmark will be considered further, in detail, below, following consideration of issues associated with income, capital and total return measurement.

5.5.1 Return measurement

Return measurement requires attention at three levels, being the REIT level, the portfolio level and the asset level. While performance at the REIT level is usually considered relative to an index, performance at the portfolio level and at the asset level are usually considered relative to a benchmark.

As noted above, at each progressively higher level, a greater range of issues impact performance that cannot be controlled by the REIT management team. At the REIT level, while strong individual asset and portfolio performance will be positive for REIT stock performance, the general trends in the equity market are likely to be key performance variables that are beyond the control of the REIT management team.

However, at the individual asset level, the REIT management team can exercise a considerable level of control over key performance variables that may contribute to strong individual asset and portfolio performance, thereby providing a positive contribution to REIT performance. It is, therefore, essential that the Asset Management Team undertake ongoing Performance Monitoring and Performance Measurement at the individual asset level given that the individual asset level performance is a key building block for portfolio level and REIT level performance.

As with selection of an appropriate index for relative Performance Measurement at the REIT level, it is also important to select an appropriate benchmark for relative Performance Measurement at the asset or portfolio level with the difference between an index and a benchmark being considered further below.

The benchmark needs to be indicative or representative of the portfolio or asset that is being measured, to be statistically robust in order to be credible (Hudson-Wilson and Wurtzebach, 1994) and to be capable of offering some evidence of abnormal performance (Brown and Matysiak, 2000). By thoroughly understanding the composition of the benchmark, the Asset and Portfolio Management Teams may optimise the opportunity for outperformance. For example, the sample comprising a benchmark for offices in a given city is, by definition, a finite grouping such that the relocation of a major tenant from Property A to Property B may result in under performance of the benchmark by Property A and outperformance of the benchmark by Property B. By driving such relocation, the Asset Management Team of Property B is able to influence the returns of not only their property but also those of Property A relative to the benchmark. Accordingly, individual property returns form the core of the Performance Measurement Step and are essential building blocks for the Portfolio Analysis Step and the development of property investment strategy generally.

Concerning the appropriate basis for Performance Measurement, the rate of return is the ideal investment performance decision measure as it is scale free and so does not depend on investment size, complies with the requirements of financial models such as the Capital Asset Pricing Model and NPV decision tool which are framed in terms of returns and permits the investment characteristics of a given property asset to be described in terms of the statistical distribution of its returns (Brown and Matysiak, 2000).

The total property return for a REIT may be considered to be the sum of the returns of each of the property funds comprising the REIT which, in turn, are the sum of the returns from each of the portfolios comprising the funds which, in turn, are the sum of the returns from each of the assets comprising the portfolios. Similarly, the total return from each asset is the sum of the income and capital return with the capital return being driven by net income growth and changes in capital value, reflecting the capitalisation or discount rate, as shown in Figure 5.1.

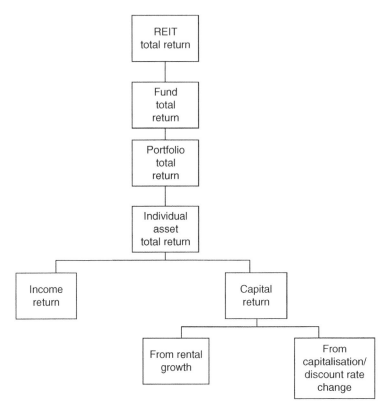

Figure 5.1   Components of total property return. Reproduced by permission of Taylor & Francis. From *Property Investment Decisions*, Hargitay & Yu, 1993 (Figure 11.2, p.195).

Past, present and future returns

Returns may typically be measured on three bases – either past, present or future (Baum, 2002). Past returns, generally referred to as *ex-post* returns, look backward in time and are historical records of past performance. They provide a useful measure of historic performance for a wide range of comparative purposes, assist in Portfolio Analysis to understand the current environment and provide a basis for estimating future performance (Geltner et al., 2007).

Present returns provide a snapshot at a point in time and do not cover a period of time. They provide a simple expression of the relativity of income to capital existing at a point in time, such as the capitalisation rate. As such, it is an explicit performance measure at a point in time with implications for returns in the future (Baum, 2002).

Future returns, generally referred to as *ex-ante* returns, look forward in time. Being framed as quantitative expressions of future return expectations, *ex ante* returns such as expected IRR are relevant for making investment decisions in the present which will have an impact on the investor in the future (Geltner et al., 2007).

While the capitalisation rate and internal rate of return are globally understood performance measures, a wide range of other performance measures exist with some being used only in certain countries and some being used in various countries but under different names. In the UK, performance measures such as reversionary yield, equivalent yield and equated yield are commonly used with free and clear return, accounting return and profitability index commonly used in the US, while the UK measure of year's purchase is conceptually akin to the US measure of payback period.

Target returns
The use of a target rate of return was considered in Chapter 3, with the formula for the required nominal rate of return stated as:

$$R_N = RF_R + RP + i_e \qquad \text{[Equation 3.2]}$$

where:
R_N is the required nominal rate of return
RF_R is the real risk free rate of return
RP is the risk premium
i_e is the compensation for expected inflation

This focuses attention on three elements, being the real risk free rate, the risk premium and compensation for expected inflation. In practice, the formula is generally simplified through the use of a nominal risk free rate, so combining the contributions of the real risk free rate and the compensation for expected inflation, as follows:

$$R_N = RF + RP \qquad \text{[Equation 3.3]}$$

where:
R_N is the required nominal rate of return
RF is the nominal risk free rate of return
RP is the risk premium

so focusing attention on the selection of the nominal risk free rate of return and the risk premium.

Income return
While a target return may be framed as a function of a risk free rate and a risk premium, the total return from a property investment or a property portfolio may initially be framed as a function of income return and capital

return, which may be subsequently analysed to provide an expression of the risk premium for a given risk free rate.

Accordingly, to derive accurate and reliable measures of actual return from a property investment, a range of accurate data is required. This includes the amount and timing of the initial investment, of each of the net income cash flows and capital expenditures over the relevant periods and either an appraisal of the current value of the property or the proceeds of sale (Hudson-Wilson and Wurtzebach, 1994). Net income cash flows may be those received or receivable, with care taken to ensure clarity concerning that which is adopted, with net income being gross rental revenue less any ongoing property outgoings or expenses. The timing of capital expenditure relative to the period of measurement is also important, with a given level of capital expenditure having a proportionately greater impact on income returns over shorter periods of investment.

The income return from a property investment represents the relationship between the net income cash flows received over the measurement period and the capital value of the property at the beginning of the period (Hoesli and MacGregor, 2000):

$$IR_t = \frac{NI_t}{CV_{t-1}}$$ [Equation 5.1]

where:
  IR_t is the income return for period t
  NI_t is the income received during period t
  CV_{t-1} is the capital value at the start of period t (being the end of period $t-1$)

While income return is a static measure at a point in time, it is informative of future expectations of income growth and risk. The capital value of a real estate investment, CV_{t-1}, may be represented as the expected future growing income stream discounted or capitalised at an appropriate discount or capitalisation rate to reflect risk. Therefore, when CV_{t-1} is expressed relative to the current level of net income, the income return may provide a proxy for future expectations of income growth and risk as illustrated in Table 5.1.

For example, Asset A in Table 5.1 offers a static or no growth income stream with an uncertain future cash flow whereas Asset B offers a static or no growth income stream with a certain future cash flow. Reflecting this risk, the future cash flow from Asset A would be discounted by the market at a higher rate than that for Asset B, producing a lower present value. This results in Asset A having a higher income return than Asset B.

Asset C offers a growing income stream with a certain future cash flow. Reflecting greater growth and lower risk, the future cash flow from Asset C

Table 5.1   Income, growth and risk inference from income returns.

Asset	Exp. inc. Year 1	Exp. inc. Year 2	Exp. inc. Year 3	Exp. inc. Year 4	Exp. inc. Year 5	Future cash flow	Income yield
A	10	10	10	10	10	Uncertain	9%
B	10	10	10	10	10	Certain	7%
C	10	15	20	25	30	Certain	5%

From the Author and Hoesli and MacGregor (2000). *Property Investment: Principles and Practice of Portfolio Management* (Table 3.7, p.41). © 2000 Longman, a Pearson company. Reproduced by permission.

would be discounted by the market at a lower rate than that for Asset B, producing a higher present value. This results in Asset C having a lower income return than Asset B.

Accordingly, all other things being equal, income return may be used to infer something about market expectations of income growth and risk to the investor. The higher the income growth expectation, the lower the income return and the higher the risk expectation, the higher the income return.

Capital return
The capital return from a property investment or a property portfolio represents the relationship between the capital value in a given period and the capital value in a preceding period, adjusted for any capital expenditure undertaken.

Capital return may be expressed as (Hoesli and MacGregor, 2000):

$$CR_t = \frac{CV_t - CV_{t-1}}{CV_{t-1}}$$ [Equation 5.2]

where:
  CR_t is the capital return in period t
  CV_t is the capital value at the end of period t
  CV_{t-1} is the capital value at the end of period t–1

The equation may be adjusted to reflect capital expenditure for repair, refurbishment, extension or alteration:

$$CR_t = \frac{(CV_t +/- C_t) - CV_{t-1}}{CV_{t-1}}$$ [Equation 5.3]

where:
  C_t is the positive or negative capital expenditure incurred at the beginning of period t

with the equation requiring restatement if capital expenditure is incurred at any other time during period t. An increasingly commonly adopted heuristic approach, for relatively small levels of capital expenditure incurred over the course of the period, is to assume an amount equating to half of the total for the period was incurred at the beginning of the period.

In some cases, minor capital expenditure may be paid from net income, rather than from a capital account. In such cases, the income return would be understated and the capital return overstated, with great care required in the interpretation and application of the return data generated (Baum, 2002).

A critical issue for calculating property returns is, of course, the assessment of capital value at the beginning and end of the period. In the absence of a sale/purchase transaction of the subject property or portfolio, an appraised value may be used though this creates a range of Performance Measurement issues considered further below.

Total return

The total return from an individual property asset or a property portfolio represents the relationship between the capital value in a given period, the capital value in a preceding period and the net income received during the period, adjusted for any capital expenditure incurred during the period.

Total return may be expressed as the sum of income and capital return (Hoesli and MacGregor, 2000):

$$TR_t = \frac{(CV_t - CV_{t-1}) + NI_t}{CV_{t-1}}$$ [Equation 5.4]

where:

   TR_t is the total return in period t
   CV_t is the capital value at the end of period t
   CV_{t-1} is the capital value at the end of period t−1
   NI_t is the net income during period t

with capital expenditure more accurately reflected as follows (Hoesli and MacGregor, 2000):

$$TR_t = \frac{(CV_t - CV_{t-1} - C_t) + NI_t}{CV_{t-1} + kC_t}$$ [Equation 5.5]

where:

   TR_t is the total return in period t
   CV_t is the capital value at the end of period t
   CV_{t-1} is the capital value at the end of period t−1

C$_t$ is the capital expenditure during period t
NI$_t$ is the net income during period t
k   is the fraction of the period over which the capital expenditure was applied

As noted before, an increasingly commonly adopted heuristic approach, for relatively small levels of capital expenditure incurred over the course of the period, is to assume an amount equating to half of the total for the period was incurred at the beginning of the period. This may be included within the equation for total return as follows (Baum, 2002):

$$TR_t = \frac{\left(CV_t - \left(CV_{t-1} + (0.5 \times C_t)\right)\right) + NI_t}{CV_{t-1} + (0.5 \times C_t)}$$ [Equation 5.6]

where:
TR$_t$ is the total return in period t
CV$_t$ is the capital value at the end of period t
CV$_{t-1}$ is the capital value at the end of period t–1
C$_t$ is the capital expenditure during period t
NI$_t$ is the net income during period t

Total return, considered in this way for a single period, may be measured as or considered to be the Money Weighted Rate of Return (MWRR), which is also a single period Internal Rate of Return (IRR), with the equation being restated as (Hoesli and MacGregor, 2000):

$$\left[\frac{CV_t}{1+TR_t} + \frac{NI_t}{1+TR_t}\right] - CV_{t-1} = 0$$ [Equation 5.7]

where:
CV$_t$ is the capital value at the end of period t
CV$_{t-1}$ is the capital value at the end of period t–1
NI$_t$ is the net income during period t
TR$_t$ is the total return, measured by the MWRR or the single period IRR

The MWRR is defined as that interest or discount rate which equates the sum of all realised cash flows and the capital value of the asset at the end of a holding period to the initial capital outlay or the capital value of the asset at the beginning of the holding period (Hargitay and Yu, 1993). As such, the single period expression mirrors the definition of the IRR, being that rate which discounts all future cash flows to a net present value of zero.

Accordingly, the above bases may be adopted to calculate the income return, capital return and total return for a property or portfolio over a single specified period. Single period Performance Measurement is particularly useful for comparing the relative performance between individual properties or between portfolios and relative to performance against benchmarks or the performance of single period development projects. However, many properties or portfolios are held for extended periods, with real estate generally being characterised as a long term investment, such that Performance Measurement over multiple periods is also of considerable relevance.

Multi period return
The most commonly adopted forms of multi period return measurement are the time weighted rate of return (TWRR) and the internal rate of return (IRR).

The TWRR is defined as the geometric mean of the rates of return achieved over each sub period contained in the holding period (Hargitay and Yu, 1993). The TWRR calculates the return up to the period of the capital injection and then 'chain links' or compounds these separate period returns to calculate the average return over a longer period (Hoesli and MacGregor, 2000):

$$\text{TWRR} = \left[\prod(1 + TR_i)\right]^{1/t} - 1 \qquad\qquad \text{[Equation 5.8]}$$

where:
   TR_i is the total return in period i
   $\prod$ is the mathematical symbol, pi, indicating that the individual values of $(1+R_t)$ have to be multiplied
   t   is the number of periods

The TWRR is capable of reflecting changes in the capital value of a property or portfolio during the periods of measurement. Adoption of an opening capital value for a property in an early period which is carried forward and only replaced by an updated capital value, through appraisal or sale, in a later period leads to the resulting TWRR being an approximation only. To calculate the TWRR exactly in the absence of a sale of the property, an appraisal of the property should be undertaken for each of the periods, being precisely dated in order to produce an accurate measure of return (Brown and Matysiak, 2000).

As the TWRR measures the individual returns for each sub period as a series of discrete units of time, it is not influenced by the magnitude or timing of cash flows. For individual properties or portfolios, the Asset Management and Portfolio Management Teams have some control over the magnitude and timing of cash flows, such as major capital expenditure, thereby being in a position to influence capital and total returns through the timing of such cash flows. Accordingly, the alternative multi period performance measure of IRR is generally considered to be more suitable for property Performance Measurement.

With the IRR being that rate which discounts all future cash flows to a net present value of zero, there is no direct solution to determining the IRR and an iterative process must be adopted based on the NPV formula (Whipple, 1995):

$$NPV = \Sigma \frac{CF_j}{(1+i)^i} - CF_0 \qquad \text{[Equation 5.9]}$$

where:

NPV   is the net present value

Σ is the mathematical symbol, sigma, being an instruction to take the sum

CF_j is the cash flow for each of the jth periods

CF_0 is the cash outlay at the beginning of the first period

i   is the internal rate of return, being that rate which results in a NPV of zero

j   is the number of periods

Conveniently, most financial calculators and financial software now have a pre-programmed iterative process to determine the IRR, removing the need for long hand iteration based on the NPV formula.

Over the last 20 years, concerns with the IRR formula have moved from theoretical concerns over reinvestment issues and alternative equations, such as the financial management rate of return (FMRR) and modified internal rate of return (MIRR), to practical concerns arising from application by practitioners. In addition to very high sensitivity to the magnitude and timing of cash flows, the IRR calculation is also heavily influenced by the interaction of growth and risk through the assessment of key input variables, as considered in Chapter 3.

Income, capital and total return measurement provides a large amount of information concerning the performance of individual properties and of portfolios. This may be combined with information ascertained from risk measurement, considered further below in the Portfolio Analysis Step.

Use of sale prices and appraised values in capital
return measurement

The measurement of property, portfolio, fund and REIT total return individually or for inclusion in a benchmark or index necessitates the measurement of both income return and capital return. Given the rare occurrence and therefore usual absence of a sale of the subject property from which to measure capital return, capital value is usually adopted and proxied by Independent Appraisal. However, capital value determined by Independent Appraisal is subject to a range of influences including appraisal basis, appraisal smoothing, appraisal accuracy and appraiser behaviour considered in Chapter 4.

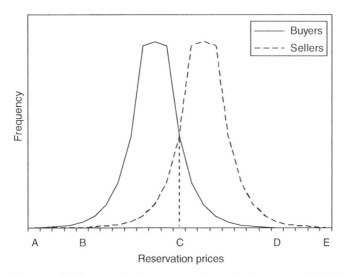

Figure 5.2   Buyer and seller populations: reservation price frequency distributions. From the author and Geltner, Miller, Clayton and Eichholtz (2007). *Commercial Real Estate Analysis and Investment (with CD-ROM)*, 2E. © 2007 Delmar Learning, a part of Cengage Learning, Inc. Reproduced by permission. www.cengage.com/permissions.

Where data on the capital value of a property asset at the start or end of the period based on a transaction of the property is available, it is generally preferred as an indicator of the markets current value of a property, though it is not without issues.

As shown in Figure 5.2, transaction price represents a point of overlap where the buyer's reservation price is at least as high as the seller's reservation price at a given point in time. Potential transaction prices may range between B and D, tending to be distributed around that value labelled C which represents the classic economic concept of equilibrium value or market clearing price. The difference between the observable transaction price and the unobservable true value may be referred to as transaction price noise or transaction price error, with error, by definition, being unbiased and equally likely to be on the high side or the low side as long as time is held constant. Accordingly, even when indexes or benchmarks are based on transaction prices, performance data should be interpreted having regard to transaction price noise or transaction price error (Geltner et al., 2007).

In the absence of transaction data for the property, periodic Independent Appraisals are relied upon for the determination of capital value and capital returns, though it should be acknowledged that appraisals are subject to a range of issues as considered in Chapter 4. Ideally, the frequency of appraisal mirrors the frequency of the relevant index or benchmark, with annual appraisals of property for an annual index or benchmark, quarterly apprais-als for a quarterly index or benchmark and so forth.

Appraisal basis

For the assessment of capital return for Performance Measurement or for an index or benchmark to have rigour, those appraisals comprising base data for the calculation of capital returns must be undertaken on a consistent and transparent basis. The method of appraisal adopted, be that capitalisation of income, discounted cash flow or another method, is of lesser relevance than the basis of appraisal. To accord with International Financial Reporting Standards, the International Valuation Standards Committee definition of market value is commonly adopted as the basis of appraisal, being:

> *The estimated amount for which a property should exchange on the date of valuation between a willing buyer and a willing seller in an arm's-length transaction after proper marketing wherein the parties had each acted knowledgably, prudently, and without compulsion.* (IVSC, 2003)

With the International Valuation Standards Committee definition of market value being adopted by RICS for their globally applicable Red Book and also commonly adopted by national valuation standard setters around the world, it may be considered to be the default basis of appraisal. Accordingly, when comparing data from indexes or benchmarks, care should be taken to ensure that the basis of appraisal adopted is common to each (Hoesli and MacGregor, 2000).

Appraisal smoothing

The issue of appraisal smoothing has received an enormous amount of attention in real estate research, reflecting the potential significance of its impact on understanding real estate returns. Direct property indexes or benchmarks are generally argued to be smoothed, meaning that they understate the variability of returns due to the use of appraisals. Such smoothing due to appraisals is usually attributed to two sources, being infrequent transactions and an aggregation effect. Infrequent transactions mean appraisers have limited information to work with in determining open market value, so transactional information is often combined with past appraised values to reach an opinion of value. Accordingly, current time, objective value evidence from transactions is influenced by prior period, subjective value evidence from appraisals which imputes all of the issues associated with prior appraisal processes into the current appraisal. This creates smoothing at the individual asset or disaggregated level, which is then compounded by the smoothing resulting from the aggregation of property appraisals at the portfolio, fund or index level (Hoesli and MacGregor, 2000).

Appraisal based indexes thus present smoothed versions of the underlying price series that would be evident if every property in the sample were to be transacted at the relevant date. Methods for correcting the impact of smoothing have been developed at a theoretical level (Blundell and Ward, 1987; Ross and Zisler, 1991) but are yet to be adopted in practice, with de-smoothed property indexes showing significantly higher levels of risk for real estate when measured by standard deviation (being a range of multiples of nearly two times (MacGregor and Nanthakumaran, 1992), 3.44 times (Brown, 1991) or 3–5 times (Ross and Zisler, 1991)). Accordingly, an awareness of the issue and the likely contributors to its having a significant impact on portfolio, benchmark and index returns are required in the interpretation of portfolio, benchmark and index data.

Indexes and benchmarks of direct property returns may also suffer from the smoothing effect of temporal lag, which does not diversify out at the portfolio level and has an impact similar to a moving average. Where a progressive appraisal policy is adopted and a portion of the properties within a portfolio are appraised each period, a portion of the portfolios appraised capital values are always behind the balance leading to a smoothing effect which lags behind the unobservable true return. Over a very long or infinite period, this would have no effect on average returns across time but, for short or finite periods, conditional bias will be evident with the direction of the bias depending on the direction in which the returns are trending.

Accordingly, in a rising market returns may be biased upward or, conversely, downward in a falling market which will also reduce the apparent volatility of observable returns leading to the apparent beta of lagged returns being less than the beta of non-lagged returns. Therefore, an awareness of the issue and the likely contributors to its having an impact on portfolio, fund, benchmark and index returns are required in the interpretation of portfolio, fund, benchmark and index data (Geltner et al., 2007). A move to quarterly appraisal of all assets within the portfolios and funds of all REITs would be highly commendable and contribute significantly to addressing the impact of appraisal smoothing.

Appraisal accuracy
For an appraisal to be useful in determining capital returns, it must be an effective proxy for the likely selling price of an asset. Accordingly, it is necessary to be confident that an appraisal is an accurate estimation of the likely selling price.

Extensive academic research has been undertaken in several countries including the UK (Brown, 1985; Drivers Jonas, 1988), USA (Miles et al., 1992) and Australia (Newell and Kishore, 1998) comparing the sale prices of large samples of properties to recent appraisals of the same properties and identifying a very close relationship. This suggests that, at the broadest

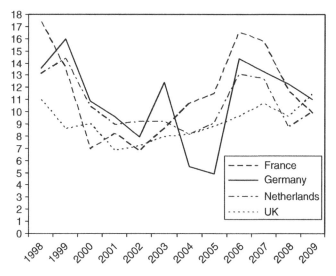

Figure 5.3 Weighted average absolute valuation/price differences, %pa, 1998–2008. Reproduced by permission of IPD (2010).

level, appraisals are an effective proxy for likely selling price and so provide a useful input into determining capital returns.

The usefulness of appraisals as an effective proxy for most likely selling price may, however, be expected to be reduced in periods of rapid value rises or falls when appraisers, reliant on evidence from recent transactions, tend to lag the market and in periods of no transactional activity. This is graphically illustrated in Figure 5.3 based on ongoing research by IPD to measure the difference between appraisals and sale prices, which vary significantly over time and in different markets. Accordingly, awareness that, during such periods, capital returns may be under or over stated is essential and the use of such return data should be approached with appropriate caution.

Appraiser behaviour

The appraisal process is based, implicitly, on an assumption that appraisers are rational and act in an optimal manner when undertaking an appraisal. Whether or not this is the case is the subject of a growing body of academic research in behavioural finance (Brown and Matysiak, 2000).

A wide range of behavioural issues arise from the fact that appraisers are faced with the practical problem of preparing an appraisal in a market that is not frequently traded and for which, therefore, information may be incomplete. Different appraisers may be expected to react to this problem in different ways with the form and nature of the reaction potentially impacting the results of the appraisal (Brown and Matysiak, 2000).

Academic research has identified a range of behavioural issues concerning appraisers and the appraisal process. The impact of client influence on appraisers has been found to be linked to the type of client, the characteristics of the appraiser, the purpose of the appraisal and the relative levels of information held by the appraiser and the client (Levy and Schuck, 1999; Levy and Schuck, 2005). Appraisers have been found to be subject to a range of client influences including expert power, information power, reward and coercive power and procedural power as considered in Chapter 4 (Levy and Schuck, 2005).

For the Asset Management Team and the Portfolio Management Team, such behavioural issues provide an ethical challenge. Being aware of the nature of influences that may impact an appraiser may entice the Asset Management Team and the Portfolio Management Team to implicitly or explicitly seek to use same to influence an appraisal. This would, however, be unethical and contrary to the principles of openness and transparency discussed in Chapter 1.

There are, however, other behavioural issues impacting appraisers that are not influenced by the client. Anchoring a current appraisal on a previous appraisal, rather than being a purely stand-alone assessment based on new information, is a common trait among appraisers together with a herding tendency whereby the appraiser follows the general upward or downward trend being exhibited by other appraisers or investors rather than being reliant solely on the facts of the appraisal at hand. Further, the appraisal profession is susceptible to adopting a range of procedural short cuts and rules of thumb in the appraisal process that may impact the quantum of the final appraised value.

Appraisers have also been found to have a bias towards recent information to which greatest weight is attached and to be prone to confirmation bias, whereby a preliminary value judgment is formed and evidence then sought to support this judgment. Asking prices have also been found to have an anchoring role in the appraisal process with knowledge of same influencing the appraiser's judgment (Black et al., 2003).

The combined effect of such behavioural issues may be to distort the appraisal above or below that number which it may otherwise have been. If the appraisal is then adopted for the purposes of capital return assessment or inclusion in an index or benchmark, the capital return may be influenced upwards or downwards and, if there is significant change from period to period, the resulting assessment of risk may also be impacted.

In the interest of openness, transparency and accuracy, it is important that appraisers are afforded the opportunity to be rational and to act in an optimal manner. An awareness by the Asset Management Team and the Portfolio Management Team of the ways in which such an opportunity may be diminished should serve to avoid them occurring to the extent controllable by each.

Return measurement

As both the REIT portfolio management profession and academic research into property portfolio management have advanced, the issues surrounding the quantitative measurement of returns have started to become better understood. Recognition of an issue comprises the initial step, followed by the identification of solutions to the issue by academic research, followed by awareness of the issue by the REIT portfolio management profession in practice, but with adoption of the solution by the profession usually a considerable period after its proposal by academic research.

As with all aspects of REIT portfolio management, an equal focus on each of the risk and return aspects of Performance Measurement is essential. Having considered the return aspects of Performance Measurement above, the risk aspects are considered further below.

5.5.2 *Performance relative to an index or benchmark*

Considerable care is required in selecting the index or benchmark for use in Performance Measurement, the difference between each being considered further below. Either needs to be indicative or representative of the REIT that is being measured, to be statistically robust in order to be credible (Hudson-Wilson and Wurtzebach, 1994) and to be capable of offering some evidence of abnormal performance (Brown and Matysiak, 2000). By thoroughly understanding the composition of the index or benchmark, the Asset and Portfolio Management Teams may optimise the opportunity for relative abnormal performance. For example, relative abnormal performance compared to other REITs constituting the index or benchmark may be achievable through acquiring properties that appear mis-priced (Brown and Matysiak, 2000) or by bringing forward appraisals of properties to increase capital returns in a given period.

In Performance Measurement, the differing levels at which Performance Measurement may be undertaken are inextricably linked. Performance Measurement may be undertaken at the individual property asset level, at a portfolio level such as real estate sector or geography, at the fund level or at the REIT level. Further, assets may be grouped as core, specialised, development (Hudson-Wilson and Wurtzebach, 1994) or by other common feature such as age or tenant profile (Pagliari, 1995) for the purposes of Performance Measurement. Whichever approach is adopted, Performance Measurement usually starts at the individual asset level and is then aggregated upwards. Accordingly, asset level Performance Measurement data not only forms a useful input into the decision making process concerning a specific asset (Hudson-Wilson and Wurtzebach, 1994), but also between different assets, in portfolio rebalancing and at the fund and overall REIT level (Brown and Matysiak, 2000).

The real estate sector was probably the last sector of the capital markets to develop indexes and benchmarks for Performance Measurement. Stocks and bonds have indexes dating back to the late 1800s but it wasn't until 1978 that the US NCREIF Property Index was created with various other indexes following thereafter (Geltner et al., 2007). As with all aspects of REIT portfolio management, equal focus on each of the risk and return aspects of Performance Measurement is essential, both of which are considered further below. While return measurement is usually a quantitative exercise focusing on income return, capital return and total return, risk measurement may be a mixture of qualitative and quantitative assessment (Geltner et al., 2007).

Indexes and benchmarks
Though the terms are often used interchangeably, an index measures return for a defined segment of the capital market and a benchmark reflects how a specific participant or group of participants performed within that market segment (Hudson-Wilson and Wurtzebach, 1994). Therefore, the Dow Jones US Total Stock Market Index measures the performance of all equity securities issued by US companies that have readily available price data, while the Dow Jones Equity All REIT Index measures the performance of all publicly traded US equity REITs, providing a benchmark reflecting the performance of a participant sector within the index. Consequently, the performance of sector specific REITs such as office REITs, shopping centre REITs and so forth could then be benchmarked against the relevant sectoral index, the Dow Jones Equity All REIT Index.

For a less clearly or undefined universe, a fundamental decision arises in index construction concerning the extent of the universe to be covered by the index. This may be decided to be the entire universe or a subset or sample of the universe only, the decision on sample size being a trade off between accuracy and the cost and availability of data (Hoesli and MacGregor, 2000).

The direct property market is a typical example of a less clearly or undefined universe. The property market in its entirety includes all sectors, all geographic areas and all forms of ownership – hypothetically ranging from the smallest apartment or car parking space to the largest office tower or the biggest cathedral. However, in many cases, it is a subset of the entire direct property market that is of interest, such as institutional grade commercial real estate for investment purposes, though this, in itself, provides challenges with different real estate sectors being considered institutional grade in different countries.

The relative size of properties within the index sample may also have a significant impact on the information provided by the index. As the size of the sample increases, the risk from individual assets in the sample is reduced through diversification and the risk of the sample will approach market risk.

However, several unusually large properties within the sample may increase the level of risk within the sample and so adversely affect its approximation of market risk.

When comparing data provided by different indexes, it is, therefore, essential to clearly understand the nature of the sample upon which the index is based (Hoesli and MacGregor, 2000). For example, the IPD UK Annual Property Index provides a measure of institutional grade commercial real estate in the UK real estate market based on a very large sample of over 11 000 properties, but it cannot represent the entire UK commercial real estate market as the sample does not include all of the properties in that market. As such, the index is not indicative of the entire underlying real estate market but that section of the market as defined by those properties held within the sample (Geltner et al., 2007). A sample comprising an index may, therefore, bear no relationship in value weighted terms to the underlying real estate market.

However, as the IPD UK Annual Property Index sample is very large, idiosyncratic or specific asset risk may be considered diversified and the index may be considered to approach market risk, so acting as an effective proxy for the UK commercial real estate market with the balance of properties not included in the sample unlikely to significantly change the risk-return performance as measured. Similar to the equity market, within the direct property market the performance of the office sector, retail sector and so forth may be benchmarked against the index, with the performance of individual office or retail properties being benchmarked against the office or retail market subsets of the index.

Unlike the equity market, the real estate market makes the development of index replicating portfolios particularly challenging. An equity manager seeking a passive investment management style replicating the returns of the Dow Jones US Total Stock Market Index would create a portfolio that held stocks in exactly the same weights as they represented in the Dow Jones US Total Stock Market Index. Such an equity manager would be able to achieve replication identically through direct investment in IBM, Boeing, BHP and so forth. However, a Fund Management Team seeking a passive investment management style replicating the returns of the IPD UK Annual Property Index could not create a portfolio that held properties in exactly the same weights as they represented in the IPD UK Annual Property Index as those properties are already held by other parties. The Fund Management Team may proxy the holdings in the IPD UK Annual Property Index by holding the same proportion of office property in one city or retail property in another city as the index but, because the individual buildings held would be different and so have different idiosyncratic or specific risk profiles, the performance of the index could not be replicated exactly.

Indexes as measures of return for defined segments of the capital market provide useful data for a range of purposes. By calculating returns over a given period, it is possible to then calculate the average return, standard deviation and correlation coefficient between pairs of returns which provide the building blocks for the development of Property Portfolio Strategy and Strategic Asset Allocation (Hoesli and MacGregor, 2000), as considered in Chapter 2.

5.5.3 Risk measurement

As with return measurement, risk measurement requires attention at several levels including the REIT level, the portfolio level and the individual property level. While performance, in terms of both return and risk, at the REIT level is usually considered relative to an index, performance at the portfolio level and at the individual property level is usually considered relative to a benchmark.

As considered in Chapter 2, return and risk are inextricably intertwined so it is essential to consider risk adjusted returns. Though high returns are intuitively attractive, they are insufficient alone unless accompanied by a clear understanding of the level of risk accepted. The most commonly adopted concept of risk is variation in returns or spread of distribution, measured by standard deviation, as considered in Chapter 2. Standard deviation measures the spread of actual returns achieved around the mean, with a greater spread indicating a greater level of risk (Hoesli and MacGregor, 2000) and may be used to measure risk at the REIT level, at the fund level, at the portfolio level and at the individual property level.

Risk adjusted returns

While standard deviation provides a measure of risk that can be considered in isolation and compared to that for other assets, portfolios, funds or REITs, it is not particularly informative about the level of risk relative to return. Simple risk adjusted returns at either the REIT, fund, portfolio or individual property level may be determined by dividing the average return by the standard deviation of that return (Baum, 2002). This provides a basic indication of risk-return relativity that works for several levels including the REIT, fund, portfolio and individual property but does not address different types of risk from a capital market theory viewpoint.

Return measurement, as considered above, implicitly assumes that all properties lie within the same risk class and that each property is as risky as the index or benchmark (Brown and Matysiak, 2000). Accordingly, one approach to risk management would be to constrain investment to only those assets that are essentially of equal risk to the index or benchmark, so avoiding the need to adjust for risk quantitatively and allowing the direct comparison of unadjusted returns (Geltner et al., 2007). However, given the real estate market limitations of homogeneity and supply, such an approach is challenging to implement in practice.

To appreciate the relativity between risk and return from a capital markets perspective, the three most common measures adopted are the Sharpe Ratio, Treynor Index and Jensen Measure which each provide a single number that can then be used for ranking purposes (Brown and Matysiak, 2000).

The Sharpe Ratio comprises the average risk premium for a portfolio, being the total return less the risk free rate, divided by its total risk or standard deviation, providing a return premium per unit of risk. This allows ranking of alternatives in risk-return terms rather than just in total return terms with higher Sharpe Ratios indicating more desirable portfolios. As the Sharpe Ratio is only effective for diversified portfolios that do not contain any unsystematic risk, it is not appropriate for ranking the performance of individual properties and requires great care when used for property portfolios given the probability of latent unsystematic risk (Brown and Matysiak, 2000).

The Treynor Index focuses on systematic risk rather than total risk, being total return less the risk free rate divided by beta. Given its basis in systematic risk, the Treynor Index is useful to evaluate both property portfolios and individual properties (Brown and Matysiak, 2000). Similarly, the Jensen Measure uses the security market line to focus on abnormal performance by measuring desirability as the vertical distance of the portfolio above or below the security market line. With its reliance on systematic risk, the Jensen Measure can be applied to both portfolios and to single assets and offers the greatest potential usefulness for risk-return ranking in real estate (Brown and Matysiak, 2000).

While the Sharpe Ratio, Treynor Index and Jensen Measure offer theoretically elegant solutions to the challenge of accurately measuring risk adjusted returns, each are limited by practical problems in risk measurement for real estate and even greater theoretical and practical difficulties in applying formal quantitative risk adjustment to investment in real estate, including data problems and the applicability of the single index Capital Asset Pricing Model to real estate (Geltner et al., 2007). Accordingly, in practice, more qualitative approaches to risk-return analysis are often adopted.

Expectations

Risk at the REIT, fund, portfolio, and individual asset levels may be explicitly addressed within the *ex ante* return forecasting process referred to in Chapter 3. The forecast return and forecast risk for each property and at the portfolio, fund, REIT and index level may be estimated for the nominated future period based on expectations, providing a basis for comparative analysis following measurement of the actual outcome of each at the end of the period (Brown and Matysiak, 2000).

Prior to acquisition, the Advanced Financial Analysis Step included consideration of risk expectations which were then subject to review against actual risk observations in the Post Audit Step as considered above. Each set of forecasts prepared in the Performance Monitoring Step represents an implicit or explicit statement of risk expectation with the actuality being the subject of risk measurement.

The sources of differences in actual returns from expected returns are given in Equation 5.5, being differences in the capital value at the end of the period, capital expenditure during the period, net income during the period and/or the timing of each. Within each of these is a wide range of downstream expectations that may or may not be realised such as rental growth rates based on assumed market conditions, capitalisation or discount rates based on assumed capital market conditions and so forth. If any of these differ in actuality to that expected in the forecast, a difference in return will result with the magnitude of the difference being measurable as risk.

REIT management teams, like other investors, are principally concerned with downside risk (Hargitay and Yu, 1993) or the probability of actual returns being less than expected returns. Upside risk, or the probability of actual returns being greater than expectation, generally receives much less attention. If the distribution of possible returns is symmetrical around the expected return (or mean), then the measure of total risk may also be a measure of downside risk. However, if the distribution is not symmetrical, a separate measure of downside risk is required. While there is evidence to suggest that asset returns are not symmetrical, there is little reason to con-clude that this makes a substantial difference to most analyses (Hoesli and MacGregor, 2000).

Risk measurement
While recognition by Portfolio Management Teams of issues associated with return measurement may be increasing, recognition of issues associated with risk measurement remains in its infancy. An awareness of standard deviation as a measure of risk and its use at the REIT, fund and portfolio level may be increasing, but risk measurement at the individual property level remains unusual.

Again, recognition of an issue comprises the initial step, followed by the identification of solutions to the issue by academic research followed by awareness of the issue by the REIT portfolio management profession in practice but with adoption of the solution by the profession usually a con-siderable period later.

5.5.4 Performance Measurement

The ongoing process of the Performance Monitoring, Performance Measurement and Portfolio Analysis Steps not only applies to each asset but also to portfolios, funds and to the REIT as a whole.

With the Performance Monitoring Step considering the process of plan-ning and monitoring the management of the portfolio in order to achieve the

Goals and attain the Vision of the REIT, the Performance Measurement Step seeks to quantify the level of performance achieved. This may be considered through two lenses, being the lens of the respective entities for performance (REIT, fund, portfolio and individual asset) and the lens of the risk-return relationship.

The importance of index or benchmark selection was considered, together with issues associated with index and benchmark construction in real estate and the management of the portfolio in cognizance of the index or benchmark.

Though there has been extensive academic research into issues associated with real estate return and risk measurement, implementation of such research in property portfolio management practice is generally slow. While some of the larger, global real estate investment management businesses lead the way in adoption of more sophisticated real estate return and risk measurement techniques, a large proportion of REIT managers are slow adopters continuing to rely heavily on heuristics and simple techniques.

The ongoing process of the Performance Monitoring and Performance Measurement Steps provides the extensive source data required for the next Step in the REIT real estate investment decision making process, the Portfolio Analysis Step.

5.6 Portfolio Analysis

The Performance Measurement Step addresses only past or delivered returns and may be distinguished from the Portfolio Analysis Step which is concerned with the present (Baum, 2002). Essentially, having measured returns from the REIT, fund, portfolio or individual property, the Portfolio Analysis Step seeks to determine the exact source of such returns which assists with both diagnosis and evaluation.

Diagnosis provides information on the sources and causes of performance which may provide an insight into the Asset Management Team's and the Portfolio Management Team's ability to consistently maintain such performance levels. Evaluation provides information allowing comparison of performance with that of other managers permitting informed judgment on whether, where and to what extent the Asset Management Team and the Portfolio Management Team added value compared to their peer group (Geltner et al., 2007).

As with the Performance Monitoring Step and the Performance Measurement Step, the Portfolio Analysis Step not only applies to each asset but also to groups of assets or portfolios, funds and to the REIT as a whole and may be considered to comprise two aspects. The first aspect concerns the ongoing, recurrent analysis of individual properties, the portfolio, the fund and the REIT as a whole on a perpetual basis with the second aspect concerning analysis of discrete, time specific projects.

5.6.1 Recurrent analysis

An individual property, a portfolio, a fund or a REIT may be subject to ongoing recurrent analysis on a perpetual basis which seeks to diagnose and evaluate the data obtained from the Performance Measurement Step in order to determine whether, where and to what extent the Asset Management Team and the Portfolio Management Team has added value. Comparison of the REIT level, fund level or portfolio level returns with benchmark or index returns will provide a measure of under or out performance of the benchmark or index, but will not explain the sources of such under or out performance.

At the REIT level, fund level or portfolio level, analysis of tracking error provides useful information on manager volatility. Tracking error is the standard deviation of return relative to an index. A REIT may have low absolute volatility but high tracking error and vice versa, so the analysis of tracking error provides useful information on manager performance (Baum, 2002).

At the individual property, portfolio, fund or REIT level, a macro approach to performance analysis may be adopted to parse or break down the performance into identified components. The total return measured for a property may be broken down into:

- the **initial yield** received;
- the **growth in net cash flow** during the Performance Measurement period, which may be divided into rental growth and operating expense growth; and
- the impact of **changes in the gap** between the capitalisation rate at the beginning of the period and that at the end of the period (Geltner et al., 2007).

While parsing can be applied at an individual property, portfolio, fund or REIT level and provides some useful information on the sources of return, it does not provide information on the extent to which the Asset Management Team and the Portfolio Management Team added value to an actively managed REIT portfolio through market timing and allocation, stock or property selection or diversification which may be determined through attribution analysis.

5.6.2 Attribution analysis

While attribution analysis is becoming of growing importance in REIT portfolio management and starting to feature in the design of Goals and Objectives and performance linked remuneration, there is surprisingly little academic research into attribution analysis for real estate investment returns (Baum, 2002).

Attribution analysis seeks to apportion returns between different sources relative to the benchmark or index to allow identification of where and to what extent the Strategy Team and the Portfolio Management Team added value and whether this was an occasional event or consistent over time. To adopt a nautical analogy:

"Essentially, performance attribution seems to provide a finer screen of assessment beyond the concept that "a rising tide raises all boats" by giving consideration to which type of boat was selected, which particular boat was chosen, which course was charted, and how well the boat was skippered." (Hudson-Wilson and Wurtzebach, 1994)

Generally, attribution analysis seeks to identify two components of return relative to the benchmark or index, being that component of relative return due to segment structure and that due to stock selection. Segment structure concerns the return attributable to the allocation of portfolio weights to segments of the market, usually defined as sector or geography, with different average rates of return. Stock selection concerns the return attributable to the choice of individual assets within each market segment that deliver returns above or below averages for that market segment (Baum, 2002).

The aim is to identify the relative contributions of each decision and so provide an indication of how much was attributable to manager performance and how much was attributable to forces beyond the control of the manager (Pagliari, 1995). Such information may then be used by the Strategy Team and Portfolio Management Team to improve real estate investment decision making by learning from those decisions that added value and focusing on those that deducted value (Brown and Matysiak, 2000).

The principal approach to attribution analysis comprises benchmark attribution analysis, comparing the performance of different parts of a fund with similar groupings in a benchmark which addresses risk in a general way by assuming each grouping represents a particular risk class. An alternative approach, theoretically purer though more challenging to implement practically, would be to adopt an explicit allowance for risk in order to evaluate the Strategy Team and Portfolio Management Team's selection and diversification skills (Brown and Matysiak, 2000).

As with many aspects of real estate investment decision making, theoretical and statistical purity has to be balanced against the pragmatic limitations of the real estate asset class and the real estate market (Baum, 2002). Theoretically, the segmentation of the portfolio should be matched with the segmentation of the benchmark used for analysis, which may be different for each REIT portfolio. For example, the benchmark may segment by region while the portfolio segments by city within region for which performance may be very different.

Further, statistically, each segment should contain a sufficient number of properties for the average return to be reasonably robust, so that each segment ideally only reflects systematic risk with the optimum segmentation of the market being that which statistically explains the most variance in individual property returns.

However, practically, there are relatively few benchmarks available leading to effectively standardised segmentation for the purposes of attribution analysis for all portfolios. Reflecting the development of benchmarks using data from existing portfolios, the segments adopted in the benchmarks tend to mirror those adopted by the existing portfolios with most segments covering those markets for which relevant information is readily available to support analysis and forecasting. Effectively, benchmark segments follow generally accepted divisions of the real estate market in a country, usually resolving to sectoral divisions of office, retail, industrial and so forth and geographical divisions relevant to that country.

As considered in Chapter 2, a Portfolio Management Team may deliberately adopt a different Strategic Asset Allocation position or make a Tactical Asset Allocation weighting to a particular sector or geographic area that differs from the benchmark as part of the search for outperformance. A different Strategic Asset Allocation position may reflect a theme of the Portfolio Management Team's investment approach which fine tunes the Strategic Asset Allocation position (Baum, 2002). Alternatively, reflecting the indivisibility or lumpiness of real estate, a Portfolio Management Team may be left with an over or under weight position to the benchmark due to a recent acquisition, development or disposal.

In a large portfolio, expected return attributable to stock selection should be zero due to the impact of diversification on eliminating unsystematic and idiosyncratic risk. However, in smaller portfolios, stock risk may be expected to be greater and dependent on the number and value of the constituent properties, with the risks being idiosyncratic and specific to individual buildings and so uncorrelated (Hoesli and MacGregor, 2000).

However, the impact of segment structure, being the allocation of portfolio weights to segments of the market, has the greatest impact on variations in returns when the scale of difference in performance between segments is greatest, such as when the market generally is booming or contracting but different segments are changing at significantly different rates (Baum, 2002).

Whether or not the impact of stock selection, being the choice of individual assets within each market segment, comprises the balance of the return or whether a portion of return is attributable to a third variable, being a cross product term between segment structure and stock selection, is currently unresolved (Baum, 2002; Brinson et al., 1995). Differing data service providers adopt either a two or three variable approach to attribution analysis, such that the Portfolio Management Team should carefully read the supporting information provided by the data service provider to clearly understand the basis of performance attribution adopted.

Two variable approach

Currently, the most common approach to attribution analysis is that adopting a two variable approach. This approach uses the ratio of segment structure and stock selection variables to explain the performance of a REIT portfolio against a benchmark based on relative return (Baum, 2002):

$$\text{Relative Return} = ((1 + \text{Portfolio Return})/(1 + \text{Benchmark Return}) - 1)$$
[Equation 5.10]

For example, if the portfolio return was 10% against a benchmark of 5%, the relative return would be 4.8%:

$$\text{Relative Return} = ((1.10)/(1.05) - 1) = 0.0474 \text{ or } 4.8\% \text{ rounded}$$
[Equation 5.11]

The construction of the formula ensures that the components of the return and returns annualised over periods of years maintain consistent relative results, which would not occur if simple differences were used to compare returns.

Attribution scores may be built up from the comparison of weights and returns in each segment of the market, with separate segment structure and stock selection scores summed across the portfolio to produce portfolio level segment structure and stock selection scores that account for the relative return (Baum, 2002).

The segment structure score may be calculated as:

$$\text{Segment Structure Score} = (\text{Portfolio Weight} - \text{Benchmark Weight}) \times \text{Benchmark Return}$$
[Equation 5.12]

and the stock selection score, based on the commonly adopted two variable approach, then calculated as:

$$\text{Stock Selection Score} = \text{Portfolio Weight} \times ((1 + \text{Portfolio Segment Return})/(1 + \text{Benchmark Segment Return}) - 1)$$
[Equation 5.13]

with the segment structure score and the stock selection score than summing to a weighted contribution to the relative return (Baum, 2002).

Thus, attribution analysis allows the Strategy Team and Portfolio Management Team to clearly understand where value was added, whether this was through segment structure decisions (to allocate an overweight or underweight position to a particular sector or geography) or whether it was through stock selection decisions (to overweight or underweight particular assets or themes) or a combination of both. Importantly, attribution analysis assists in identifying where underperformance occurred and to what degree, providing vital data for consideration by the Portfolio Management Team in the next Stage of real estate investment decision making, the Optimising Stage.

When attribution analysis is repeated over time, it provides useful information concerning the effectiveness of the Strategy Team and Portfolio Management Team's real estate investment decision making process. Occasional outperfomance due to either segment structure decisions or stock selection decisions or both may indicate that the Strategy Team and Portfolio Management Team were lucky whereas consistent outperformance over time may be likely to indicate the effectiveness of the teams' real estate investment decision making process.

REIT Strategy Teams, Portfolio Management Teams and investors benefit from consistent presentation of attribution analysis over time and between REITs. The adoption of common reporting approaches by all REITs allows comparison of attribution scores between REITs providing beneficial information to REIT management teams and investors, with the adoption of tailored reporting approaches by individual Portfolio Management Teams limiting performance comparisons with other managers and so limiting the information benefit to investors (Hudson-Wilson and Wurtzebach, 1994).

5.6.3 Recursion

Recursion is one of the most logically intuitive but often overlooked aspects of the Portfolio Analysis Step. Recursion concerns a discrete, time specific project such as a refurbishment or redevelopment project, where the Advanced Financial Analysis Step was undertaken prior to the project being approved by the Governing Entity and where the project is currently underway. As part of the ongoing portfolio management process, the performance is monitored and measured with reference to the forecast developed in the Advanced Financial Analysis Step and adopted in the Governing Entity report in the Governance Decision Step.

Following Performance Monitoring and Performance Measurement, the project may be found to now be running ahead of or behind schedule, to be under or over budget or to face an unexpected event. Having determined this, the Portfolio Management Team will then analyse the event impact, often a time or budget difference, in order to understand the source and implications, together with identification of alternative forms of remedial action. It is likely that each alternative form of remedial action or scenario will have an impact on the expected return and risk for the project, which then each require explicit analysis.

Effectively, a further Advanced Financial Analysis forecast should be undertaken for each potential remedial action scenario and the resulting forecast risk-return determined for comparison to the original forecast from that Advanced Financial Analysis upon which the original decision to proceed was based. This will permit evaluation of the revised forecast risk-return from each scenario against the decision criteria to determine which, if any, of the scenarios is optimal. It may transpire that the remedial action needs to be varied, usually to be faster or cheaper, if the forecast risk-return from the original Advanced Financial Analysis is to be achieved. Alternatively, it may become apparent that the original forecast risk-return will not be achieved with something less now forecast.

Following completion of an updated Advanced Financial Analysis based on the optimal remedial action scenario, the project should be again subject to the approval process outlined in the Governance Step of the Executing Stage, allowing an explicit decision to be made about proceeding in the direction proposed. Depending upon the nature of the revised forecast risk-return, the Governing Entity then has the opportunity to either confirm the recommendation of the Portfolio Management Team or intervene to require further analysis, stop the project or take such other action as it considers appropriate in the best interests of unitholders. This ensures that the decision making process is both transparent and explicit, so avoiding the project progressing to either an unexpected late completion or significant budget over run which may not be in the best interests of unitholders.

By adopting a policy of recursion in the event of time change, budget change or unexpected event impact, the original Advanced Financial Analysis for a discrete, time specific project is regularly revisited by the Portfolio Management Team for project control through the Portfolio Analysis Step, following the Performance Monitoring and Performance Measurement Steps as part of the usual, ongoing portfolio management process.

5.6.4 *Portfolio Analysis*

Following the Performance Monitoring and Performance Measurement Steps that address the past or delivered returns, the Portfolio Analysis Step addresses the present. Essentially, having measured returns from the REIT, fund, portfolio or individual property asset, the Portfolio Analysis Step seeks to determine the exact sources of such returns which assists with both diagnosis and evaluation. Portfolio Analysis may be project discrete through recursion or recurrent through attribution analysis of asset, portfolio, fund or REIT performance and provides both a diagnosis and an evaluation of measured performance as the foundation for the ensuing Optimising Stage.

5.7 Super REIT

Having completed the Envisioning Stage, Super REIT has developed a Vision to be the premier diversified REIT on the stock exchange, interdependent with its adopted generic and specific investment management Style which is active, top down, growth and value added, respectively. To attain this Vision, Super REIT has identified four Goals including to be within the top quartile return performance with lowest quartile tracking error of the stock exchange REIT index every year. Consistently, Super REIT's Strategic Plan focuses on return optimisation at the REIT, portfolio and property level together with effective risk management, supported by a large number of specified Objectives encompassing all REIT management executives in the respective Teams and so aligning the motivations and actions of all REIT management executives with the attainment of Super REIT's Vision.

On completion of the Planning Stage, Super REIT has developed a Property Portfolio Strategy with a Strategic Asset Allocation comprising a sectoral allocation (50% retail, 40% office, 10% industrial) and geographic allocation (60% northern, 40% southern states), enhanced by a Tactical Asset Allocation of 2.5% to the office sector in the northern city of Metropolis for a period of two years reflecting a forecast undersupply of office accommodation. Within the allocation to the office sector, Super REIT has developed Stock Selection criteria specifying lots of around $375 million each, being freehold title in prime office locations within the downtown precincts of specified cities and A grade, high rise, modern office towers that are less than ten years old, being principally leased to corporate tenants.

Having completed the Dealing Stage, Super REIT has identified a specific asset for acquisition, Superman Tower, that is considered mis-priced by a significant extent over both a three- and ten-year holding period and so capable of generating abnormal returns. At a portfolio level, Superman Tower was confirmed to be acceptable for acquisition at $385 million on the basis of the commercial and funding structure proposed.

On completion of the Executing Stage, Super REIT has summarised the findings of the pricing process to secure the requisite internal and external approvals for the acquisition to proceed and negotiated Transaction Closure and Documentation. Super REIT has also undertaken Due Diligence to verify information relied upon in the Dealing Stage and commissioned an Independent Appraisal to support the assumptions made in the Dealing Stage.

Entering the Watching Stage, Super REIT now needs to complete the Settlement Step, after which Superman Tower is incorporated into the REIT portfolio and subject to Post Audit and ongoing Performance Monitoring, Performance Measurement and Portfolio Analysis.

5.7.1 Settlement

Having contracted to acquire Superman Tower after 90 days for $385 million, on a 40% debt and 60% equity basis, Super REIT must now settle the commercial and funding transactions.

Having liaised with the solicitors for Super REIT and for the vendor and the debt providers in the period leading up to Settlement, the Portfolio Management Team arrange a trial Settlement two days before the Settlement date which runs smoothly and identifies only a minor issue concerning the location of lift warranty certificates that is quickly resolved.

Accordingly, on the day of Settlement all runs smoothly and Super REIT becomes the owner of Superman Tower which is then included in the REIT portfolio with the onus now upon the Portfolio Management Team to deliver that which has been promised.

5.7.2 Post Audit

The acquisition of Superman Tower by Super REIT comprised a Tactical Asset Allocation to Metropolis for a period of two years to benefit from forecast short term outperformance due to a temporary office accommodation supply/demand imbalance.

Accordingly, therefore, Post Audit of the acquisition of Superman Tower should be undertaken as soon as practically possible given the short anticipated holding period. While Post Audit after three months may be too early to identify differences between assumptions adopted in the pricing process and emerging reality, Post Audit after six months may be optimal as this will be approximately 25% of the way through the anticipated holding period and so allow time for remedial action if necessary.

Having undertaken Post Audit, the Portfolio Management Team establish that the forecasts for office accommodation supply and demand in Metropolis were generally accurate, but that the forecast for rental growth was understated with a higher rental growth rate found to be applicable.

5.7.3 Performance Monitoring

For Superman Tower, the asset management plan proposed within the Governing Entity report prior to acquisition may be anticipated to form the basis for the annual asset management plan and budget, which will then be subject to Performance Monitoring for the balance of the year.

Reflecting the understated rental growth forecasts identified in the Post Audit Step, the forecasts for Superman Tower are amended by the Portfolio Management Team for inclusion in portfolio, fund and Super REIT performance forecasts.

Now being part of the REIT portfolio, Super REIT's management team will monitor the performance of Superman Tower on an ongoing basis through the cyclical process of budgeting, comparative analysis and forecasting to maintain awareness of whether or not the forecasts for the property will contribute to Super REIT achieving its Goals and so attaining its Vision.

5.7.4 Performance Measurement

Following completion of the Envisioning Stage, Super REIT has a Goal to be within the top quartile return performance of the stock exchange REIT index every year. Such a Goal requires a relevant index against which performance may be measured with Super REIT adopting the Dow Jones Equity All REIT Index. For consistency, when considering the performance of Superman Tower at the property level, Super REIT adopts a relevant office property benchmark for analysis.

For Super REIT, the acquisition of Superman Tower comprised a Tactical Asset Allocation to Metropolis for a period of two years to benefit from forecast short term outperformance due to a temporary office accommodation supply/demand imbalance. Accordingly, while Super REIT will measure income returns on a monthly basis in common with the balance of the portfolio, it may decide to commission an Independent Appraisal of Superman Tower on a quarterly or half-yearly basis to not only measure capital returns but also to maintain a close focus on the market in order to optimise the target disposal date given the short anticipated holding period.

5.7.5 Portfolio Analysis

Reflecting the acquisition of Superman Tower as a Tactical Asset Allocation to Metropolis for a period of two years to benefit from forecast short term outperformance due to a temporary office accommodation supply/demand imbalance, if such a forecast was valid the periodic attribution analysis of the performance of Superman Tower should indicate the source of returns to be principally segment structure with stock selection providing a lesser contribution.

5.7.6 Outcomes of implementing the Watching Stage

On completion of the Executing Stage, Super REIT had summarised the findings of the pricing process to secure the requisite internal and external approvals for the acquisition to proceed and negotiated Transaction Closure and Documentation. Super REIT had also undertaken Due Diligence to verify information relied upon in the Dealing Stage and commissioned an Independent Appraisal to support the assumptions made in the Dealing Stage.

Having completed the Watching Stage, Super REIT has exchanged unitholder capital for legal title to Superman Tower and the rights and responsibilities associated therewith. Reflecting the Tactical Asset Allocation for a period of two years, Super REIT undertakes Post Audit after six months with the learning incorporated as changes to the real estate investment decision making process. Thereafter, Superman Tower is included within Super REIT's portfolio and subject to ongoing, cyclical Performance Monitoring, Performance Measurement and Portfolio Analysis to maintain awareness of whether or not the forecasts for the property will contribute to Super REIT achieving its Goals and so attaining its Vision.

Following completion of the Watching Stage, Super REIT now embarks upon the Optimising Stage, being the final Stage of the third and final Phase, the Observing Phase.

5.8 Summary

The first Phase of the REIT real estate investment decision making process, the Preparing Phase, comprised the Envisioning Stage (considered in Chapter 1) and the Planning Stage (considered in Chapter 2). On completion of the Preparing Phase, the REIT has articulated where it is going and how it is going to get there, providing unitholders with a clear understanding of the risk-return profile to expect from the managers investment of their funds.

The second Phase of the REIT real estate investment decision making process, the Transacting Phase, comprised the Dealing Stage (considered in Chapter 3) and the Executing Stage (considered in Chapter 4). On completion of the Transacting Phase, the REIT manager has implemented the outcomes of the Preparing Phase through the creation of a tangible property portfolio.

The third and final Phase of the REIT real estate investment decision making process, the Observing Phase, comprises the Watching Stage (considered in this chapter) and the Optimising Stage (considered in Chapter 6).

The Watching Stage comprises the Steps of Settlement, Post Audit, Performance Monitoring, Performance Measurement and Portfolio Analysis that allow the REIT management team to watch whether or not the REIT's Goals will be achieved and hence the Vision attained.

The first Step of Settlement is a critical transition, being the transfer point from the vendor into the REIT management structure and inclusion of the acquired property within the REIT portfolio. Post Audit is, as the name suggests, an audit process that offers the opportunity for independent review.

As such, Post Audit provides a useful check point that should not be ignored by the Strategy Team and the Portfolio Management Team in the rush to the next transaction as the optimality of the next transaction may benefit from the findings of a thorough Post Audit.

Performance Monitoring, Performance Measurement and Portfolio Analysis are perpetual, ongoing cyclical processes whereby the REIT plans for the future, measures the past and then replans for the future. Being continual activities, they risk becoming tedious and perfunctory which then risks totally undermining their usefulness in the REIT real estate investment decision making process. As such, the Portfolio Management Team needs to ensure that the requisite level of attention is given not only to the preparation but also to the consideration of the data provided.

It is only through careful planning and objective measurement that the Portfolio Management Team can remain in control of REIT portfolio performance and identify the need for corrective action early, with such vigilance being fundamental to the nature of the fiduciary duty between the REIT management team and unitholders. Performance Monitoring, Performance Measurement and Portfolio Analysis can provide much useful information for the Portfolio Management Team but the benefits may only be realised if the Portfolio Management Team first undertake such activities, then study the results and finally learn from them and apply that learnt to the ongoing management of the REIT.

Completion of the Watching Stage may result in the REIT being able to clearly determine whether or not the Goals will be achieved and hence the Vision for the REIT will be attained, leading into the Optimising Stage of the REIT real estate investment decision making process where the REIT takes corrective action, if necessary, which is considered in the next chapter.

Completion of the Watching Stage and the Optimising Stage then mark completion of the third and final of the three Phases, the Observing Phase, wherein the REIT ensures that its performance will achieve its Goals and so attain its Vision, thereby completing the cyclical process of REIT real estate investment decision making.

5.9 Key points

- The Watching Stage is the first Stage of the **Observing Phase**, following successful completion of the Preparing Phase (comprising the Envisioning and Planning Stages) and the Transacting Phase (comprising the Dealing and Executing Stages).
- The **Watching Stage** comprises the Settlement, Post Audit, Performance Monitoring, Performance Measurement and Portfolio Analysis Steps, being a cyclical ongoing process without end.

- The Watching Stage includes the involvement of the **Compliance and Risk Management Team** whose principal contribution is to facilitate the mitigation of risk by the REIT.
- **Settlement** represents that point at which the rights and responsibilities for a property investment transition from the vendor to the REIT management team and the property becomes part of the REIT portfolio.
- **Post Audit** offers a process to consider the validity of assumptions made and forecasting approaches adopted, providing an opportunity to implement improvements, if required.
- **Performance Monitoring** is a continuous, dynamic, cyclical process of asset, portfolio, fund and REIT planning and budgeting prospectively together with reporting against such plans and budgets retrospectively.
- **Performance Measurement** provides the means for an objective, retrospective assessment of whether a REIT is achieving its targets and/or Goals in both risk and return dimensions, providing essential data for Portfolio Analysis. Within Performance Measurement for real estate, there are a range of issues including appraisal basis, smoothing, accuracy and appraiser behaviour that impact upon reported returns and thus risk of which the Portfolio Management Team should be aware in interpreting returns, benchmark and index data.
- **Portfolio Analysis** seeks to determine the exact sources of return, through asset, portfolio, fund or REIT attribution analysis or project discrete recursion, to assist with both the diagnosis and evaluation of measured performance as a foundation for the Optimising Stage.
- Completion of the Watching Stage may result in the REIT being able to clearly determine whether or not the **Goals will be achieved** and hence the Vision for the REIT will be attained.
- The Watching Stage is followed by the **Optimising Stage**, wherein the REIT takes such action as may be necessary to address any forecast underperformance identified in the Watching Stage, with completion of the Watching Stage and the Optimising Stage completing the third and final Phase, the Observing Phase.

References

Further information concerning issues considered in this chapter may be found in the following texts:

Baum, A.E. (2002) *Commercial Real Estate Investment*, Estates Gazette, London.
Black, R.T., Brown, M.G., Diaz, J., Gibler, K.M. and Grissom, T.V. (2003) Behavioural Research in Real Estate: A Search for the Boundaries, *Journal of Real Estate Practice and Education*, **6**(1), p.85.

Blundell, G. and Ward, C.W.R. (1987) Property Portfolio Allocation: A Multi Factor Model, *Land Development Studies*, **4**, p.145.

Brinson, G.P., Hood, R. and Beebower, G.L. (1995) Determinants of Portfolio Performance, *Financial Analysts Journal*, **51**(1), p.133.

Brown, G. (1985) The Information Content of Property Valuations, *Journal of Valuation*, **3**(4), p.350.

Brown, G.R. (1991) *Property Investment and the Capital Markets*, Chapman and Hall, London.

Brown, G.R. and Matysiak G.A. (2000) *Real Estate Investment: A Capital Market Approach*, Financial Times Prentice Hall, Harlow.

Drivers Jonas (1988) *Technical Appendix to the Variance in Valuations*, IPD, London.

Farragher, E.J. and Kleiman, R. (1995) Investment Decision Making Practices of Equity REITs, *Real Estate Finance*, **12**(2), p.48.

Geltner, D.M., Miller, N.G., Clayton, J. and Eichholtz, P. (2007) *Commercial Real Estate Analysis and Investment*, Thomson South-Western, Mason.

Hargitay, S. and Yu, S.-M. (1993) *Property Investment Decisions: A Quantitative Approach*, E&FN Spon, London.

Hoesli, M. and MacGregor, B. (2000) *Property Investment – Principles and Practice of Portfolio Management*, Longman, Harlow.

Hudson-Wilson, S. and Wurtzebach, C. (1994) *Managing Real Estate Portfolios*, Irwin, Burr Ridge.

IPD (2010) *IPD Index Research and Development Review January 2010*, IPD, London.

International Valuation Standards Committee (2003) *International Valuation Standards*, International Valuation Standards Committee, London.

Levy, D. and Schuck, E. (1999) The Influence of Clients on Valuations, *Journal of Property Investment and Finance*, **17**(4), p.380.

Levy, D. and Schuck, E. (2005) The Influence of Clients on Valuations: the Clients' Perspective, *Journal of Property Investment and Finance*, **23**(2), p.182.

MacGregor, B.D. and Nanthakumaran, N. (1992) The Allocation of Property in the Multi Asset Portfolio: the Evidence and Theory Reconsidered, *Journal of Property Research*, **9**(1), p.5.

Miles, M., Guilkey, D., Webb, B. and Hunter, K. (1992) *An Empirical Evaluation of the Reliability of Commercial Appraisals 1978–1990*, Prudential Real Estate Investors, Parsippany.

Newell, G. and Kishore, R. (1998) Are Valuations an Effective Proxy for Property Sales?, *The Valuer and Land Economist*, **35**(2), p.150.

Pagliari, J.L. (ed.) (1995) *The Handbook of Real Estate Portfolio Management*, Irwin, Chicago.

Ross, S.A. and Zisler, R. (1991) Risk and Return in Real Estate, *Journal of Real Estate Finance and Economics*, **4**(2), p.175.

Whipple, R.T.M. (1995) *Property Valuation and Analysis*, Law Book Company Limited, Sydney.

6

Optimising

Chapter 1 outlined the Envisioning Stage of the REIT real estate investment decision making process comprising the Steps of development of a Vision, Goals, Style, Strategic Plan and Objectives for the REIT. On completion of this Stage, the REIT should have a clearly articulated destination together with a high order route map by which to get to the destination and some measurable outcomes to determine whether or not the REIT has arrived at the destination.

Having completed the Envisioning Stage, Super REIT has developed a Vision to be the premier diversified REIT on the stock exchange, interdependent with its adopted generic and specific investment management Style which is active, top down, growth and value added, respectively. To attain this Vision, Super REIT has identified four Goals including to be within the top quartile return performance with lowest quartile tracking error of the stock exchange REIT index every year. Consistently, Super REIT's Strategic Plan focuses on return optimisation at the REIT, portfolio and property level together with effective risk management, supported by a large number of specified Objectives encompassing all REIT management executives in the respective teams and so aligning the motivations and actions of all REIT management executives with the attainment of Super REIT's Vision.

Chapter 2 then outlined the Planning Stage of the REIT real estate investment decision making process comprising the Steps of development of the Property Portfolio Strategy, Strategic Asset Allocation, Tactical Asset Allocation, Stock Selection and Asset Identification. On completion of this Stage, the REIT should have converted its Vision into an

Global Real Estate Investment Trusts: People, Process and Management,
First Edition. David Parker.

identified target list of specific property assets for potential acquisition that meet the Stock Selection criteria and may be mis-priced.

On completion of the Planning Stage, Super REIT has developed a Property Portfolio Strategy with a Strategic Asset Allocation comprising a sectoral allocation (50% retail, 40% office, 10% industrial) and geographic allocation (60% northern, 40% southern states), enhanced by a Tactical Asset Allocation of 2.5% to the office sector in the northern city of Metropolis for a period of two years reflecting a forecast undersupply of office accommodation. Within the allocation to the office sector, Super REIT has developed Stock Selection criteria specifying lots of around $375 million each, being freehold title in prime office locations within the downtown precincts of specified cities and A grade, high rise, modern office towers that are less than ten years old, being principally leased to corporate tenants.

Completion of the Envisioning Stage and the Planning Stage mark completion of the first of the three Phases, the Preparing Phase, wherein the REIT articulates where it is going and how it is going to get there, providing unitholders with a clear understanding of the risk-return profile to expect from the managers investment of their funds.

Having completed the Preparing Phase, the REIT then moves into the second of the three Phases, the Transacting Phase, comprising the Dealing Stage and the Executing Stage. Chapter 3 then outlined the Dealing Stage of the REIT real estate investment decision making process comprising the Steps of Preliminary Negotiation, Preliminary Analysis, Structuring, Advanced Financial Analysis and Portfolio Impact Assessment. On completion of this Stage, the REIT should have converted a target list of specific assets for potential acquisition into an in-principle transaction for the acquisition of a nominated asset.

Having completed the Dealing Stage, Super REIT has identified a specific asset for acquisition, Superman Tower, that is considered mis-priced by a significant extent over both a three- and ten–year holding period and so capable of generating abnormal returns. At a portfolio level, Superman Tower was confirmed to be acceptable for acquisition at $385 million on the basis of the commercial and funding structure proposed.

Chapter 4 then outlined the Executing Stage of the REIT real estate investment decision making process comprising the Steps of the Governance Decision, Transaction Closure, Documentation, Due Diligence and Independent Appraisal. On completion of this Stage, the REIT should have verified all information relied upon and assumptions made in the pricing process and reflected this in the Documentation necessary to protect the interests of unitholders at Settlement.

On completion of the Executing Stage, Super REIT has summarised the findings of the pricing process to secure the requisite internal and external approvals for the acquisition to proceed and negotiated Transaction Closure and Documentation. Super REIT has also undertaken Due Diligence to verify information relied upon in the Dealing Stage and commissioned an Independent Appraisal to support the assumptions made in the Dealing Stage.

Completion of the Dealing Stage and the Executing Stage mark completion of the second of the three Phases, the Transacting Phase, wherein the REIT manager seeks to implement the outcomes of the Preparing Phase through the creation of a tangible property portfolio.

Having completed the Transacting Phase, the REIT then moves into the third and final of the three Phases, the Observing Phase, comprising the Watching Stage and the Optimising Stage. Chapter 5 then outlined the Watching Stage of the REIT real estate investment decision making process comprising the Steps of Settlement, Post Audit, Performance Monitoring, Performance Measurement and Portfolio Analysis. On completion of this Stage, the REIT should be able to clearly determine whether or not the Goals for the REIT will be achieved and hence the Vision attained.

Having completed the Watching Stage, Super REIT has exchanged unitholder capital for legal title to Superman Tower and the rights and responsibilities associated therewith. Reflecting the Tactical Asset Allocation for a period of two years, Super REIT undertakes Post Audit after six months with the learning incorporated as changes to the real estate investment decision making process. Thereafter, Superman Tower is included within Super REIT's portfolio and subject to ongoing, cyclical Performance Monitoring, Performance Measurement and Portfolio Analysis to maintain awareness of whether or not the forecasts for the property will contribute to Super REIT achieving its Goals and so attaining its Vision.

This chapter outlines the Optimising Stage of the REIT real estate investment decision making process being those Steps comprising the continuous cycle of Asset Management, Property Management and Facilities Management together with a focus on Transformation at the individual asset level and Portfolio Rebalancing at the portfolio level with potential Disposal. On completion of this Stage, the REIT should have taken such action as may be necessary to ensure that the Goals for the REIT will be achieved and hence the Vision attained.

Completion of the Watching Stage and the Optimising Stage mark completion of the third and final of the three Phases, the Observing Phase, wherein the REIT ensures that its performance will achieve its Goals and so attain its Vision, thereby completing the cyclical process of REIT real estate investment decision making.

Accordingly, by the end of this chapter, the reader should understand:

- the role of the Asset Management Team in the management of **idiosyncratic risk**;
- the **customer service role** of the Property Management Team and the Facilities Management Team, including the importance of prompt resolution of issues, communication, courtesy and user satisfaction;
- the ability to significantly change the **risk-return forecast** at the individual property level through Transformation;
- the role of Portfolio Rebalancing in implementing Strategic Asset Allocation at the portfolio level and addressing **performance issues** at the property level; and
- the rationale for Disposal being the **final step of last resort** in addressing under performance at the property level.

6.1 People

While the Asset Management Step involves the Asset Management Team and the Property and Facilities Management Step involves the Property Management Team and the Facilities Management Team, the Transformation and Rebalancing Steps require the additional involvement of the Research, Strategy and Portfolio Management Teams with the Disposal Step also requiring the involvement of the Capital Transactions Team.

6.1.1 Asset Management Team

The role of the REIT Asset Management Team is to manage the assets within the portfolios, with the principal purpose of the role being to optimise the risk-return balance at the asset level and the scope of the role usually comprising either one very large asset, a small number of larger assets or a large number of smaller assets within one or more portfolios.

The Asset Management Team usually reports to the Portfolio Management Team, with direct reports including the Property Management Team.

The principal contribution of the Asset Management Team is the implementation of the asset management plan, with the functions of the role including:

- preparation of an **asset management plan** for each asset in the portfolio, including targets for achievement;
- **budgeting and forecasting** at the asset level;
- undertaking data collection, implementation and completion of larger tenant **rent reviews and lease renewals**;

- co-ordination of leasing agents and negotiation for **leasing** of larger areas of vacant accommodation;
- co-ordination of major **refurbishment and redevelopment** projects;
- co-ordination of provision of summary **income data** for performance measurement and analysis at the asset level;
- co-ordination of provision of information for **Independent Appraisal**;
- periodic management **reporting** at the asset level to the Portfolio Management Team; and
- continual focus on the **idiosyncratic risk** aspects of those assets comprising the portfolios.

Depending on the size of the REIT, the Asset Management Team may be arranged as generalists by portfolio or fund or as specialists by function for the REIT itself. Given the continuously increasing size and level of complexity and sophistication of REIT property assets, a general trend is emerging towards Asset Management Teams that specialise sectorally and geographically with the role and number of generalists diminishing.

6.1.2 Property Management Team

The role of the REIT Property Management Team is to manage the properties within the portfolios, with the principal purpose of the role being to optimise financial efficiency at the individual property level and the scope of the role usually comprising either one very large property, a small number of larger properties or a large number of smaller properties within one or more portfolios.

The Property Management Team usually reports to the Asset Management Team, with direct reports including the Facilities Management Team and external service providers.

The principal contribution of the Property Management Team is to achieve the net income targets within the property budget, with the functions of the role including:

- preparation of a gross and net income **budget and forecast** at the property level;
- **collection** of all income, management of arrears and payment of all operational expenses;
- undertaking data collection, implementation and completion of smaller tenant **rent reviews** and **lease renewals**;
- co-ordination of leasing agents and negotiation for **leasing** of small areas of vacant accommodation;
- completion and management of lease and licence **documentation**;
- co-ordination of minor refurbishment projects and redevelopment projects;

- prepare specifications, call tenders and document **service provider contracts** for lift maintenance, air conditioning maintenance, security services and so forth;
- general, ongoing **administration** of the properties under management;
- tenant liaison and maintenance of **harmonious lessor-lessee relations**; and
- periodic management **reporting** at the property level to the Asset Management Team.

Whether managing a small number of larger properties or a large number of smaller properties within one or more portfolios, the level of complexity and sophistication of REIT property assets is again resulting in a general trend emerging towards Property Management Teams that specialise sectorally and geographically with the role and number of generalists diminishing.

6.1.3 Facilities Management Team

The role of the REIT Facilities Management Team is to manage the facilities (such as washrooms, car parks, foyer areas) and services (such as lifts, air conditioning and security) within the properties, with the principal purpose of the role being to optimise operational efficiency at the individual property level and the scope of the role usually comprising either one very large property, a small number of larger properties or a large number of smaller properties within one or more portfolios.

The Facilities Management Team usually reports to the Property Management Team, with direct reports comprising employees such as concierges/superintendents, janitors, security staff and/or a wide range of external service providers including cleaning, lift maintenance, air conditioning maintenance and security service providers.

The principal contribution of the Facilities Management Team is the maintenance of occupier satisfaction, with the functions of the role including:

- **supervision** of employees;
- management of **service provider** contracts and supervision of maintenance;
- calling quotes and supervising **tradesmen**, repairs and minor works;
- maintaining **key/access device** registers and provision to occupiers; and
- **customer service**, being the initial point of contact for occupiers concerning day to day occupancy issues.

The combination of Asset Management, Property Management and Facilities Management Teams provides the engine room for the day to day control, management and operation of the REIT property portfolio under a general principle of quiet achievement whereby the absence of tenant complaints is usually demonstrative of effective Facilities Management and Property Management outcomes.

6.2 Asset Management

Completion of the Envisioning Stage resulted in the REIT having a clearly articulated destination, being its Vision, together with a high order route map by which to get to the destination, being its Strategic Plan, and some measurable outcomes to determine whether or not the REIT has arrived at the destination, being its Goals.

Reflecting the underlying asset base of the REIT business being income producing real estate, the Vision, Strategic Plan and Goals often include elements reliant upon income return and capital return for achievement. Further, given that capital return is largely a function of income return, capital expenditure and the capitalisation rate or discount rate, the importance of both income return and capital expenditure to the fulfilment of the Strategic Plan, achievement of Goals and attainment of Vision is self-evident.

The Asset Management Step and the Property and Facilities Management Step are instrumental in ensuring that the income return and capital expenditure are managed effectively with the clear focus being on the asset rather than on the portfolio. The role, purpose, scope, principal contribution and functions of the Asset Management Team were summarised above and may be considered to be the administration of property assets, excluding the cash or gearing and not taking account of the structure of the portfolio as a whole, with the objective of maximising the financial performance of each asset (Baum, 2002), essentially focusing on:

- **maintenance and enhancement of net income** – management of the Property Management Team to ensure rent collection and outgoings payment together with undertaking larger tenant rent reviews and lease renewals and leasing larger areas of vacant accommodation, being part of the Transformation Step; and
- **control and management of capital expenditure** – supervision of major capital expenditure together with co-ordinating major refurbishment and redevelopment projects, also being part of the Transformation Step,

through reactive and proactive management components which are considered further below.

The Asset Management Step includes the principal focus on the management of idiosyncratic risk within the REIT real estate investment decision making process, through the attention given to the management of issues unique to each property. While diversification is generally argued to significantly reduce the impact of idiosyncratic risk at the portfolio level, active management of the tenant and physical building aspects of each property may contribute the potential for further reduction in idiosyncratic risk impact. For example, maintaining a range of rent review bases within the tenancy profile or ensuring that the building structure is compliant with disability regulations are activities that may be undertaken by the Asset Management Team in the Asset Management Step that contribute to reduction in idiosyncratic risk.

6.2.1 Proactive components

Proactive asset management strategies comprise those strategies which are explicitly addressed and in-built within the ongoing portfolio planning process. For a newly acquired property, the asset management plan formed a key component of the report supporting the proposal for acquisition provided to the Governing Entity in the Governance Decision Step of the Executing Stage.

For those properties within the existing portfolio, the cyclical process of planning, comparative analysis and reporting, comprising the Performance Monitoring Step in the Watching Stage, includes annual portfolio management, asset management and property and facilities management plans working from the individual property level up to the portfolio level.

The asset management plan focuses on larger rent reviews, lease renewals, letting vacancies, capital expenditure and so forth, providing input for the net income budget and producing an asset management capital budget and forecast for each property. While the Property Management Team and Facilities Management Team provide recurrent gross income and outgoings expense data for the net income budget, the variable inputs are provided by the Asset Management Team.

Such variable inputs may include those surrounding rent reviews, leasing renewals, vacancies and capital expenditure. Depending on the size of each, such inputs may be considered within the Transformation Step, below, such as whole building tenant rent reviews, lease renewals or the leasing of large areas of vacant accommodation which have the capacity to transform the income returns of the property.

If not considered within the Transformation Step, the Asset Management Team will give consideration in the asset management plan to such issues as rent reviews, lease renewals, letting vacancies and capital expenditure which will not only contribute to the expected performance of the REIT but may also provide the Objectives for use in the performance plans for the respective members of the Asset Management Team.

Rent reviews

Where a larger rent review is to open market rental value or similar, the Asset Management Team will have regard to current and forecast market conditions and estimate the likely level of rental achievable on exercise of the open market rent review together with the management strategy to be adopted for its negotiation. For example, if the open market rent review is mid-lease term, the management strategy may be to negotiate aggressively to obtain the highest possible rent, whereas if the lease expiry is at the end of the review period, the management strategy may be more conciliatory with a view to fostering an environment conducive to lease renewal. For the purposes of gross income budgeting, the most likely expected rental may be included with the negotiation process commencing at a higher level with an expectation that the budget will be at least achieved if not exceeded.

Lease renewals

Careful tenancy management should ensure that larger lease renewals for multiple tenancies within a property investment are staggered over time so as not to all occur simultaneously, therefore effectively managing idiosyncratic risk. Where there is only one or a small number of larger lease renewals, the potential market rent may be determined by the Asset Management Team in the same way as for rent reviews but with regard to conditions in the letting market. Such conditions may require that a tenant be offered some form of incentive, such as a rent free period, fit-out allowance or staggered rent, which will require reflection in the income or capital budget.

The Asset Management Team also needs to attach an estimate of probability to the lease renewal, particularly where there are a large number of lease renewals. If the Asset Management Team is confident that all lease renewals will be successfully completed, then 100% of the anticipated revenue may be included in the income budget. If, however, the Asset Management Team is not confident that all lease renewals will be successfully completed, then less than 100% of the anticipated revenue should be included in the income budget.

It is particularly important for the Asset Management Team to be cognisant of the compounding effect of assumptions made for larger rent reviews and lease renewals in income budgeting. Pessimistic open market rental estimates coupled with pessimistic lease renewal probability assumptions will compound to result in lower estimates of income for the property and for the portfolio if replicated across all properties. This may have the effect of causing the Portfolio Management Team and the Fund Management Team to then unnecessarily pursue other strategies to achieve the Goals and attain the Vision of the REIT.

Conversely, optimistic open market rental estimates coupled with optimistic lease renewal probability assumptions will compound to result in higher estimates of income for the property and for the portfolio if replicated across all properties. This may have the effect of causing the Portfolio Management Team and the Fund Management Team to be complacent or consider it not necessary to pursue other strategies to achieve the Goals and attain the Vision of the REIT. If the Asset Management Team then either under delivers or over delivers on the estimate of income, the repercussions of such outcomes may impact across the entire REIT.

Accordingly, a considered and careful approach to the estimate of open market rentals for larger rent reviews and lease renewals and probabilities of lease renewals is essential for effective budgeting and REIT management.

Letting vacancies
As with lease renewals, a small number of vacancies of small areas of accommodation may require a different management approach in planning to a large number of vacancies of small areas of accommodation or a large area of vacant accommodation (considered further in the Transformation Step, below).

As with larger lease renewals, regard will be required to conditions in the letting market but with specific regard to the need to attract potential tenants to the building which may be distinguished from lease renewal where the tenant is already in the building and has some sunk costs in the tenancy such as fit-out, known location of the business, printed stationery and so forth. Accordingly, particular regard is required to any likely requirement to offer some form of incentive, such as a rent free period, fit-out allowance or staggered rent, which will require reflecting in the income or capital budget.

The Asset Management Team will have careful regard to the state of the letting market and the relative levels of supply and demand of accommodation in determining the rent likely to be achieved, the period likely to be required to lease the vacant accommodation, the level of incentive likely to be required and the level of inducement, commission or remuneration likely to be required by the leasing agent whom the Asset Management Team will select and then supervise. While this is less problematical in under-supplied or balanced markets, it is a major issue in over-supplied markets to the point where, in heavily oversupplied markets, the Asset Management Team may consider withdrawing larger areas of vacant accommodation from the market and waiting for conditions to improve, rather than paying substantial up front leasing commissions and tenant incentives in return for relatively low levels of rental.

As with larger lease renewals, it is particularly important for the Asset Management Team to be cognisant of the compounding effect of assumptions made for letting larger vacancies in income budgeting. Optimistic or pessimistic assumptions for time taken to lease, rental achieved or incentives and agent costs required will impact on the achievement of Goals and attainment of Vision for the REIT as a whole. Accordingly, a considered and careful approach to estimating is essential for effective budgeting and REIT management.

Capital expenditure
Ongoing capital expenditure is a feature of real estate investment and may sometimes have a direct income effect, such as refurbishment of a vacant office suite resulting in a higher rent being achieved, or an indirect income effect such as replacement of an air-conditioning chiller not necessarily resulting in an immediate rent increase but having an indirect effect through tenant retention and enhanced future rental growth.

Capital expenditure will have a direct impact on capital and total return from the property and may be expected to have a funding implication for the REIT. Accordingly, high levels of capital expenditure across the portfolio may dampen returns if not accompanied by commensurate income return enhancement and so may be deferred by the Portfolio Management Team in order to achieve the Goals and so attain the Vision of the REIT.

Generally, minor capital expenditure will be estimated by the Asset Management Team for inclusion in the capital budget for the property together with an assessment of potential return and deferability. Minor capital expenditure for which a high level of return will be achieved or essential capital expenditure for safety purposes will be less likely to be deferred than that for which there is limited or no direct return or which is non-essential.

It is not uncommon for a *'shopping list'* of minor capital expenditure items, for which there is limited or no direct return or which are non-essential, to be repeatedly deferred from year to year until the portfolio budget indicates a year in which such capital expenditure can be accommodated without detriment to achieving the Goals of the REIT. Similarly, it is not uncommon for capital expenditure budgeted for late in the REIT's financial year to be deferred if events during the course of the year appear likely to result in the REIT not achieving its Goals.

From a practical viewpoint, the Asset Management Team may alternatively seek to include some such minor capital expenditure items within a major capital expenditure project for which there is a demonstrable return and which may be considered within the Transformation Step, below.

Monitoring and reporting
Having prepared the asset management plan and provided inputs into the net income and capital budgets for each property in the portfolio, the Asset

Management Team then manage the properties on an ongoing basis and collate performance data to contribute to the Performance Monitoring Step of the Watching Stage through comparative analysis on a monthly basis with the preparation of forecasts for the balance of the financial year as the year progresses.

The Asset Management Team forecast is then used by the Portfolio Management Team to update forecast returns for the respective properties and the cumulative portfolio as the year progresses and for provision to appraisers for periodic Independent Appraisal of the property. Such comparative analysis and updated forecasts are usually reported upward through the REIT management structure to the Fund Management Team, CEO and Governing Entity as part of the REIT's ongoing operational performance reporting process.

While closely watching monthly data, the Asset Management Team will work with the Portfolio Management Team on a formal quarterly review of the asset management plan for each property to determine whether performance is in line with, running ahead of or slipping behind that forecast in the asset management plan and so identifying if remedial action is required to achieve the REIT's Goals and so attain its Vision.

6.2.2 Reactive components

Reactive asset management components comprise those which are not explicitly addressed, nor in-built within the cyclical portfolio planning process and that may arise within expected events or as unexpected events.

Expected events
As considered above, the asset management plan includes assumptions concerning a range of expected events such as the leasing of vacant accommodation or replacement of an air conditioning chiller. Reactive asset management strategies occur when that which was expected and planned for does not occur as planned. For example, rather than remaining stable as assumed, the local economy may deteriorate resulting in decreased tenant demand for accommodation and a longer letting up period, lower rental achieved on letting, larger incentive or higher agent leasing costs.

The Asset Management Team would need to determine how to react to such an event and what action, if any, to take having regard to achieving the Goals of the REIT. Reaction to such changes may be required between the quarterly periodic reviews or may wait until the next review, with changes to expected events generally likely to be incremental and resulting in small potential changes to budget or forecast returns that may be balanced or offset by other changes to expected events.

Unexpected events

Reactive asset management components occur when an unexpected event happens that was not planned for in the asset management plan. For example, the deterioration in the economy may result in the unexpected collapse of a major retail chain leading to an unexpected vacancy, loss of budgeted gross income and further loss of income through unrecoverable outgoings in one or more properties within the portfolio.

The Asset Management Team would need to determine how to react to such an event and what action, if any, to take having regard to achieving the Goals of the REIT. Reaction to such changes may be likely to be required between the quarterly periodic reviews and not wait until the next review, with unexpected events generally likely to be significant and resulting in large potential changes to budget or forecast returns that are unlikely to be balanced or offset by other changes to expected events.

Depending on the significance of the unexpected event, the REIT may be required to make an announcement to the stock exchange and unitholders which may trigger an impact on the REIT's trading price. Accordingly, scenario modelling around the unexpected event and remediation strategies by the Asset Management Team and Portfolio Management Team are required to provide information on possible impacts for use by the CEO and Investor Interface Team in informing the market and managing the possible downside effect of such an unexpected event.

In common with downside risk events generally, the greater the amount of information that can be provided to the market concerning the nature of the unexpected event and its possible impact on the REIT's earnings, distributions and other characteristics, the greater the confidence of the market in the REIT management team and the lesser the potential impact on the REIT's stock price.

6.2.3 Asset Management

The Asset Management Step is a critical part of and should be fully integrated within the REIT real estate investment decision making process. The achievement of Objectives by the Asset Management Team should contribute to the achievement of the REIT's Goals and hence the attainment of its Vision.

With a large portfolio comprising many properties for which larger rent reviews, lease renewals, letting of vacant accommodation and capital expenditure are continually occurring, the scope for small shortfalls in performance in many buildings to sum to a large shortfall in performance at the portfolio level, fund level and REIT level is significant with continuous monitoring, reporting and remedial action, where appropriate, essential.

Accordingly, the outcomes of effective asset management are not only return optimisation but also management of idiosyncratic risk at the individual property level.

6.3 Property and Facilities Management

The role, purpose, scope, principal contribution and functions of the Property Management Team and the Facilities Management Team were summarised separately above but, for some REITs, may both be undertaken by the same group though, in either scenario, may be considered further as follows.

6.3.1 Property Management

Property Management may be distinguished from Facilities Management by the former having a greater emphasis on process and the latter having a greater emphasis on people. Property Management is concerned with the day to day minutiae of matters arising from the occupation of property under lease such as the obligation to pay rent, provide quiet enjoyment, repair and maintain, comply with statutory and regulatory requirements and so forth.

As such, Property Management focuses on the administration of the property asset, not necessarily with the objective of maximising financial performance for the REIT beyond the efficient and prompt collection of rent and payment of outgoings (Baum, 2002). Reflecting the range of functions referred to above, the Property Management Team require a wide range of skills with Wurtzebach et al. (1994) noting the need to be part lawyer to understand the lease, part engineer to make sure the services work, part marketer to sell the tenant on the quality of the services and part accountant to report it all to the owner.

While the Asset Management Team focus on larger rent reviews, lease renewals and letting of vacant accommodation, the Property Management Team administer the fixed and index linked rent reviews together with smaller open market rent reviews, lease renewals for smaller tenants and the coordination of leasing agents for the leasing of smaller areas of vacant accommodation.

In common with the Asset Management Team, the Property Management Team undertakes proactive and reactive components of management. Within the cyclical process of planning, comparative analysis and reporting comprising the Performance Monitoring Step in the Watching Stage, the Property Management Team contribute to provision of recurrent gross income and outgoings expense data for the net income budget at the individual property level.

Following ongoing day to day management of the property, the Property Management Team then undertakes comparative analysis on a monthly basis with the preparation of forecasts for the balance of the financial year as the year progresses for provision to the Asset Management Team for inclusion in the updated forecasts prepared by the Portfolio Management Team.

6.3.2 Facilities Management

Facilities Management may be distinguished from Property Management by the former having a greater emphasis on people and the latter having a greater emphasis on process, with Facilities Management being concerned with the management and operation of the physical building environment from the viewpoint of end user satisfaction through the cleanliness of toilets, temperature of the air conditioning and so forth.

As such, Facilities Management focuses on the physical operation of building facilities, contributing to maximising financial performance through the provision of a stable and functional working environment within the property. Management of the air conditioning, lifts, fire services and so forth, together with the repair and maintenance of the building, cleaning, security, rubbish removal, landscaping, painting and other user facing services, directly impact the physical building environment, the quality of the occupation experience and the tenant's goodwill towards the property and its owner, the REIT.

In addition to administering the maintenance and other services provided by outsourced service providers, the Facilities Management Team may also administer the preparation of policies, procedures and manuals and co-ordinate building wide activities such as fire evacuation drills, moving in/out protocols and so forth. However, the increasing level of computerisation, automation and sophistication in the operation of building plant generally and that for green buildings specifically is significantly changing the profile of skills required within the Facilities Management Team.

The Facilities Management Team and the Property Management Team overlap in various aspects of their role, purpose, scope, contribution and functions. The process of administering service contracts (from specification, through tendering, awarding and monitoring) may be shared between the Teams, together with such responsibilities as the fixing of minor, on the spot problems, annual tenancy inspections and the general promotion of harmony with tenants. In common with the Asset Management Team and the Property Management Team, the Facilities Management Team undertakes proactive and reactive components of management.

Within the cyclical process of planning, comparative analysis and reporting comprising the Performance Monitoring Step in the Watching Stage, the

Facilities Management Team contribute to provision of recurrent gross income and outgoings expense data for the net income budget at the individual property level.

Following ongoing day to day management of the property, the Facilities Management Team then undertakes comparative analysis on a monthly basis with the preparation of forecasts for the balance of the financial year as the year progresses for provision to the Property Management Team and the Asset Management Team for inclusion in the updated forecasts prepared by the Portfolio Management Team.

6.3.3 Outsourcing Property and Facilities Management

While Property Management and Facilities Management may be provided internally by a REIT, sectoral specialisation and/or geographic diversity in a REIT portfolio often result in the use of external or outsourced service providers, usually under the control of a national management structure.

While single tenanted property may not require external management, with the tenant often liaising directly with the REIT head office regarding such issues, external management of multi-tenanted property offers the benefits of local market knowledge and local contacts, from local tenants seeking small areas of accommodation to local plumbers to fix dripping taps and local lift service contractors to free trapped lift occupants.

For other sectors, the specialist nature of the property may mean that it is preferable for a REIT to adopt external management. For example, hotels and apartment buildings or major shopping centres require specialist management skills that, unless the REIT is a sector specialist with an economy of scale, may be optimally accessed through external management.

For many smaller tenants in REIT portfolios and for some larger tenants, the Property Management Team and the Facilities Management Team are the only point of contact with and the public face of the REIT. Accordingly, for both internal and external or outsourced Property Management and Facilities Management Teams, key performance indicators around tenant satisfaction, prompt resolution of issues, communication, courtesy and so forth are essential. In common with the airline check-in and supermarket check-out, the willingness of tenants to engage with the REIT and pay higher rent, renew their leases and generally co-operate in the management of a property will be heavily influenced by their interaction with the Property Management and Facilities Management Teams.

The Facilities Management, Property Management and Asset Management Teams together with the Portfolio Management Team are each significant contributors to the cyclical process of planning, comparative analysis and reporting comprising the Performance Monitoring Step in the Watching Stage which provides continual monitoring of whether the Goals of the REIT are being achieved so that the Vision may be attained. The involvement of all Teams allows day to day operational and management issues to be acknowledged in performance forecasting for the REIT and ensures intimate knowledge of each property in the portfolio by each of the respective teams.

However, the ongoing cyclical process of the Watching Step also permits the teams to maintain awareness of and actively plan for the Transformation, Portfolio Rebalancing and Disposal Steps, if required, within the Optimising Stage.

6.4 Transformation

The cyclical process of planning, comparative analysis and reporting comprising the Performance Monitoring Step in the Watching Stage alerts the Asset Management Team and the Portfolio Management Team to upcoming events that may adversely impact on the forecast return and/or risk from a property potentially impacting the REIT's ability to achieve its Goals and so attain its Vision. In such a scenario, the REIT has a choice between three possible responses, being Transformation at the property level, Portfolio Rebalancing at the portfolio level or, in the event of neither of the foregoing being optimal, Disposal.

Such upcoming events with an impact of forecast return and/or risk may include a major or whole building rent review, lease expiry, option exercise or vacancy, looming major capital expenditure, the potential for a property to lose competitive advantage and suffer decreasing rents due to the need for refurbishment or the opportunity for redevelopment. The actions taken by the Asset Management Team and the Portfolio Management Team in response to such opportunities provide the ability to transform the forecast return and/or risk from such a property and may be undertaken in the Transformation Step.

Reflecting the various costs associated with Disposal, considered further below, in the event that the forecast risk-return from a property is considered likely to potentially impact the ability of the REIT to achieve its Goals and so attain its Vision, it is important that the Teams thoroughly investigate all alternative forms of Transformation prior to contemplating Disposal. Such alternative forms of Transformation may include refurbishment or redevelopment and mandatory or optional lease related issues.

6.4.1 Refurbishment Transformation

Refurbishment may take many forms including whole or part building, common areas or tenancy areas, cosmetic or integral and so forth. Generally, the Performance Monitoring Step will highlight a catalyst for the consideration of refurbishment which may include an upcoming major lease renewal, large vacancy or other event that will force an explicit comparison of the subject property to others in the market with the prospect of losing competitive advantage and so suffering decreasing rents and/or vacancy.

The extent of refurbishment and the consequent return and risk are exceptionally difficult to quantify. For example, if a major lease renewal is coming up, the REIT may consider undertaking a cosmetic refurbishment of common areas including repainting foyer and lift lobby walls and new signage together with repainting toilet walls, installing new mirrors and changing to new tap fittings. Such a refurbishment will have a return impact and a risk impact, both of which may be expected to be relatively low. While an increased rent may be expected, this may not be significant and risks such as delay and cost over runs may be expected to be minimal in such a project.

However, if the REIT were to also replace the floor coverings and raise the ceilings with new lighting in the foyer and lift lobbies and also replace the floor covering and hand basins in the toilets, the increased rent may be expected to be greater but the risk may be expected to be significantly greater with a longer project time, greater costs, increased disruption to tenants and so forth. Exactly how much more rent and how much more risk arise from each are exceptionally difficult to quantify and are always relative to taking no action at all with the risk that the major lease may not be renewed or may be renewed at a lesser rent.

Effectively, in contemplating refurbishment, the REIT management teams undertake those Steps comprising the Dealing Stage and the Executing Stage. The Preliminary Negotiation Step may include discussions with a major tenant facing lease renewal or a tenant contemplating leasing a large area of vacant accommodation in the property concerning the nature of refurbishment that they may be seeking and the indicative rentals that they may be prepared to pay. In the Preliminary Analysis Step, simplistic, single period analyses may be applied to the proposed refurbishment, including undertaking a short form residual or hypothetical appraisal (valuation), to assist with shaping the transaction in the Structuring Step.

The Advanced Financial Analysis Step is essential in determining the acceptable profile of refurbishment to be undertaken. A range of scenarios should be considered including at least three capital cost, income and capital return and risk scenarios (low, most likely and high) together with a 'do nothing' scenario. The use of discounted cash flow provides a flexible approach to modelling changes in expected costs, rents and time allowing an explicit analysis of the risk-return outcomes for each scenario and a comparison of the expected return from the refurbishment project with the REIT's target or required rate of return.

The Portfolio Impact Assessment Step then facilitates an assessment of the impact of the proposed refurbishment project on the REIT portfolio as a whole, being particularly significant if the refurbishment project requires a substantial amount of funding and/or may result in an extended period of no incoming cash flow for the REIT.

Having completed the Dealing Stage, the REIT may then embark upon the Executing Stage of the REIT real estate investment decision making process for the proposed refurbishment project. The Governance Decision Step of the Executing Stage is undertaken in which the refurbishment proposal is submitted as a formal proposal for acceptance or rejection by the Governing Entity, followed by the Transaction Closure Step and the Documentation Step which may be likely to include a lease document and the principal building contract. In the context of a refurbishment project, the Due Diligence Step may be expected to focus on the verification of all information relied upon, such as formalising contracts for goods and services for which quotes or estimates were previously obtained, with the Independent Appraisal Step focusing on the verification of support for all assumptions relied upon by the Portfolio Management Team in the Dealing Stage.

Having completed the Dealing Stage and the Executing Stage, the refurbishment project will be undertaken and monitored generally through the Steps comprising the Watching Stage and specifically through recursion in the Portfolio Analysis Step considered in Chapter 5. Recursion is particularly important for a discrete, time specific project such as a refurbishment project allowing the original Advanced Financial Analysis for the refurbishment project to be regularly revisited by the Portfolio Management Team in the event of schedule change, budget change or unexpected event impact, so facilitating effective risk management.

While refurbishment Transformation may include a range of activities from the minor cosmetic upgrade of one small part of a building to a more major project involving the whole building, it may be catalysed by an event that will force an explicit comparison of the subject property to others in the market with the prospect of losing competitive advantage and suffering decreasing rents and/or vacancy. As such, the property may be likely to remain within the same sector and within the REIT portfolio on an ongoing basis which may be distinguished from redevelopment Transformation where the property may be redeveloped to another sector or for the purposes of Disposal from the REIT portfolio.

6.4.2 Redevelopment Transformation

Generally, use of the term redevelopment suggests potentially significantly greater risk-return than may arise from use of the term refurbishment. Accordingly, those REITs that specifically refer to redevelopment in their publicly stated Strategic Plan or Goals signal to both existing and potential unitholders that the REIT is willing to accept significantly greater risk in pursuit of returns and such unitholders may then make an informed decision regarding investment in such a REIT.

Those REITs adopting a core investment management Style may generally be expected to undertake a modest amount of refurbishment with those adopting a value added (or core plus) investment management Style expected to undertake a greater amount of refurbishment and possibly some redevelopment, while those that adopt an opportunistic investment management Style may be expected to undertake considerable redevelopment. Again, specific reference to redevelopment in their publicly stated investment management Style permits unitholders to make an informed decision regarding investment in such a REIT.

For the purposes of REITs, redevelopment may be considered to be the Transformation of a property into another sector (such as the redevelopment of an office property as an apartment building) or for the purposes of Disposal from the REIT portfolio. As with refurbishment, the cyclical activities of the Performance Monitoring Step will have alerted the REIT management teams to an event that will force an explicit comparison of the subject property to others in the market with the prospect of losing competitive advantage and so suffering decreasing rents, potential vacancy or the prospect of the property being unlettable. Given the magnitude of such an event, it is likely to be considered well ahead of time with redevelopment Transformation being an alternative to Disposal for those REITs adopting a value added (or core plus) investment management Style and an ideal scenario for those REITs adopting an opportunistic investment management Style.

On the assumption that the REIT explicitly referred to redevelopment in the Steps comprising the Envisioning Stage such that unitholders are expecting same, the investment decision making process for redevelopment Transformation of a property within the REIT portfolio will follow that for refurbishment Transformation through the Steps of the Dealing Stage, the Executing Stage and the Watching Stage. However, given the very significantly greater range of risks inherent in redevelopment, the scenario analysis and sensitivity analysis undertaken in the Advanced Financial Analysis Step and during recursion in the Portfolio Analysis Step may be expected to be much more extensive than those for refurbishment Transformation.

With the outcome of redevelopment Transformation generally being that a property may be redeveloped into another sector or for Disposal from the REIT portfolio, the Portfolio Rebalancing Step and Disposal Step, referred to below respectively, usually require consideration in parallel with the Transformation Step in the case of redevelopment Transformation.

6.4.3 *Mandatory lease related Transformation*

A mandatory lease related Transformation comprises a situation where an unavoidable upcoming lease event may adversely impact on the forecast risk-return from the property and so potentially impacts the ability of the REIT to achieve its Goals and so attain its Vision. Such an event may be, for example, a request for assignment of lease, a request for lease surrender or an upcoming major lease expiry which is going to happen and the REIT has no choice but to address the event.

By addressing a mandatory lease related event as a Transformation opportunity, the REIT has the ability to convert what might otherwise be a source of adverse impact into a source of enhanced impact on the forecast risk-return from the property. The cyclical activities of the Performance Monitoring Step may have alerted the REIT management teams to a mandatory lease related event, such as a lease expiry, whereas other events such as assignment or surrender requests may arise unexpectedly.

A mandatory lease related Transformation event may be discussed between the Asset Management Team and the Portfolio Management Team and a range of possible scenarios developed. For example, the Teams may discuss a range of scenarios where the terms of a lease may be varied to benefit the REIT on assignment or where refurbishment may be contemplated with a surrender premium on lease surrender or at lease expiry with potential lease renewal. Accordingly, a mandatory lease related event may provide the Teams with an opportunity to enhance the forecast returns of the REIT and/or decrease the forecast risk through the identification of an optimal solution.

The investment decision making process for a mandatory lease related Transformation of a property within the REIT portfolio will also follow that for refurbishment Transformation through the Steps of the Dealing Stage, the Executing Stage and the Watching Stage. As the event catalysing the Transformation is unavoidable, the Portfolio Management Team and the Asset Management Team have to develop a response that is not only acceptable to the REIT but also to the tenant, with the latter requiring particular focus on the Portfolio Impact Assessment Step of the Dealing Stage. In the event that the response is to redevelop the property, the Portfolio Rebalancing Step and Disposal Step, referred to below respectively, may require consideration in parallel with the Transformation Step.

6.4.4 *Optional lease related Transformation*

An optional lease related Transformation comprises a situation where an upcoming lease event may offer the opportunity to positively impact on the forecast risk-return from the property and so potentially enhance the ability of the REIT to achieve its Goals and so attain its Vision. Such an event may be, for example, a fixed rent review for a major tenant which, if exercised, will have the effect of raising the rent to a level far in excess of current open market rental value or the opportunity to widen the user clause in a retail lease to include the right to sell a new and popular high profit margin product.

Such an event provides the REIT with an option to choose whether it wishes to address the event as a Transformation opportunity for the benefit of the REIT. The cyclical activities of the Performance Monitoring Step may have alerted the REIT management teams to an optional lease related event, such as a rent review, whereas other events, such as the opportunity to widen the user clause in a retail lease, may arise unexpectedly.

The key distinction from a mandatory lease related Transformation is that the REIT has the choice to either do something or do nothing about an optional lease related Transformation, such that the decision to do something should provide a significantly superior risk-return outcome for the REIT than the *'do nothing'* scenario which will prevail for the REIT anyway.

An optional lease related Transformation event may be discussed between the Asset Management Team and the Portfolio Management Team and a range of possible scenarios developed. For example, the teams may discuss a range of scenarios where the rent on review or user clause may be varied to benefit the REIT through agreement by the tenant to an extended lease term. Accordingly, an optional lease related event may provide the teams with an opportunity to enhance the forecast returns of the REIT and/or decrease the forecast risk through the identification of an optimal solution.

The investment decision making process for an optional lease related Transformation of a property within the REIT portfolio will also follow that for a mandatory lease related Transformation through the Steps of the Dealing Stage, the Executing Stage and the Watching Stage. As the event catalysing the Transformation is an optional opportunity, the Portfolio Management Team and the Asset Management Team have to develop a response that is not only beneficial in terms of return but also does not significantly increase risk placing greater emphasis on the prevailing forecasts which comprise the *'do nothing'* scenario in the Advanced Financial Analysis Step and the Portfolio Impact Assessment Step.

6.4.5 *Transformation*

The Transformation Step comprises one of three possible responses by the REIT to a forecast which indicates that it may not achieve its Goals and so not attain its Vision. The other two possible responses, being subsequent to the Transformation Step at the property level, are either the Portfolio Rebalancing Step at the portfolio level or, if neither of the foregoing are optimal, the Disposal Step.

The cyclical process of planning, comparative analysis and reporting comprising the Performance Monitoring Step in the Watching Stage alerts the Asset Management Team and the Portfolio Management Team to upcoming events that may provide opportunities for the Transformation of a property asset. Transformation of a property asset through refurbishment, redevelopment, the response to a mandatory lease related event or the opportunity afforded by an optional lease related event provides the REIT management team with the possibility to increase property and portfolio returns while actively managing risk.

6.5 Portfolio Rebalancing

While the Transformation Step is a possible response to adverse forecast returns at the property level, the Portfolio Rebalancing Step provides a possible response at the portfolio level.

Similar to the Asset Management Step, there are both proactive and reactive components to the Portfolio Rebalancing Step, undertaken by the Portfolio Management Team, wherein the REIT's portfolio composition is modified to better suit the achievement of the Strategic Plan and Goals and the attainment of the Vision.

6.5.1 Proactive components

Proactive Portfolio Rebalancing components comprise those components which are explicitly addressed within the ongoing portfolio planning process and may arise from top down influences such as changes to the Strategic Plan or Goals following periodic review and/or from bottom up influences arising from the ongoing Performance Monitoring Step.

Within the Envisioning Stage, it was noted that a REIT's Vision and Style would not require review more than five yearly with the Strategic Plan and Goals being subject to review every two to three years. Accordingly, therefore, the REITs Vision and Style should not be expected to change more often than the five-yearly proactive review, limiting the repercussions for the Strategic Plan and Goals, unless there is an unexpected event or a change in the Governing Entity's risk tolerance, time horizon or view as to where the REIT is going.

However, the two to three yearly periodic proactive review of the strategic environment by the Fund Management Team may result in changes to the Strategic Plan or Goals which may then have an impact on the Property Portfolio Strategy. The Property Portfolio Strategy Step within the Planning Stage comprised the process by which the REIT's Strategic Plan is converted into property assets through the Strategic Asset Allocation, Tactical Asset

Allocation, Stock Selection and Asset Identification Steps. Within the Strategic Asset Allocation Step, the entire real estate market was analysed through a series of risk-return lenses to identify the optimal investment in different sectors or geographic areas.

Therefore, the Property Portfolio Strategy may be subject to review if the Strategic Plan is subject to change and/or if there are changes in the various sectors and geographic areas of the real estate market necessitating change to the Strategic Asset Allocation. Simultaneously, the formal annual review of the real estate market, with informal review quarterly or in the event of significant change in economic or real estate market conditions, undertaken by the Strategy Team and Research Team, provides a basis for the assessment of changes in the various sectors and geographic areas of the real estate market as input to a review of the Strategic Asset Allocation and the Property Portfolio Strategy.

The top down influences of changes in Governing Entity direction, time frame or risk tolerance, changes in the Strategic Plan or changes in real estate market conditions and Strategic Asset Allocation complement the bottom up influences of the Performance Monitoring Step. The cyclical process of planning, comparative analysis and reporting comprising the Performance Monitoring Step in the Watching Stage alerts the Portfolio Management Team to risk-return forecasts which indicate that the REIT may not achieve its Goals and so not attain its Vision, thus prompting potential review of the Property Portfolio Strategy.

Regardless of the top down or bottom up direction of the influence, one of the outcomes of a review of the Property Portfolio Strategy may be to undertake Portfolio Rebalancing wherein the REIT's portfolio composition is modified to better suit the achievement of the Strategic Plan and thus achievement of the Goals and attainment of the Vision. It should be noted that top down influences of changes in Governing Entity direction, time frame or risk tolerance are unusual and rare and major changes in the Strategic Plan or in market conditions impacting Strategic Asset Allocation are few and infrequent with bottom up influences often addressed through the Transformation Step, such that REIT Portfolio Rebalancing may not be expected to be a regular occurrence.

Review of the Property Portfolio Strategy by the Strategy Team and the Research Team may lead to variation in the Strategic Asset Allocation of the REIT between sectors and geographies (such as increasing the allocation to retail from office or to north from south) or within sectors or geographies (such as increasing the allocation to regional shopping centres from convenience centres), the Stock Selection criteria of the REIT (such as from minimum ten year lease terms to minimum five year lease terms) or to simply replacing one property with another of like kind but different characteristics (Pagliari, 1995).

A key benefit of the Portfolio Rebalancing Step following a change in Strategic Asset Allocation is the potential to implement the revised Strategic Asset Allocation through Transformation and acquisition rather than through Disposal. However, while an amended Property Portfolio Strategy may be theoretically robust, the ability to convert this into practice may be constrained by the financial and executive costs of transactions, the suitability of timing for sale of certain existing assets (such as those with an imminent major rent review or those undergoing refurbishment) and the prevailing conditions in the target sale or acquisition markets (Hoesli and MacGregor, 2000).

In addition to the proactive components of the Portfolio Rebalancing Step undertaken by the Portfolio Management Team, events may arise that necessitate further reactive components in the Portfolio Rebalancing Step.

6.5.2 Reactive components

Similar to the Asset Management Step, reactive Portfolio Rebalancing components comprise those which are not explicitly addressed nor in-built within the cyclical proactive process and which may arise within expected events or as unexpected events.

Expected events
As considered above, the REIT Strategic Plan, Property Portfolio Strategy and Strategic Asset Allocation are premised on forecasts and expectations for the risk-return trade off based on a range of market and other variables. In the event of the actual change in any such variables being significantly different to that which was forecast or expected, the risk-return trade off may change and each of the REIT Strategic Plan, Property Portfolio Strategy and Strategic Asset Allocation may require review with the potential for a Portfolio Rebalancing outcome.

Unexpected events
In addition to change in forecasts and expectations, the REIT Strategic Plan, Property Portfolio Strategy and Strategic Asset Allocation may be impacted by unexpected events such as natural disaster or significant change in regulation or law. Reactive Portfolio Rebalancing occurs when an unexpected event happens that was neither forecast nor expected and is of sufficient significance to impact the REIT Strategic Plan, Property Portfolio Strategy and Strategic Asset Allocation leading to review with the potential for Portfolio Rebalancing.

For example, unexpected major flooding within a CBD office area may cause disruption to the forecast supply of and demand for office accommodation for the next two to three years such that a review of the Strategic

Asset Allocation to that CBD may be required with the potential to require Portfolio Rebalancing through acquisition elsewhere.

6.5.3 *Portfolio Rebalancing*

While a proactive approach to the Portfolio Rebalancing Step is prudent to fulfil the REIT management team's fiduciary obligations, by maintaining an awareness of unitholder objectives and constraints and sectoral and geographic real estate market conditions, the likelihood of changes to the REIT Strategic Plan, Property Portfolio Strategy and Strategic Asset Allocation significant enough to justify action through Portfolio Rebalancing resulting in Disposals is low. However, as the real estate derivatives market develops around the world, the prospect of managing the Portfolio Rebalancing Step through the use of derivatives promises to become an increasingly attractive proposition.

The Portfolio Rebalancing Step at the portfolio level comprises one of three possible responses by a REIT to a forecast that the REIT may not achieve its Goals and so attain its Vision, with the response at the property level being the Transformation Step. In the event that neither the Transformation Step nor the Portfolio Rebalancing Step may be an optimal solution to an adverse performance forecast, the REIT may have no alternative but to consider the Disposal Step as a matter of last resort.

6.6 Disposal

The Disposal of a property by a REIT may be expected to be a rare event and when it occurs may be expected to be intentional. Disposal should only occur when:

- the Performance Monitoring Step indicates that the forecast risk-return from a property will **not achieve the Goals to attain the Vision** of the REIT and after alternatives, such as Transformation and Portfolio Rebalancing, have been investigated and deemed inappropriate; or
- the Disposal is the **intended conclusion** of a Tactical Asset Allocation decision.

In each case, the decision to dispose should be the result of a rigorous decision making process and the process of Disposal should be carefully planned to optimise returns to unitholders. The REIT management team should manage the REIT portfolio such that the situation should never arise where the REIT is an unexpected vendor of a property asset and forced to bring the asset to market inadequately prepared for sale or with an inappropriate or insufficient marketing campaign resulting in sub-optimal returns to unitholders.

While the Performance Monitoring Step includes the preparation of annual property and facilities management, asset management and portfolio management plans, care is required that these not only focus on the detail of the property itself but also have regard to the property in context. In addition to changes in the tenancy profile and other property specific characteristics and to changes in the real estate market over time, a number of other influences also change gradually over time but are less immediately visible, including:

- **obsolescence** – in its various forms including physical, structural, functional, design and so forth;
- **location** – new developments in the surrounding area or changes in the road layout may adversely impact a property;
- **planning** – a series of minor changes to planning may have a significant cumulative effect on a property and may change its development potential;
- **demographic** – population growth or decline within sub-markets may progressively impact demand over time;
- **fashion** – changes in aesthetics and design may gradually render some building materials or finishes less attractive over time; and
- **legislative, government and fiscal measures** – economic development initiatives or building regulations may render other sub-markets or other properties more attractive than the subject.

It is, therefore, important for the Portfolio Management, Strategy and Research Teams to be cognisant of the gradual change in such influences and to address these in asset and portfolio planning in order to avoid any surprises.

> A survey of 54 UK property fund managers found nearly 90% of decisions to dispose of assets were due to the expected return of an individual asset being less than target return. (MacCowan and Orr, 2008)

Given the enormous sunk and arising costs for the REIT in Disposal of an asset, it is essential that the REIT management team be certain that Disposal is the only alternative following a rigorous decision making process.

6.6.1 Disposal process

A property may be identified for potential Disposal through completion of the Performance Monitoring Step in the Watching Stage, which alerts the REIT management team to that property for which the forecast risk-return appears unlikely to achieve the Goals and so attain the Vision of the REIT or through completion of a Tactical Asset Allocation.

Commencing with the Preliminary Negotiation Step of the Dealing Stage, the Capital Transactions Team may discuss the potential Disposal and Structuring with market participants to gauge the level of interest and perceptions of worth. By then using this information to undertake the Preliminary Analysis Step, the Structuring Step, the Advanced Financial Analysis Step and the Portfolio Impact Step, the Portfolio Management Team will confirm the findings of the Performance Monitoring Step supporting Disposal and identify the preferred form of Disposal to optimise returns to unitholders. The preferred form of Disposal may be sale of a 100% interest in the property, sale of a partial interest in the property, vending the property into another managed fund and so forth.

Having completed the Dealing Stage, the Portfolio Management Team are in a position to prepare a Governing Entity report recommending Disposal within a given price range and time frame for consideration by the Governing Entity in the Governance Decision Step of the Executing Stage. Having obtained a mandate for Disposal, the Capital Transactions Team will co-ordinate the marketing of the property for Disposal (considered further below) with a view to obtaining several offers to purchase from market participants.

Thereafter, in the Transaction Closure Step and the Documentation Step, the iterative process of negotiation and Documentation will lead to exchange of contracts for sale with the successful purchaser. The Due Diligence Step may then focus on the provision of information for verification to the purchaser with the Independent Appraisal Step providing verification and support for the assumptions relied upon by the Portfolio Management Team in the Dealing Stage.

With the Executing Stage completed, funds from the Disposal of the property may be received in the Settlement Step of the Watching Stage with completion of the Post Audit Step providing a process to consider the validity of the assumptions made and the forecasting approaches adopted and offering an opportunity to implement improvements, if required.

Accordingly, the Steps in the real estate investment decision making process through the Dealing Stage, Executing Stage and into the Watching Stage may be applied to a range of real estate investment decisions including acquisitions, disposals and other transactions with a portfolio risk-return impact for the REIT.

6.6.2 Disposal method

Having determined the preferred form of Disposal in the Structuring Step (being a 100% interest, partial interest or other form) and having obtained a mandate for Disposal in the Governance Decision Step, the

Capital Transactions Team is tasked with coordinating the marketing of the property for Disposal with a view to obtaining several offers to purchase from market participants. As Pyhrr et al. (1989) succinctly comment: *'Methods of disposal are limited only by the imagination, the law, and economic and financial feasibility.'* (Pyhrr et al., 1989)

The principal alternative methods of Disposal usually considered by REITs include:

- sale by **private treaty** – where the property is offered for sale publicly, bids are taken privately and the property may be sold to the optimal bidder;
- sale by **tender** – where the property is offered up for tender publicly through a private process, bids are taken privately and the property may be sold to the optimal bidder; and
- sale by **auction** – where the property is offered up for bid in a public forum, bids are taken publicly and the property may be sold to the highest bidder.

The preferred method of Disposal will have regard to the condition of the property and the condition of the market. Fully leased, income producing property may lend to sale by private treaty whereas a property with vacancy may lend to sale by tender or auction to maximise the competitive tension between potential purchasers with differing views of the upside from leasing the property. Similarly, very buoyant market conditions may lend to sale by tender or auction to maximise the competitive tension between potential purchasers whereas a stable market may lend to sale by private treaty.

Depending on the nature of the property and the target market, the Capital Transactions Team may offer the property to the market directly themselves or may prefer to use a brokerage agent or an investment bank to assist with marketing the property and soliciting offers to purchase. Sales of large and complex assets that may appeal to the REIT, unlisted fund and sophisticated purchaser market may lend better to sale by an investment bank whereas smaller assets with wide appeal to a range of sectors of the market may lend better to effective sale through one or more brokerage agents.

6.6.3 Disposal Step

As may be expected, many of the Steps identified in the Dealing, Executing and Watching Stages of the real estate investment decision making process may be commonly applied to various forms of transaction including acquisition, disposal and other activities. However, whereas acquisitions may be the result of starting with the Envisioning and Planning Stages and working progressively forwards through the decision making process, Disposals may be the result of completion of the Performance Monitoring Step in the Watching Stage and then stepping back to repeat the Dealing, Executing and Watching Stages sequentially.

Given the enormous sunk and arising costs for the REIT in Disposal of an asset, a critical aspect of the Disposal Step is that it must be intentional and planned being, other than as a result of Tactical Asset Allocation, the only remaining response to an adverse risk-return forecast after all others have been investigated and discarded.

6.7 Observing Phase

Completion of the Optimising Stage may result in the REIT taking such action as may be necessary to address any forecast underperformance identified in the Watching Stage, with completion of the Watching Stage and the Optimising Stage resulting in completion of the third and final Phase, the Observing Phase.

Having completed the Observing Phase, the REIT has ensured that its performance will achieve its Goals and so attain its Vision, thereby completing the cyclical process of REIT real estate investment decision making.

6.8 Super REIT

Having completed the Envisioning Stage, Super REIT has developed a Vision to be the premier diversified REIT on the stock exchange, interdependent with its adopted generic and specific investment management Style which is active, top down, growth and value added, respectively. To attain this Vision, Super REIT has identified four Goals including to be within the top quartile return performance with lowest quartile tracking error of the stock exchange REIT index every year. Consistently, Super REIT's Strategic Plan focuses on return optimisation at the REIT, portfolio and property level together with effective risk management, supported by a large number of specified Objectives encompassing all REIT management executives in the respective Teams and so aligning the motivations and actions of all REIT management executives with the attainment of Super REIT's Vision.

On completion of the Planning Stage, Super REIT has developed a Property Portfolio Strategy with a Strategic Asset Allocation comprising a sectoral allocation (50% retail, 40% office, 10% industrial) and geographic allocation (60% northern, 40% southern states), enhanced by a Tactical Asset Allocation of 2.5% to the office sector in the northern city of Metropolis for a period of two years reflecting a forecast undersupply of office accommodation. Within the allocation to the office sector, Super REIT has developed Stock Selection criteria specifying lots of around $375 million each, being freehold title in prime office locations within the downtown precincts of specified cities and A grade, high rise, modern office towers that are less than ten years old, being principally leased to corporate tenants.

Having completed the Dealing Stage, Super REIT has identified a specific asset for acquisition, Superman Tower, that is considered mis-priced by a significant extent over both a three and ten year holding period and so capable of generating abnormal returns. At a portfolio level, Superman Tower was confirmed to be acceptable for acquisition at $385 million on the basis of the commercial and funding structure proposed.

On completion of the Executing Stage, Super REIT has summarised the findings of the pricing process to secure the requisite internal and external approvals for the acquisition to proceed and negotiated Transaction Closure and Documentation. Super REIT has also undertaken Due Diligence to verify information relied upon in the Dealing Stage and commissioned an Independent Appraisal to support the assumptions made in the Dealing Stage.

Having completed the Watching Stage, Super REIT has exchanged unitholder capital for legal title to Superman Tower and the rights and responsibilities associated therewith at Settlement. Reflecting the Tactical Asset Allocation for a period of two years, Super REIT undertakes Post Audit after six months with the learning incorporated as changes to the real estate investment decision making process. Thereafter, Superman Tower is included within Super REIT's portfolio and subject to ongoing, cyclical Performance Monitoring, Performance Measurement and Portfolio Analysis to maintain awareness of whether or not the forecasts for the property will contribute to Super REIT achieving its Goals and so attaining its Vision.

Entering the Optimising Stage, Superman Tower is now part of Super REIT's portfolio for Asset Management, Property Management and Facilities Management purposes as well as being an asset for which Transformation may be considered and part of a portfolio which may be subject to Portfolio Rebalancing, together with consideration for Disposal reflecting the defined time frame basis of acquisition.

6.8.1 Asset Management

The Asset Management Team will include Superman Tower within the ongoing, cyclical asset management processes applied to all properties held within Super REIT's portfolios.

However, reflecting the Tactical Asset Allocation basis for the acquisition of Superman Tower, the Asset Management Team may be expected to focus on optimising the rental achieved at larger rent reviews and lease renewals as well as keeping the property in a continued state of readiness for possible Disposal at short notice.

6.8.2 Property Management and Facilities Management

Similar to the Asset Management Team, the Property Management and Facilities Management Teams will include Superman Tower within the ongoing, cyclical property and facilities management processes applied to all property held within Super REIT's portfolios, as well as keeping the property in a continued state of readiness for possible Disposal at short notice.

6.8.3 Transformation

Reflecting the Tactical Asset Allocation to Metropolis to benefit from a forecast undersupply of office accommodation, Transformation in Superman Tower may be expected to focus on optimising the rents achieved at rent review and lease renewal, together with endeavouring to convert any mandatory lease related events into a source of enhanced forecast risk-return impact for the property.

Further, reflecting the Tactical Asset Allocation timeframe, the asset management plan for Superman Tower is unlikely to include refurbishment or redevelopment which may otherwise have been undertaken in the Transformation Step.

6.8.4 Portfolio Rebalancing

Having recently stated its Vision and Style, Super REIT may not consider it necessary to review either at this time. However, Super REIT's Goals and Strategic Plan should be subject to review very two to three years and its Property Portfolio Strategy every year.

Super REIT's Goals for return, risk, people and the environment were broadly stated such that the need for regular change should be limited. Similarly, Super REIT's Strategic Plan focuses on return optimisation at the REIT, portfolio and property level, measures for effective risk management at each level, steps to significantly improve the appeal of the REIT as an employer and a commitment to substantial capital expenditure to improve the environmental friendliness of several identified properties within the portfolio, which are also broadly stated and so limiting the need for regular change.

However, Super REIT's Property Portfolio Strategy is premised on assumptions and forecasts regarding the real estate market and the individual properties within the portfolio necessitating annual review and possible amendment to reflect changes in either.

Accordingly, following review and reflecting limited change in real estate market conditions generally, Super REIT considers it is not currently necessary to amend its Goals, Strategic Plan or Property Portfolio Strategy such that no requirement arises for Portfolio Rebalancing.

6.8.5 Disposal

Disposal may, however, be considered more readily for Superman Tower in Metropolis as the property was acquired as part of a Tactical Asset Allocation to benefit from a temporary imbalance in the office market supply/demand.

Optimising returns from such a Tactical Asset Allocation is highly sensitive to timing based on the state of the office market in Metropolis, placing significant emphasis on the quarterly asset management plan review. Give the short time frame of the Tactical Asset Allocation and the potential for relatively fast changes to the supply/demand balance for office accommodation in Metropolis, Super REIT will need to rigorously undertake quarterly reviews in a timely manner and carefully forecast each following quarter in order to ensure sufficient time to undertake the requisite decision making Steps and then adequately market Superman Tower for sale and finally complete the transaction before the market starts to decline.

Accordingly, therefore, in the Optimising Stage, Super REIT is simultaneously managing several different review timelines including three- to five-yearly Vision and Style review, two- to three-yearly Goals and Strategic Plan review, annual Property Portfolio Strategy, portfolio management plan and asset management plan review, quarterly asset management plan review and monthly net income and capital expenditure budget review and forecasting which each provide a significant contribution to the cyclical, ongoing process of real estate investment decision making.

6.8.6 Outcomes of implementing the Optimising Stage

Having completed the Watching Stage, Super REIT has exchanged unitholder capital for legal title to Superman Tower and the rights and responsibilities associated therewith. Reflecting the Tactical Asset Allocation for a period of two years, Super REIT undertakes Post Audit after six months with the learning incorporated as changes to the real estate investment decision making process. Thereafter, Superman Tower is included within Super REIT's portfolio and is subject to ongoing, cyclical Performance Monitoring, Performance Measurement and Portfolio Analysis to maintain awareness of whether or not the forecasts for the property will contribute to Super REIT achieving its Goals and so attaining its Vision.

On completion of the Optimising Stage, Superman Tower will have been subject to Super REIT's ongoing cyclical Asset Management, Property Management and Facilities Management processes. Reflecting the Tactical Asset Allocation to Metropolis to benefit from a forecast undersupply of office accommodation, Transformation in Superman Tower focuses on optimising the rents achieved at rent review and lease renewal. Recent development of a Vision, identification of Goals and development of a Strategic Plan and Property Portfolio Strategy by Super REIT may preclude the requirement for Portfolio Rebalancing but Disposal is continuously under consideration reflecting the two year Tactical Asset Allocation timeframe.

Accordingly, completion of the Watching Stage may result in Super REIT being able to clearly determine whether or not its Goals will be achieved and hence its Vision attained. This then leads to the Optimising Stage of the REIT real estate investment decision making process where Super REIT takes such action as may be necessary to address any forecast underperformance, identified in the Watching Stage, that may prevent it from achieving its Goals and attaining its Vision. Having completed the Watching Stage and the Optimising Stage, Super REIT has now completed the Observing Phase being the third and final Phase, thereby completing the cyclical process of REIT real estate investment decision making.

6.9 Summary

The first Phase of the REIT real estate investment decision making process, the Preparing Phase, comprised the Envisioning Stage (considered in Chapter 1) and the Planning Stage (considered in Chapter 2). On completion of the Preparing Phase, the REIT has articulated where it is going and how it is going to get there, providing unitholders with a clear understanding of the risk-return profile to expect from the managers investment of their funds.

The second Phase of the REIT real estate investment decision making process, the Transacting Phase, comprised the Dealing Stage (considered in Chapter 3) and the Executing Stage (considered in Chapter 4). On completion of the Transacting Phase, the REIT manager has implemented the outcomes of the Preparing Phase through the creation of a tangible property portfolio.

The third and final Phase of the REIT real estate investment decision making process, the Observing Phase, comprised the Watching Stage (considered in Chapter 5) and the Optimising Stage (considered in this chapter).

The Optimising Stage comprises the Asset Management Step and the Property and Facilities Management Step wherein the day to day management and operation of the properties is undertaken to ensure that the income return and capital expenditure are managed effectively with the clear focus being on the asset rather than on the portfolio. The reactive components of both the Asset Management Step and the Property and Facilities Management Step address changes to expected events and unexpected events which, together with the proactive components, provide input into the Performance Monitoring Step in the Watching Stage, alerting the Portfolio Management Team to forecast underperformance which may contribute to the REIT not achieving its Goals and so not attaining its Vision.

The Transformation Step provides an opportunity, at the individual property level, to transform the forecast risk-return from a given property through either or a combination of refurbishment, redevelopment and/or a mandatory or optional response to a lease related event. Similarly, the Portfolio Rebalancing Step provides an opportunity, at the portfolio level, to change the forecast risk-return from the portfolio either proactively through the portfolio monitoring process or reactively in response to changes to expected events and unexpected events. Both the Transformation Step and the Portfolio Rebalancing Step provide the REIT management team with opportunities to address forecast performance at the asset level and at the portfolio level which appears unlikely to achieve the Goals of the REIT and which may then preclude it from attaining its Vision.

The final Step, being the Step of last resort in addressing forecast under performance, comprises the Disposal Step where those properties whose risk-return forecast cannot be addressed through Transformation or Portfolio Rebalancing and those properties comprising part of a Tactical Asset Allocation are sold into the market.

Completion of the Optimising Stage may result in the REIT taking such action as may be necessary to address any forecast underperformance identified in the Watching Stage. Completion of the Watching Stage and the Optimising Stage mark completion of the third and final of the three Phases, the Observing Phase, wherein the REIT ensures that its performance will achieve its Goals and so attain its Vision, thereby completing the cyclical process of REIT real estate investment decision making.

6.10 REIT real estate investment decision making process

This book sought to explain the real estate investment decision making process by which a real estate investment trust, or REIT, converts $1 of unitholder capital into $1 of investment property. This process is not only a sequence of Phases, Stages and Steps but also a fusion of 'how' with 'why' and interdependency both with and between a range of people.

The *how* of what activities to undertake in which order contributes transparency, explicability and repeatability to the REIT real estate investment decision making process, but will be limited in its effectiveness without a clear understanding of the *why*, being the real estate theory, capital market theory and finance theory that underpins real estate investment management.

Similarly, the individual people involved in the REIT real estate investment decision making process each have a specific contribution to make, but the effectiveness of their joint contribution will be limited without overlap, interaction and teamwork.

However, it is in the combination of people and process that REIT real estate investment decision making may be at its most effective. While real estate theory, capital market theory and finance theory may offer a range of tools to use in real estate investment decision making, such use will only be optimised when combined with the intuition and judgment that come from years of practical experience.

6.11 Key points

- The Optimising Stage is the second and final Stage of the **Observing Phase**, following successful completion of the Preparing Phase (comprising the Envisioning and Planning Stages), the Transacting Phase (comprising the Dealing and Executing Stages) and the Watching Stage (being the first Stage of the Observing Phase).
- The **Optimising Stage** comprises the Asset Management, Property and Facilities Management, Transformation and Portfolio Rebalancing Steps together with, potentially, the Disposal Step.
- Principal participants in the Optimising Stage are the **Asset Management, Property Management** and **Facilities Management Teams** who provide the engine room for the day to day control, management and operation of the REIT property portfolio.
- **Asset Management** addresses various aspects of idiosyncratic risk, which may impact on income and capital returns, through a focus on larger rent reviews, lease renewals, letting vacancies and capital expenditure at the individual property level together with an ongoing contribution to the cyclical performance monitoring process.
- **Property Management and Facilities Management** are focused at the individual property level, having an emphasis on process (through the operation of the property asset) and people (through the maintenance of user satisfaction), respectively.

- **Adverse risk-return forecasts** arising from the Performance Monitoring Step may be addressed through Transformation, Portfolio Rebalancing or, as a last resort, Disposal.
- **Transformation** offers the opportunity, at the individual property level, to transform the forecast risk-return from a given property through either or a combination of refurbishment, redevelopment and/or a mandatory or optional response to a lease related event.
- At the portfolio level, **Portfolio Rebalancing** offers the opportunity to modify the REIT's portfolio composition, reflecting Strategic Asset Allocation decisions and/or forecast under performance at the individual property level, in order to achieve the Goals and so attain the Vision of the REIT.
- **Disposal** of a property asset should only be contemplated as an intended conclusion of a Tactical Asset Allocation decision or a last resort response to forecast under performance at the individual property level.
- Completion of the Optimising Stage may result in the REIT taking such action as may be necessary to **address any forecast underperformance** identified in the Watching Stage.
- Completion of the Watching Stage and the Optimising Stage mark completion of the third and final Phase, the Observing Phase, wherein the REIT ensures that its **performance will achieve its Goals** and so **attain its Vision**, thereby completing the cyclical process of REIT real estate investment decision making.

References

Further information concerning issues considered in this chapter may be found in the following texts:

Baum, A.E. (2002) *Commercial Real Estate Investment*, Estates Gazette, London.

Hoesli, M. and MacGregor, B. (2000) *Property Investment – Principles and Practice of Portfolio Management*, Longman, Harlow.

MacCowan, R.J. and Orr, A.M. (2008) A Behavioural Study of the Decision Process Underpinning Disposals by Property Fund Managers, *Journal of Property Investment and Finance*, **26**(4), p.342.

Pagliari, J.L. (ed.) (1995) *The Handbook of Real Estate Portfolio Management*, Irwin, Chicago

Pyhrr, S.A., Cooper, J.R., Wofford, L.E., Kapplin, S.D. and Lapides, P.D. (1989) *Real Estate Investment: Strategy, Analysis, Decisions*, John Wiley and Sons, Inc., New York.

Wurtzebach, C.H., Miles, M.E. and Cannon, S.E. (1994) *Modern Real Estate*, John Wiley & Sons, Inc., New York.

Glossary

Active Style   An investment management style where a manager seeks to actively manage an individual investment or portfolio in order to add value and enhance returns above those achieved by a benchmark or index within a stated risk tolerance.

Appraisal   The term commonly used in the USA to indicate what is termed in Commonwealth countries as a valuation (Real Estate Institute of Australia et al., 2007).

Appraisal Accuracy   The extent to which an appraisal is an effective proxy for the likely selling price of an asset.

Appraisal Smoothing   Potential understatement of the variability of capital returns due to the use of appraisals, attributable to infrequent transactions providing limited information in the appraisal process and an aggregation effect at the portfolio level.

Asset Identification   The process of identifying potential assets for transaction that meet the criteria identified in stock selection.

Asset Management   The management of assets within a portfolio, with the principal purpose being to optimise the risk-return balance at the asset level.

Attribution Analysis   The process whereby a manager's investment judgements are seen to be attributable to the return on stock (or real estate) selection or sector allocation (Real Estate Institute of Australia et al., 2007).

Bottom Up Style   An investment management style where the manager seeks to specifically consider the investment attributes of a nominated individual asset and their acceptability as the basis for acquisition, potentially disregarding other than local economic and real estate market conditions.

Capital Asset Pricing Model   A model for describing the way prices of individual assets are determined in an efficient market, based on their relative riskiness in comparison with the return on risk free assets (Real Estate Institute of Australia et al., 2007).

Global Real Estate Investment Trusts: People, Process and Management,
First Edition. David Parker.
© 2011 David Parker. Published 2011 by Blackwell Publishing Ltd.

Capitalisation Rate   Any divisor (usually expressed as a percentage) that is used to convert income into value. The rate or yield at which the annual net income from an investment is capitalised to ascertain its capital value at a given date. The calculations are as follows: real estate value estimate = net operating income ÷ capitalisation rate (Real Estate Institute of Australia et al., 2007).

Core Style   An investment management style that seeks to provide a risk adjusted return that is approximately equal to the market but through the holding of only a small portfolio of high quality properties with limited leverage.

DCF   Discounted Cash Flow, being a method of analysing investment opportunities in which annual cash flows are discounted to arrive at their Net Present Value or Internal Rate of Return (Real Estate Institute of Australia et al., 2007).

Discount Rate   The interest rate used to discount future cash flows to determine present value (Real Estate Institute of Australia et al., 2007).

Debt   Short or long term borrowings. An obligation or liability to pay or render money, goods or services to another party. (Real Estate Institute of Australia et al., 2007).

Due Diligence   A process of information verification, comprising an investigation of the legal, financial and physical nature and characteristics, including the entitlements and liabilities attaching to and arising from a real estate asset or assets, usually for acquisition or compliance purposes (Real Estate Institute of Australia et al., 2007).

Efficient Market   A market in which security prices reflect all information about securities, with levels of market efficiency usually defined as weak form, semi strong form or strong form (Real Estate Institute of Australia et al., 2007).

Equity   The interest or value that an owner or investor has in an asset over and above the debt against the asset (Real Estate Institute of Australia et al., 2007).

Facilities Management   The management of facilities and services within the properties in a portfolio, with the principal purpose being to optimise operational efficiency at the individual property level.

Growth Style   An investment management style where the manager consistently focuses on constructing a portfolio comprising assets that offer the potential for growing income, capital and/or total returns over an undefined but usually longer future timeframe.

Heuristics   Simple measures, such as rules of thumb or commonly understood ratios or metrics.

Index   A statistical indicator providing a representation of the value of investments over time (Real Estate Institute of Australia et al., 2007).

Indexation   An investment management style where a manager seeks to replicate or follow a benchmark or index and so approximate the risk-return of that benchmark or index (also known as passive style).

IPD   Investment Property Databank, the world leader in performance analysis for the owners, investors, managers and occupiers of real estate.

IRR   Internal Rate of Return, being the discount rate that equates the present value of the net cash flows of a project with the present value of the capital investment. It is the rate at which the Net Present Value (NPV) equals zero (Real Estate Institute of Australia et al., 2007).

Landlord (Lessor)   The owner of a property who transfers the right to occupy and use property to another by way of lease agreement (Real Estate Institute of Australia et al., 2007).

Lease Renewal   The entering into of a new lease by the lessor and lessee following the expiry of a prior lease.

Lessee (Tenant)   A person or legal entity who receives the right to occupy and use a property under the terms of a lease (Real Estate Institute of Australia et al., 2007).

Lessor (Landlord)   The owner of a property who transfers the right to occupy and use property to another by way of lease agreement (Real Estate Institute of Australia et al., 2007).

Market Value   The estimated amount for which a property should exchange on the date of valuation between a willing buyer and a willing seller in an arm's-length transaction after proper marketing wherein the parties had each acted knowledgeably, prudently, and without compulsion (IVSC, 2007).

Modern Portfolio Theory   The theoretical constructs that enable investment managers to classify, estimate and control the sources of risk and return. In popular usage, the term encompasses all notions of modern investment, as well as portfolio theory. The end objective is to select optimal combinations of assets to produce the highest return for a given level of risk, or the least risk for a given level of return (Real Estate Institute of Australia et al., 2007).

NPV Net Present Value, being the measure of the difference between the discounted revenues, or inflows, and the costs, or outflows, in a DCF analysis (Real Estate Institute of Australia et al., 2007).

Opportunistic Style An investment management style that seeks to achieve outperformance through a wide spectrum of multiplicative risk approaches including higher risk real estate assets and greater leverage.

Passive Style An investment management style where a manager seeks to replicate or follow a benchmark or index and so approximate the risk-return of that benchmark or index (also known as indexation).

Post Audit The process of comparing and reconciling the assumptions made pre-acquisition against the actual observations post-acquisition.

Price A term used for the amount asked, offered or paid for a good or service (IVSC, 2007).

Property Management The management of properties within a portfolio, with the principal purpose being to optimise financial efficiency at the individual property level.

Recursion The process of monitoring and measuring actual performance with reference to forecast performance and with remedial action, if appropriate, being usually undertaken for a discrete, time specific project.

Redevelopment Where existing development is to be replaced by new development (Real Estate Institute of Australia et al., 2007).

Refurbishment The upgrading of a building's fabric and services with the aim of enhancing its ability to attract tenants, improve rental growth and maximise market value (Real Estate Institute of Australia et al., 2007).

REIT A Real Estate Investment Trust or Listed Property Trust (LPT), being a collective investment vehicle which holds a portfolio of real property and is listed on a stock exchange (Real Estate Institute of Australia et al., 2007).

Rent Review   A periodic review of rental under a lease using a predetermined method. For example, increase in line with inflation (such as a Consumer Price Index) or in accordance with a market valuation (Real Estate Institute of Australia et al., 2007).

RICS   The Royal Institution of Chartered Surveyors, the world's leading professional body for qualifications and standards in land, real estate and construction.

Risk Premium   The amount that investors require above the risk free rate (generally taken as the long term central government bond rate) to compensate them for the uncertainty of an investment (Real Estate Institute of Australia et al., 2007).

Stock Selection   The process of identifying and specifying real estate characteristics such as lot size, preferred location, real estate style, asset age, tenant profile and so forth, as the basic criteria for asset identification.

Strategic Asset Allocation   Analysis of the entire real estate market through a range of risk-return lenses, including the different real estate sectors or geographic areas, to identify target sectoral and geographic weightings.

Style   Investment style is the approach to investment management adopted to reflect a stated risk tolerance.

Tactical Asset Allocation   Identification of target markets offering significant potential outperformance for over-weight allocation for a limited time period.

Tenant (Lessee)   A person or legal entity who receives the right to occupy and use a property under the terms of a lease (Real Estate Institute of Australia et al., 2007).

Top Down Style   An investment management style where a manager sequentially considers the global economy, national economy, regional economies and local economies and then considers the global real estate market, national real estate market, regional real estate markets and local real estate markets to identify optimal geographic areas and/or real estate sectors for investment, then seeking assets within such areas and sectors for acquisition.

Tracking Error   The difference between the return of a portfolio and the return on the benchmark index to which the portfolio's performance is compared (Real Estate Institute of Australia et al., 2007).

Valuation   The process of estimating value. The term commonly used in Commonwealth countries to indicate what is termed in the USA as an appraisal (Real Estate Institute of Australia et al., 2007).

Value Added Style   An investment management style that seeks to achieve outperformance by identifying opportunities to add value using mixed quality real estate assets and moderate leverage.

Value Style   An investment management style where the manager consistently focuses on seeking assets that are significantly mis-priced and offer the potential for abnormal income, capital and/or total returns over a defined future timeframe.

Weighted Average Cost of Capital   A measure of the cost of capital for a given entity, comprising both debt and equity, which is required to service debts and to maintain a return on equity and thus maintain solvency (Real Estate Institute of Australia et al., 2007).

Worth   The value of a property to a particular investor, or a class of investors, for identified investment objectives (IVSC, 2007).

Yield   The derived percentage return of a property assessed from the net income and the market value or price. It is calculated by dividing the net income by the opening market value or price (Real Estate Institute of Australia et al., 2007).

References

International Valuation Standards Committee (2007) *International Valuation Standards,* Eighth Edition, International Valuation Standards Committee, London.
Real Estate Institute of Australia, Australian Property Institute and Property Council of Australia (2007) *Glossary of Property Terms,* Sydney.

Index
